Governance in
Immigrant Family Businesses

Governance in Immigrant Family Businesses

Enterprise, Ethnicity and Family Dynamics

DAPHNE HALKIAS and
CHRISTIAN ADENDORFF

 Routledge
Taylor & Francis Group

LONDON AND NEW YORK

First published 2014 by Gower Publishing

2 Park Square, Milton Park, Abingdon, Oxfordshire OX14 4RN
52 Vanderbilt Avenue, New York, NY 10017

Routledge is an imprint of the Taylor & Francis Group, an informa business

First issued in paperback 2020

Gower Applied Business Research
Our programme provides leaders, practitioners, scholars and researchers with thought provoking, cutting edge books that combine conceptual insights, interdisciplinary rigour and practical relevance in key areas of business and management.

British Library Cataloguing in Publication Data
A catalogue record for this book is available from the British Library

Library of Congress Cataloging-in-Publication Data
Halkias, Daphne.
 Governance in immigrant family businesses : enterprise, ethnicity and family dynamics / by Daphne Halkias and Christian Adendorff.
    pages cm
 Includes bibliographical references and index.
  ISBN 978-1-4094-4557-9 (hardback) -- ISBN 978-1-4094-4558-6 (ebook) -- ISBN 978-1-4724-0239-4 (epub) 1. Family-owned business enterprises--Cross-cultural studies. 2. Corporate governance--Cross-cultural studies. 3. Entrepreneurship--Cross-cultural studies. 4. Immigrant families. I. Adendorff, Christian. II. Title.
 HD62.25.H34 2014
 338.6--dc23

2013042242

ISBN 13: 978-1-4094-4557-9 (hbk)
ISBN 13: 978-0-367-60540-7 (pbk)

Contents

List of Figures

List of Tables

About the Authors

Daphne Halkias, PhD is a distinguished academic, researcher, published author, and consultant in the areas of immigrant entrepreneurship, family business, coaching and mentoring family businesses, organizational psychology, education and sustainable entrepreneurship. She is a Fellow at the Institute of Coaching, McLean Hospital at Harvard Medical School; Research Affiliate at the Institute for Social Sciences, Cornell University; Research Associate at the Center for Comparative Immigration Studies, University of California, San Diego; and Senior Research Fellow at The Center for Youth and Family Enterprise, University of Bergamo. Dr Halkias is CEO of Executive Coaching Consultants, and Editor of *International Journal of Teaching and Case Studies* and *International Journal of Social Entrepreneurship and Innovation*. She is a Member of the Family Firm Institute.

Christian Adendorff, PhD has been a business entrepreneur since 1985 and developing a family business that is owner-managed internationally. He has an MS and a PhD in Commerce from Rhodes University, and an MPhil and DBA in Future Studies from Stellenbosch University with specializations in research methodology, corporate governance, and turnaround strategies. Prof. Adendorff is on the faculty of Nelson Mandela Metropolitan University (NMMU) Business School teaching future studies, family businesses, entrepreneurship, and research methodology. He serves as Associate Editor of *International Journal of Teaching and Case Studies* and on the editorial board of various international peer-reviewed journals. He is a published author and researcher in the areas of governance and immigrant entrepreneurship, future studies, family business, technological entrepreneurship, culture, strategic management, demographics, systems management, and turnaround strategies and a Member of the Family Firm Institute and International Family Enterprise Research Academy.

Notes on
Case Study Contributors

Ms. Shehla Riza Arifeen is Associate Professor of Marketing and Management at the Business School of Lahore School of Economics, Pakistan.

Dr. Mary Barrett is Professor of Management at the School of Management & Marketing, University of Wollongong, Australia.

Dr. Nina Gorovaia is Assistant Professor of Management at the Department of Business Administration, Frederick University, Cyprus.

Ms. Maryam Khazaeli is a graduate student in management at the School of Management & Marketing, University of Wollongong, Australia.

Dr. Melquicedec Lozano is Director of Research and Special Projects at the Center for Entrepreneurship Development, Universidad Icesi in Cali, Colombia.

Dr. Leann Mischel is Associate Professor and founder of the Entrepreneurship program at Susquehanna University, United States of America.

Dr. Meenakshi Rishi is Associate Professor of Economics at the Albers School of Business and Economics at Seattle University in Seattle, United States of America.

Dr. Claire Seaman is Director of the Scottish Forum for Family Business Research at Queen Margaret University in Edinburgh.

Prof. Paul W. Thurman is Clinical Professor, School of International and Public Affairs, Mailman School of Public Health, Columbia University in New York, United States of America.

Dr. Athanasia Tziortzi is Lecturer of Marketing at the Department of Business Administration, Frederick University, Cyprus.

Dr. Franco Vaccarino is Senior Lecturer of Cross-Cultural Communication at the School of Communication, Journalism and Marketing, Massey University in Palmerston North, New Zealand.

Dr. Ioannis Violaris is Dean of the School of Economic Sciences and Administration, Frederick University, Cyprus, Associate Professor of Economics, and Doctoral Adviser for the Middlesex University's Work-based program in Cyprus.

Acknowledgements

The realization of this book lies squarely in the lap of my good friend and respected colleague at Nelson Mandela Metropolitan University, Dr. Christian Adendorff, who spent two years on a groundbreaking and vast research project on corporate governance in immigrant family businesses of South African Greeks. Plainly put, this work would have never come to fruition without Chris's original research. It is my honour to publish this book with him where we now break new theoretical ground in the area of sustainable immigrant family business. Chris's original conceptual model, *The Model of Perceived Good Governance in Immigrant Family Business*, which he originally published in 2005, has since evolved and extended through Chris's continued scholarly work over the past decade. In this book we present the latest version of Chris's original theoretical model, now termed *The Sustainable Immigrant Family Business Model*. Our hope is that the next step for this model is its validation through a cross-national study, which will be the basis of our next book. Chris, it has been an amazing journey working with you and I send you my gratitude for opening this door to me so I may take part in some small way to supporting immigrant families worldwide starting business ventures in their adopted lands.

We thank our colleagues for lending to this book their valuable time and expertise through their country case study contributions. The colleagues that represented their countries or regions in this book through their case study work gave their time generously to gather the data supporting the concepts presented in each chapter. These contributing authors are researchers and scholars around the globe collaborating with us to write each country/ regional case study. From nations across the globe – Australia, Colombia, Cyprus, Greece, New Zealand, Pakistan, Philippines, South Africa, the United Kingdom (Scotland), the United Arab Emirates, and the United States of America – this applied research book is in the reader's hands today thanks to the collaborative efforts of this international network of colleagues dedicated to giving a voice to immigrant family businesses and life stories of hope, family support, work, identity, integration, and a profound love for the adopted countries and communities that welcomed them, their families, and their businesses. A special thanks to my colleague and research partner at Columbia University, Paul Thurman, who generously gave us his business acumen and insights by authoring the introductory chapter of the book: "Why Today's Global Marketplace Cares about Good Governance in Immigrant Family Businesses". Paul, it is a privilege to work with you – and your amazing mind – and I look forward to our many future research collaborations and projects.

Chris and I owe a great debt of gratitude to the book's Managing Editor, Sylva Caracatsanis. Sylva is unfailing in her work ethic and her ability to handle our little editorial emergencies and remain calm and positive throughout this process. Sylva has been integral in managing all the editing details of the final manuscript and in coordinating the international network of professionals that made this book possible. Sylva, after 18 years of working together, you know you have a special place in our hearts always!

As always, many thanks to the fine team at Gower Publishing for their continued professionalism, support, and encouragement of our research work. The team at Gower believed in this project from the very beginning and supported it in every way possible.

Daphne Halkias,
Athens, Greece

I wish to express my sincere gratitude to Prof. Daphne Halkias and all those who have assisted us in the completion of this detailed study and book. Daphne is most probably one of the most acute and driven professionals that I've had the privilege to come across. As an intellectual her knowledge on any particular field is impeccable. At the same time, she has the warm heart of a giant. I would highly recommend anyone to get to know this special lady. Daphne, the difference that you bring to this world is greatly appreciated and noted.

This is a book of inspiring and important stories for anyone interested in making the world of immigrant entrepreneurship a better place. Whether you are a CEO, student or aspiring professional, this book provides a refreshing perspective on how and why entrepreneurs around the world are pioneering innovative business solutions to immigrant entrepreneurship. This book is also a response to the authors' perception that most research into immigrant family businesses has been based on a traditional, limited view of entrepreneurship that largely ignores the ethnic and family contexts that create the culture from which entrepreneurship emerges, making it impossible to understand the complex and interdependent relationships between an owning family, its firm, its governance, and the community context in which the firm operates.

Christian Adendorff,
Port Elizabeth, South Africa

Introduction:

Why Today's Global Marketplace Cares about Good Governance in Immigrant Family Businesses

PAUL W. THURMAN

Columbia University

"A family that prays together, stays together."

This timeless adage, often heard in the Southern Baptist church – and at the dinner table – of my youth, reminds many of us that if a group of people share and remind themselves of common goals, visions, and guiding principles, long-term unity, and, perhaps by extension, success and prosperity will follow. While certainly not as deterministic (or as pious) as it may sound, there is a growing body of evidence that supports the conclusion that well thought-out and well communicated goals, plans, and processes do help create more sustainable, peaceful, and prosperous family businesses ... especially those run by families living outside the countries of their birth.

This text comprises some of the best contemporary research and data to support this claim. By even the most conservative estimates, well over half of all businesses around the world are run by families ... and as labour and family mobility increase, so too does the likelihood that something you buy or a service you receive originates from a family business whose family comes from a place – and a culture, value set, and ethnography – very different from yours. Combine this "scope" effect with the broader trend of globalization, or "scale" effect, whereby larger firms increasingly turn to lower-cost local firms, producers, and services to complement or to augment existing capabilities and staff, and we observe a striking similarity between large multinational firms and much smaller, immigrant family businesses: successful planning, business controls, and effective governance are highly predictive of ongoing success.

This is a difficult paradox to accept, at first. "Big firms", with strategic planners, controllers, and auditors, and independent (we hope) corporate boards, tend to proliferate longer-term customer value, not to mention employee morale, retention, and returns to shareholder capital, if their plans, controls, and governance are world-class. This is true even with very large family-owned businesses in competitive markets; for example, the Tata Group in India and the Koch Companies in the United States.

However, to believe that the same might be true of very small family businesses – operating outside their countries of origin – seems to be a bit of a stretch. Very few small businesses – let alone immigrant family ones – have any "strategic plans", "management consultants", or "outside board members". And since these businesses are so small – and so tightly controlled by a family operating, in some cases, far away from their cultural norms and familial environments – would any planning or governance even be possible or helpful?

As it turns out, the answer is absolutely YES! As we will demonstrate in this compendium, we have discovered several examples – provided here as case studies – that exemplify the improved economic, familial, and even social returns that immigrant family businesses can embrace when equipped with even the most basic strategic planning/visioning, goal measurement, and (structured) governance. Immigrant family firms that use outside counsel, set clear(er) goals for growth and financial improvement, and that simply *write down* and *communicate* simple processes and longer-term goals – e.g. succession plans, partnerships/alliances with other, similar firms – create economic entities that last longer, live stronger, and serve customers more successfully.

So why does any of this matter? If my local grocer, who is not from the United States but whose family has a "plan" for how succession will take place or uses outside counsel and advice-givers to help his grocery make more money, do any of these things matter on the global stage?

A great deal!

As it turns out, not only do customers notice the difference, but so do larger firms, including firms that might partner with my grocer. His suppliers might give him better pricing, and if another grocer wants to expand through acquisition, chances are that the acquiring firm may be favourably impressed with these plans and offer a higher price for my grocer's location and customer base. (And his customer base is likely to be more loyal and "lifetime valued" too.)

Good business planning and governance by immigrant family businesses – even if, in MBA terms, it is rather elementary – does make a difference. And a family or firm doesn't need a global management consulting firm hired to help it, either. The value added is not just endogenous to the firm's family owners/mangers and customers, but can also extend to exogenous stakeholders such as potential business partners, shareholders, and even civic and community leaders. And that means the world cares about this. Good governance and planning create better firms – even small family-led ones. These firms serve customers and communities better. And when globalization comes calling, these firms and business partners are simply more attractive than those without any plans or management structure.

On behalf of the editors and contributors, I hope you enjoy the case studies and trendsetting research we have in this edited volume. I think you will find some interesting prototypes and business models that even the simplest, most basic immigrant family firms can adopt – and realize value from – rather quickly. And in that way, perhaps the family business that strives together, thrives together. That sounds like a good phrase for the family business dinner table any night.

Chapter 1

The Immigrant Family Business in Today's Global Marketplace

Even the most conservative estimates put the proportion of all worldwide business enterprises owned or managed by families between 65% and 90%. The economic importance of immigrant family businesses for the economies of both the developed world and developing national economies are well documented. What often goes unnoticed in the plethora of information within the area of Family Business is that immigrant family businesses are one of the most unique, complex, and dynamic systems in modern-day society. Immigrant family business has even been dubbed by researchers "the understudied entrepreneurial experience". And, today, even the social and economic phenomena that have been classically attached to immigrant family businesses, such as cutting off all ties with their native country, emigrating due only to conditions of poverty, immigrants lacking formal education and working mostly within ethnic enclaves, have changed dramatically in many countries hosting immigrant family businesses.

The development of today's global marketplace over the past decades has altered the traditional concept of immigrant entrepreneurship. If the concept of immigrant entrepreneurship brings to most people's minds the immigrant and his family boarding a boat for a vast voyage to an unknown universe known as a host country, the Internet has taken care of dissolving that reality. The traditional immigrant entrepreneur started a business in the host country as a means of survival – and usually never returning to the native land and cutting off all familial and cultural ties. Today, the concept of the immigrant entrepreneur is heterogeneous and refers not only to immigrant entrepreneurs in the traditional sense.

Today's immigrant entrepreneur, thanks to the ease of travel and telecommunications, maintains strong ties with social and cultural capital from the homeland. Many of this new breed of immigrant entrepreneurs start their business not because of the usual obstacles faced by immigrants in the host country, but because of a known business opportunity that can generate revenue in the host country and beyond its borders. And like never before, and a factor not to be overlooked by policy makers and economists alike, at least half of these immigrant entrepreneurial ventures throughout the world are headed by women. Both this new and multivariate type of immigrant entrepreneurship and the traditional immigrant entrepreneurship model still remain phenomena of great interest for policy makers, economists, entrepreneurs, and researchers.

The arrival of immigrants in economically developed societies has increased in the last two decades with the development of transport systems and improved communications. Due to reasons ranging from poverty and war to the worldwide recession, individuals decide to emigrate searching for a supposedly better economic situation; but many of them have serious difficulties entering the labour market. While some firms use immigrant labour because of the lower salaries, and in some cases because of professional qualifications, the immigrant labour market restricts the possibility of employment and the chances of being hired in certain sectors. That problem is exacerbated in times of economic recession in developed countries. As a consequence of factors like cultural baggage or previous experience, some individuals who decide to emigrate opt for entrepreneurship after identifying opportunities that are unexploited in the host societies and perceiving that they could generate high incomes.

In previous studies on immigrant entrepreneurial processes, availability of information is one of the resources with greatest impact on the success of new enterprises created by immigrants. In that regard, the immigrant entrepreneur has a bundle of knowledge stemming from the experience of the immigration process, in which the individual has been through international experiences and situations providing them with knowledge that differs from that of most native entrepreneurs.

Firstly, the immigrant entrepreneur has the knowledge that was accumulated in their country of origin up until emigration. Depending on the moment the individual decides to leave the home country, they may have to accumulate even more specific knowledge there. Thus, immigrants import experience, training and some contacts from their home country that could be useful in creating their own firm in the host country. In fact, on many occasions individuals consider that firm creation is the only valid option for application of that knowledge due to the possible barriers in the labour market. In many cases, immigrants have access to and knowledge of the markets or industries in their home countries, which enable them to establish commercial links and take advantage of international commercial networks. The establishment of such networks is usually a much more complicated task for native entrepreneurs should they wish to establish commercial relations with other countries.

Secondly, knowledge is also acquired by the individual in the host country and will be the result of their contact with the new territory and its inhabitants, culture, and institutions. One factor that is important to new venture creation by immigrants is the length of time that they have lived in the host country: that time is essential to learn and to obtain information and social resources. In other words, it is fundamental to accumulate experience in the host country in order to make the move into business. The necessary knowledge may be acquired without discounting other sources such as education or immigrant networks. Accordingly, the knowledge acquired in the host country will be key to the business expansion, with some authors stating that the firms owned by immigrants who restrict themselves to links with their ethnic community will not be able to expand. In fact, immigrants today find themselves in a more complicated situation when they wish to access a new market but do not have previous knowledge and experience. The immigrant entrepreneurs best adapted and integrated in the host country's society will have greater probabilities of being more competitive, and that is achieved by improving skills in the host country's language and social capital.

Finally, there is the knowledge acquired in the process of transition from one country to another. The individual may pass through a series of countries or regions before deciding to locate in the country where the new venture is ultimately established. The transition process would involve all the knowledge obtained in intermediate destinations between departure from the home country and arrival in the country where the firm is created. In that regard, knowing two or more countries and, therefore, different environments, will enable the individual to exploit their knowledge by applying it to the entrepreneurial activity through, for example, opportunity detection or management techniques.

The most common form of immigrant entrepreneurial activity is the known ethnic enclave where immigrants and immigrant businesses congregate. Some immigrants possess cultural capital or all the knowledge that, despite having been obtained in the host country, is a consequence of contact and relations with individuals from the entrepreneur's country of origin. Immigrant entrepreneurs' access to this information and knowledge is a result of their origins; therefore, despite being acquired in the home country, this knowledge may be considered to have been acquired at the intersection with the intermediate processes – in other words, results of the migration process (e.g. the knowledge of a compatriot supplier with lower prices).

The focus on the geographical origin of immigrants' knowledge introduces interesting perspectives to the analysis of successful firm creation by immigrants. By knowing two different realities, immigrants possess knowledge of their home countries' industry and markets, which represents an advantage that can be commercially exploited on the strength of the contacts and information acquired in the host country. There is also a knowledge acquired in the host country that is later used in the home country in sectors such as tourism. This has been evidenced in the case of Turkish-German entrepreneurs who know the likes and preferences of the German origin market and so can successfully serve those tourists. To that end, many of today's immigrant entrepreneurs seek to bring their business skills and plans for entrepreneurial expansion to the global marketplace. And, they use their greatest social capital, families in their home countries and the social networks between the two countries, to build transnational entrepreneurial activities.

The blending of two inherently different realms – the performance-based world of business and the emotion-based domain of the immigrant family – creates a system potentially fraught with confusion and conflict. Years of research has pointed to a direct link between good governance and the prosperity and survival of all business entities over the long term. Immigrant family businesses are not an exception and certainly not today as many seek to bring their enterprise activity into the global market place. A complicating factor of the immigrant family business, whether remaining local or going global, is that the relative importance of the immigrant family in different societies varies across cultures and, therefore, one can conclude that the definition of the term immigrant family business is culture-specific. When discussing managerial practices, the field of international management often neglects specific aspects of culture in favour of a more easily defined, and less theoretically precise, parameter denoted by geopolitical boundaries.

Given the dominance of immigrant family businesses in so many national economies all over the world, their poor survival rate is a continuing source of concern. As little as three out of 10 immigrant family businesses survive into the second generation, and less than 15% survive into the third generation. A major factor in the poor survival rate of immigrant family businesses is poor governance. Within the small business sector in general and the immigrant family business sector in particular, the link between longevity and good governance is complicated by two additional factors. The first is the failure to realize that the specific operating characteristics of an immigrant family business can be a source of persistent business problems, missed opportunities, and unnecessary risks that could and should be avoided. Failure by the members of an immigrant family business to acknowledge the unique characteristics of their business could similarly have severe and lasting adverse consequences for the business. In order to allow an immigrant family business to make its rightful contribution to any country's economy or beyond to the global marketplace, it must be acknowledged that its unique nature will impact on its corporate governance and thus on its survival.

The second complicating factor is the reality that corporate governance cannot be "standardized" for all ethnic groupings that function in an economy. The way in which corporate governance is implemented has been shown to be affected by ethnic and cultural influences. Despite the acknowledgement by some authors that ethnic and cultural influences impact on immigrant family businesses, few studies have been carried out to explore the relationship between cultural influence in immigrant family businesses and its impact on corporate governance and thus ultimately on their survival and contribution to any national and international economic prosperity.

Certainly, no empirical study has been done to investigate how leveraging entrepreneurship, culture, and family dynamics contributes to governance and sustainability of the immigrant family business in today's global marketplace. This applied research book specifically addresses the aforementioned not only through ideas and business models, but also through real-life case studies of immigrant family businesses thriving in today's economies – whether they are in an ethnic enclave or have expanded beyond the host country's borders. A study of corporate governance and sustainability of this nature is of particular importance if one considers the economic influence of immigrant families in the world's economy. Therefore, the basic underlying premise of the study is that once the factors that could enhance good governance and sustainability have been identified, immigrant entrepreneurs can proceed to the effective management of governance to ensure that their family businesses can optimize their critically important contribution to the global economy.

As a significant component of the international economy, one would expect that there would be extensive debate, analysis, and attention centred on immigrant family businesses. The incongruous reality is that this sector has been largely overlooked and ignored by economists, policy makers, educators, academics, and global market commentators alike. Against this background and the economic significance of the topic, this applied research book will bring to light much needed, new scholarly and practical knowledge on how entrepreneurship, culture, and family dynamics influence the development of good governance and sustainability in immigrant family businesses.

Case Study:
The al-Awadhi Brothers:
The Story of Two Emirati Entrepreneurs

Maryam Khazaeli, Mary Barrett

For centuries, families of transnational Sunni Arabs, or Persians both Sunni and Shiite, have migrated from southern Iran to the Arab coast of the Persian Gulf. In fact, Iranian groups living on the coast of the Persian Gulf have generally looked more to the United Arab Emirates (UAE) than to Iranian groups inland (Potter, 2009). They have maintained a "dual existence", owning houses in two or more countries and speaking multiple languages (Nadjmabadi, 2010). This has been a source of economic benefit to both Iran and the UAE, at least until the recent political unrest in the region. Many Iranians and Emirati citizens of Iranian origin in Dubai and other UAE cities come from towns in the department (*shahrestân*) known as Larestan, and from towns in the Iranian province of Hormozgân. These populations are generally called Larestani, from the name of the region, or by the name of their town of origin: Evazi, Khonji, Bastaki, etc. In the UAE they are also described by the interchangeable Farsi terms: *Khodmooni* and *Achami*; the former means "of our own kind", or in a broader sense "those familiar to us". These Farsi terms emerged in the Arab areas of the Persian Gulf and show the strong mutual attachment of Larestani transnational immigrant families and UAE native families.

The Larestani's shipping skills and access to the lucrative markets of Africa and Asia have strongly shaped Dubai's economy (Davidson, 2008). By around 1900, Dubai had become the most attractive business environment in the region and accordingly benefited from a stream of skilled migrant business people from the unstable Persian coast. This UAE tradition of welcoming entrepreneurs long predates its oil exports (Davidson, 2008). Also around 1900, around 30 of the most adaptable of the immigrant Iranian family businesses in Dubai slowly developed to become global conglomerates (Jaidah, 2008).

Two brothers, Mohamed Parham al-Awadhi and Payman Parham al-Awadhi, are descendants of the entrepreneurs who travelled and traded across the Persian Gulf. The story of the business they created in 2010, Wild Peeta, shows how the family, a primary element of the UAE's collective culture, has evolved to encompass online networks. The brothers developed a gourmet *shawarma*, transforming this local Levantine dish into an international business. A *shawarma* consists of lamb, goat, chicken, beef, or mixed meats that are grilled on a spit then wrapped in pita bread. The brothers also founded Qabeela New Media, the first UAE example of a new genre of social TV.

Mohamed, aged 38, who speaks five languages and has travelled worldwide, attributes his interest and talent in business to his family origins: "I come from a line of entrepreneurs. My great grandparents were Bedouins and travellers. My grandfather had a trading business in commodities, sugar, and food. He used to trade across the Gulf, particularly the UAE, Iran, and India."

After a successful management career at an Emirati bank, Mohamed's father started his own business. Mohamed explains how it influenced the brothers' early business learning:

My father opened up the Hello Kitty stores in the Middle East. Any vacation we had he made us work with him in his shop in Bazaar, Old Souq. My vacation memories are of getting up in the morning and walking to the Bazaar and walking back to the house in the afternoon. We grew up in that business environment though we did not get paid. We did everything and learnt a lot about business concepts in practice. From a very young age we learned how to take responsibility and it was built into us to do business.

The business idea that the brothers developed also came from their family origins. As Mohamed says: "My father started making us food from the dishes he had experienced in different countries. That is how we were exposed to international cuisine."

After studying business in the United States the brothers came home and started working in the family business. However, this only lasted two years before the brothers felt the need to start their own business careers, despite the fact that their father would be displeased, their lack of experience in other areas, and the preference among international companies to employ non-Emiratis:

We had our own identity and our own ideas about strategy in the family business. But we were under my father's rule. It was his way of doing things and it was the way he did it for years. We got to a point where we asked ourselves: "What is our potential? Is it limited to working in a small family business?" That was when we started working for multinational companies. At that time every company was looking for Western nationalities, not Emiratis. I persisted until I found a job in a Dutch medical company. I did not know anything about it except marketing, which I had graduated in.

Mohamed describes how 10 years of working with international companies in different industries helped them understand big, sophisticated retailing firms in the Middle East: "We wanted to learn from hundred-year-old companies and the systems they have. How they developed over time into the way they are now ...."

It also taught them the courage and discipline needed for entrepreneurship: "We had difficult times. But that gave us not fearlessness but this attitude that you shouldn't give up. When you fail you will learn and you move up."

Their international experience and their childhood memories led them to a new vision of the humble *shawarma*:

When we walked back from my father's shop in Old Souq, we used to pass a very small shawarma *shop. It was a big part of our childhood. We started writing our business plan using everything we had learnt while working in our family business and from those big brands and international companies we worked in.*

They spent eight or nine tough years working on their business plan for Wild Peeta:

We talked to banks, family members, and friends. They either said it is not going to work or it is too risky. We did not have the money to start our company. Nobody believed in us. We were just two guys who had this silly idea of making a business out of shawarma.

Government support finally helped Mohamed and Payman get their business plan approved. Afterwards they still had to compete for retail space in the shopping malls that have replaced the *souqs* of 40 years ago:

None of the malls returned our calls. Or if they did, they said: "It is [just] a local Emirati brand; you don't have any international franchises." But we had great support from our followers on social media. Whenever we asked for help getting information they supported us.

Guided by their trader grandparents' entrepreneurial spirit, the brothers aimed to create a brand, not just sell *shawarmas*. At the time of writing, Wild Peeta had 10,000 followers on Twitter and Facebook, updating the traditional *souq* into an online customer community that give the brothers regular feedback. This sense of community also originated in their family business. Mohamed recalls a board meeting in the U.S. where every member enjoyed talking to his father, not just about business but about everything. "Business happens through relationships", Mohamed says. "Making relationships with customers is rooted in Arab business culture." Nevertheless, the brothers are astonished that Wild Peeta is among the UAE's top five social media brands:

We set up Facebook and Twitter accounts when we started the business. We were just going to use them to talk about the journey of two Emirati brothers starting their crazy shawarma place in Dubai and the experiences we went through. People started to follow us on Twitter.

Although UAE residents comprise more than 85% expatriates, there are few opportunities for them to build relationships with Emirati nationals. Wild Peeta fills this gap through its social media presence, "Open Space at Wild Peeta". This in turn develops the business:

Wild Peeta and its customers meet online on Twitter and Facebook and offline at Wild Peeta. Wild Peeta has become a focal point, a place to meet. Social media helped us a lot as we grew and grew and grew. We call the customers "our family". They are lawyers, students, teachers, CEOs, or mothers – all sorts of people but they are connected. This is the privilege of Wild Peeta – that it connects people.

Wild Peeta shows how the entrepreneurial spirit of earlier generations survives in two individuals who value the collective culture of family business. This entrepreneurial attitude is vital to the Gulf countries, which have few other resources. As Mohamed says:

The Gulf [Arab] countries are very young countries and there is no history of industry. Very few things were produced here. It was all imported; the Gulf was a trading hub for importing and exporting, as our grandparents did. Now it is time to change and evolve.

Mohamed does not aim to transfer his business to the next generation in his family. Nevertheless, he is helping the current generation develop as entrepreneurs, just as his grandfathers did with him:

We spend a lot of our time with future entrepreneurs, whether at the university or with people actually starting up a business. Any experience or information we have we pass it to them, whether in marketing or logistics or finance.

The entrepreneurial spirit of Mohamed and Payman's forebears appears to be in good shape.

Additional Reading

Davidson, M.C. 2008. *Dubai: The Vulnerability of Success*. New York: Columbia University Press.

Jaidah, M.J. 2008. Explaining Multi-Generation Family Business Success in the Gulf States. Dissertation, Harvard University, Proquest dissertations database [accessed 29 September 2012].

Nadjmabadi, S.R. 2010. Labour Migration from Iran to the Arab Countries of the Persian Gulf. *Anthropology of the Middle East*, 5(1): 18–33.

Potter, L.G. 2009. *The Persian Gulf in History*. New York: Palgrave Macmillan.

Chapter 2
The Family and the Business

Given the relative importance of family businesses in South Africa in general, as well as the considerable influence of South African-Greek family businesses in particular, the absence of empirical evidence on the relationship between cultural influences and good governance presents an important gap in the family business literature. This chapter addresses these limitations by identifying the factors that influence the family business. Once these factors have been identified, one can proceed to the effective management of governance for family businesses, to ensure that these entities optimize their critically important contribution to the South African economy.

The ownership of businesses can be divided into two broad categories, namely family-owned and non-family-owned businesses. Family businesses are a dominant form of business, and the reason why family businesses are of interest to researchers is that there is a possibility that their ownership and control structures have an effect on the way they are managed. Family businesses are different from other businesses because ownership and control of the business interests infringe on family interests, and hence conflicts occur quite often as the business and family strive to realize different objectives. As Daily and Dollinger (1991) noted, the family and business systems are not necessarily compatible; their interaction can be thought of as a built-in Achilles heel.

Researchers spanning the past five decades concur with this view and point out that possible conflicts in family businesses arise when managerial decisions are influenced by feelings about, and responsibilities towards, relatives in the business, when nepotism exerts a negative influence. Conflict also arises when a company is run more to honour a family tradition than for its own needs and purposes. Under these circumstances there is likely to be turmoil. Recognition of these circumstances may help researchers understand why many Western family businesses cease to exist after 10 years, and why only three out of 10 survive into the second generation, while less than 15% survive into the third generation. Studies also provide further insight into the reasons for failure, by pointing out that conflicts amongst family members within a family business tend to be circular and last over a long period of time because of the interaction between relationships in the workplace. In other words, a particular family conflict can impact on a subsequent business decision that, in turn, creates new sources of differences within the family.

This chapter offers a discussion of the family business, and explores its economic importance in an international context. Discussions on the structures of family business relationships are followed by the various conceptual models used to develop an understanding of the nature of family businesses and other businesses, problems facing the family business, and family business life cycles.

Defining the Family Business

Any attempt to define the family business must account for a range of configurations as well as for the factors that distinguish it from other organizations. The degree of family members' involvement in the business can range from ownership of shares to full participation in management, or somewhere in between. These factors contribute to the complexity in defining the term "family business". This definition adds another dimension to the search for a satisfactory definition. With the influence of family members comes the involvement of the attitudes of family members towards the issue of succession. Once attitudes and values are brought to the fore, it is necessary to consider the cultural context within which the family business operates. Could the very definition of what constitutes a family business be culture-specific? If a family business is defined from the perspective of the business as central, with the family as an adjunct, then it implies that the involvement of family members will not be high, and therefore attitudes and values are not a prominent influence. On the other hand, if a family business is defined from the perspective where the family is central, with the business as an adjunct, a different scenario arises.

The importance of the family in family business operations implies that family members will have substantial influence, and therefore attitudes and values become important in defining the family business. The relative importance of the family in different societies varies across cultures and, therefore, one can conclude that the definition of the term family business is *culture-specific*. It is not surprising that attempting to define the term family business can quickly become a very complicated exercise. While it appears that academics are unable to reach consensus as to its definition, there are nevertheless commonalities among most of the definitions found in the literature. These definitions generally tend to focus on ownership and/or control of the business by the family. The proposed definitions seem to suggest that the primary focus of family businesses is business and the way in which it is related to the family; the business is central and the family is an adjunct. A good example of this emphasis of business over family is Holland and Boulton's (1984) view of the family–business relationship. They studied internal and external coalition and relationships and their effects on decision making in family businesses. Using the phrases "internal" to the business, and "external" to the business, the researchers noted that the problem of managing this relationship has to do with managing both external (managing stakeholder relationships) and internal coalitions (organizational politics). The perspective is again taken from the business's point of view, confirming the point that the family business is a business with the family involved.

In an extensive review of family business literature, Chua, Chrisman, and Sharma (1999) compiled a list of 21 definitions that touch on the degree or nature of family involvement. Several observations can be made about these definitions. First, with few exceptions, the definitions do not differentiate between governance and management. Second, some require controlling ownership or family management alone, while others require both ownership and management. Thus, the definitions include three qualified combinations of ownership and management. These are:

a)   family owned and family managed;

b)   family owned but not family managed;

c)   family managed but not family owned.

All the definitions consider combination (A) to be a family business. There is disagreement, however, on the other two combinations, although most authors seem to prefer combination (B) to (C).

Third, while some definitions do not require family ownership, those that do imply controlling ownership, although they differ with respect to the acceptable patterns of controlling ownership. The list of controlling owners includes:

• an individual;

• two persons, unrelated by blood or marriage;

- two persons, related by blood or marriage;

- a nuclear family;

- more than one nuclear family;

- an extended family;

- more than one extended family;

- the public.

The definitions that are based on family ownership unanimously consider ownership by a nuclear family to be a prerequisite. They disagree, however, about all the other aspects – especially the last one, public ownership.

In summary, there appears to be total agreement that a business owned and managed by a nuclear family is a family business. Once one deviates from that particular combination of ownership pattern and management involvement, researchers hold different opinions. A definition of a family business must stipulate its uniqueness, which begs the question: What is this uniqueness? It is not the fact that the members of the family own and/or manage a business. Research has suggested that a family business is unique according to patterns of ownership, management, governance, and succession influencing a business's goals, structure, strategies, and the manner in which these are formulated, designed, and implemented.

In other words, scholars study family businesses because they believe that the family component shapes the business in a way that the family members or executives in non-family businesses do not and cannot. To illustrate this family component, one has to extend the debate on family business definitions to ownership and management, and sometimes to succession. Clearly, a business owned and managed by a nuclear family is a family business. By necessity, it will be operated with the intention of pursuing a desired future for the family in accordance with their values and preferences. Family dynamics will affect decisions and actions, and those decisions and actions will assuredly be different from the business that is not influenced by either family ownership or family management.

One needs to consider, for instance, businesses that are family owned but not family managed, or family managed but not family owned. Some of these businesses will behave in a fashion that is markedly similar to that of a business owned and managed by a nuclear family, and some will not. As a consequence, researchers might conclude that some of these businesses are family businesses and some are not. If researchers defined family businesses as only those that are family owned and managed, they would be excluding many businesses that are in fact family businesses. On the other hand, if researchers included as family businesses all businesses that are either family owned but not family managed, or family managed but not family owned they would be including many businesses that do not belong to either group. How can we tell when ownership or management by a family makes the firm a family business? A business wholly owned by a family may be treated as being at one end of the spectrum. At the other end, a family-managed but not family-owned business may be operated predominantly to pursue the aspirations of the family managing the business with corresponding benefits for that family, or it may be operated for the benefit of unrelated shareholders. Certain researchers further argue that there are no clear-cut demarcations on how much ownership or management is necessary to qualify the business as a family business. Should it be complete ownership, majority ownership, or controlling ownership? The presence or absence of a successor offers no better solution to this difficulty.

There must be a primary theoretical imperative that makes the study of family business as a unique type of organization worthwhile. If not, there is no need for differentiation from the study of other types of business. Therefore, any attempt to define a family business must start at the theoretical level and distinguish between two types of definitions: theoretical and operational. A theoretical definition should distinguish one entity or phenomenon from another, based on a conceptual foundation of how the entity, object, or phenomenon is different, and why the differences matter. An operational definition, on the other hand, merely identifies the observable and measurable characteristics that differentiate the entity, object, or phenomenon from others. For example, in the field of strategic management, differences in business strategy are theoretically defined as the varying characteristics of the match that each organization achieves or intends to achieve between its internal resources and environmental opportunities, with the belief that the nature of this match affects organizational performance. Operationally, however, differences in organizational strategies are defined by using the components of strategy, such as competitive weapons and scope, investment intensity, growth vectors, segment differentiation, and functional policies. Both types of definitions are needed to justify the study of family businesses. The theoretical definition sets the paradigm for the field of study and the standards against which the efficacy of an operational one must be measured. Without a theoretical definition and the rationale for it, there is no standard for determining the validity of any operational definition used by researchers, and such a definition becomes a matter of convenience. On the other hand, without an operational definition, the theoretical definition cannot be applied. Continuing the example, the literature on strategic management suggests that the components by which strategy has been operationalized are valid because they are a reliable means of identifying essential differences in organizational strategies, and they empirically explain why there are differences in organizational performance.

Differences between Family and Non-family Businesses

A number of studies have explored family businesses in isolation, but very few comparative studies of family and non-family businesses have been conducted. It is now apparent, however, that there is a need for more comparative studies in order to understand the differences between family and non-family businesses, as well as the relationship between the management and performance of family versus non-family businesses. Comparative studies of family and non-family businesses have generally failed to appreciate that business demographics can distort bivariate studies exploring the relationship between the management and the performance of these two groups of businesses. Previous studies focusing on the management and performance of family and non-family businesses may have identified "demographic sample" differences rather than "real" differences. Business size can be "stunted/retarded" if a family management team is reluctant to raise external funds because it fears it will entail a loss of family control – for example, by the appointment of a "stranger" to the board. Some family businesses also operate "income substitution" businesses on the sideline, with no plans to grow in size. As a result, some family businesses only grow at a pace consistent with meeting the advancement needs of organizational members in the family system.

Donckels and Frohlich (1991), in their study of small independent manufacturing businesses, noted that the highest numbers of shares owned by members of family businesses were found in the smallest employment size groups. Cromie, Stephenson, and Monteith (1995), in their study of family and non-family companies in Ireland, also found that family businesses were smaller in terms of employment and sales turnover than non-family businesses. Conversely, in the United Kingdom, Stoy Hayward (1992) found no major differences in either employment or sales revenue size between family and non-family companies. Morris et al. (1997) identified several differences between family-owned and family-managed businesses and non-family-controlled businesses. Some of the differences identified by Venter (2002) include the fact that a professional manager in a business that is not family controlled may be expected to rely on shorter time horizons, to be less personally impacted by business failure, to demonstrate more career mobility, to be motivated more by traditional personal reward, and to perceive less job security than the family members who run a family business. She also pointed out that businesses that are family controlled frequently have more centralized decision-making processes, and control systems that are less formalized, although this centralization usually changes from generation to generation. The position of a family member in the family business will influence their position in the family. Those who are respected in the business are generally also well respected by their family members. As a consequence, personal family issues will often co-mingle with business issues, affecting decision-making processes in family businesses (Venter, 2002).

Various other studies have attempted to contrast the differences between family and non-family businesses with regard to, for example, strategic behaviour, management and ownership imperatives, customer services, organizational buyer behaviour, successor development, management of human resources, business-related goals, sectors, venture capital, and attributes of owners/managers.

Unique Characteristics of Family Businesses

Family businesses make major contributions to wealth creation, job generation, and competitiveness. Several studies on Western economies have concluded that family firms account for over two thirds of all businesses. Throughout the world, studies on the United States of America (USA) have revealed that family firms generate from 40% to 60% of the gross national product (GNP).

Family businesses are an important subject for study considering that:

- the majority of independent businesses is family owned;

- the prioritizing of objectives by family business owners is likely to differ from that of owners of non-family businesses;

- family businesses are likely to be managed differently to non-family businesses;

- owners of family businesses are more likely to be concerned with transferring the business to the next generation of family members. The fiscal regime (i.e. inheritance and capital gains tax) is, therefore, of particular concern to owners of family businesses;

- to encourage competitiveness, wealth creation, and job generation, policy makers would like to know whether family businesses perform better or worse than non-family businesses. In some instances, policy makers may consider that it is appropriate to provide special support that will encourage the survival and development of family businesses.

Every unique attribute of the family business could be a source of both benefit and disadvantage to the owners, family members employed in the business, and non-family employees. Researchers label these attributes "bivalent", maintaining that the family business's success or failure depends on how well these attributes are managed. For example, the attribute of emotional involvement and ambivalence in family businesses can be an advantage in that the expression of positive feelings creates loyalty and promotes trust among family members. On the other hand, this can be a disadvantage if there is a lack of objectivity in communication, and if resentment and guilt complicate work interaction, and covert hostility develops. The advantages of family businesses have been represented primarily in a descriptive fashion, with broad theoretical and anecdotal support that cuts across traditional academic principles. A review of the literature substantiates this descriptive emphasis on the unique characteristics of family businesses and the potential they have for competitive advantage and superior performance due to the following:

- Many family businesses are less bureaucratic and less impersonal than other types of businesses. In a family-controlled business, responsibilities are usually clearly defined and the decision-making process is deliberately restricted to one or two key individuals;

- Key elements of characteristics of family businesses include trust, shared values, shared vision, determination of family members in difficult times, opportunities for personal growth, social advancement, job security and autonomy, and absence of external interference and commitments of shareholders. Family businesses also have greater independence of action, in the sense that they might have less or no takeover risk;

- Commitment and a stable culture underpin the fact that family businesses are generally very solid and reliable structures, and are generally perceived as such in the marketplace;

- Family businesses draw special strength from the shared history, identity, and common language of families. When the key managers are relatives, their traditions, values, and priorities spring from a common source, and such a family culture often serves as a great source of pride;

- Flexibility in time, work, and money may lead to a competitive advantage for family businesses. They can adapt quickly and easily to changing circumstances;

- The overriding characteristic that distinguishes most family businesses is their unique atmosphere, which creates a sense of belonging, enhancing the common purpose among the workforce;

- Knowledge handed down from generation to generation (succession), starting in very early youth, is an important strength of family businesses;

- Enthusiasm and family commitment may also develop commitment and loyalty among the workforce;

- Family owners/managers may have a different outlook than that of their employees, their customers, the community, and other important stakeholders, which may positively affect the quality of their product.

Structures of Family Business Relationships

Family businesses exist as an institution; the organization as it is named and identified could range from a small "mom-and-pop" firm to a multinational business. The ownership structure can also vary. Some researchers prefer to consider a family business as an institution, in an evolutionary context, by describing family businesses in terms of four structural phases, from entrepreneurial to post-family relationships, as illustrated in Table 2.1.

Table 2.1   Structures of the family-business relationship

Structure (Stages)	Initiated by	Relationship characterized by	Focus on relationship
I. Pre-family	Founding of business	Concentration of power in single individual	Survival, succession
II. Family	Entry of relative of founder or sole owner/manager into management and/or ownership	Power dispersed among several individuals based on family connection	Resource acquisition
III. Adaptive Family	Sale of stock to non-family members	Power based on management position and stock ownership	Performance
IV. Post-family	Liquidation of family stock holdings	Power based on ability to function in the new organization	Adjustments

Source: Holland and Boulton (1984: 17).

It could be deduced from Table 2.1 that the focus of the family business is on the start-up of a business, and only over time does this business evolve into a family business. At the pre-family stage, although the motive of setting up a family business may exist in the entrepreneur's mind it is "technically" not a family business until Stage II.

Research provides an explanation as to how family business in society came into being, by considering the motivating factors of individuals. The argument is that providing for one's family and being connected to them financially as well as emotionally is a major motivating factor for many adults. There can hardly be a better way to encompass one's personal goals and one's need for stature and accomplishment, and to shoulder responsibility for "earning a living" than to intertwine one's career aspirations with seemingly like-minded relatives who comprise the family system, and then by setting up a family business. In essence, at the pre-family stage, the issues for business are no different from the early stages of any other corporation. The concern, for the purpose of this study, arises when the business is seen to be a family business.

Figure 2.1 (based on Table 2.1) illustrates the manner, implied in the literature, in which a business evolves into a family business. Initially, the business is a start-up, and therefore is in the pre-family stage. Over time, family members become involved in the business at various levels. Once this occurs, it becomes a family business, and the issue of succession will increase in relevance as the incumbent leader of the business ages (Neubauer and Lank, 1998).

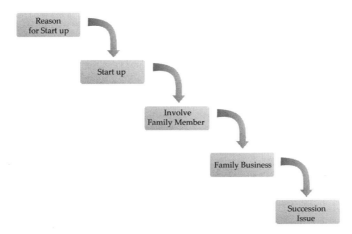

Figure 2.1   From start-up to family business to succession
Source: Researcher's own construction.

While it may seem relatively straightforward that once family members (other than the entrepreneur) are involved, a business is defined as a family business, the task of definition is complicated because each of the dimensions used to distinguish the family business from other types of organizations are not easily identified. Therefore any attempt at defining the family business must account for this range of developmental configurations as well as the factors that distinguish it from other organizations. There is also the matter of the degree of family members' involvement in the business, ranging from ownership of shares to full participation in management. All these elements contribute to the complexity of defining and understanding the term "family business". Given the close involvement of family members, the attitudes of family members towards all aspects of the family business must be considered.

In order to gain further understanding of family business and its definitions, it is logical to gain a better understanding of the importance of family businesses.

Importance of Family Businesses

Even the most conservative estimates put the proportion of all worldwide business enterprises owned or managed by families at between 65% and 90%. Their influence, as well as their numbers, can be expected to increase substantially in the future. Possible reasons for the growing importance are the ongoing rationalization of large businesses, as well as the well documented inability of the formal sector to create new jobs. Finally, and most importantly, family businesses offer powerful opportunities for economic and social empowerment in communities across the world. Internationally, the overwhelming majority of these family businesses are small or medium-sized and they remain among the most important contributors to wealth and employment in virtually every country. For this reason it is important that more care be taken by public policy makers everywhere to ensure the health, prosperity, and longevity of this type of business. Considering that family businesses are such a vital component of the global economy, one would expect that the family business sector would be the focus of extensive debate, analysis, and attention. The reality is that this sector has been largely ignored by academics and economic commentators alike in most nations.

The key difference between family businesses and other major forms of economic organization is that the business affairs of a family business are closely and intricately intertwined with the personal financial affairs of the family, and also with the power relationships, blood ties, emotional bonds, and inheritance issues within the family. Failure to understand the specific operating characteristics of a family business can be the source of persistent (business) problems, missed opportunities, and unnecessary risks that could and should have been avoided. At the same time, failure by the members of a family business to acknowledge the unique characteristics of their business could similarly have severe and lasting adverse consequences inside the business.

Research on family businesses has generally focused on experiences in the USA or, more broadly, the Western world. To study and understand the complex phenomenon of family businesses requires a multidisciplinary and cross-cultural approach. The complexity itself first stems from the nature of business. It is generally acknowledged that doing business at the beginning of the 21st century is much more complex than it was only a few decades ago. Problems include restricted resources (human resources, finances, market possibilities), a specific form of organization that often has its own unique approach to management, inadequate focus on long-term policies, vulnerability to factors in the immediate environment (government and financial institutions, interest groups), difficulty in raising outside capital, economic problems, lack of aid, state and local taxes, and recruiting and retaining properly qualified and responsible workers. In addition to all these factors, the familial character of family businesses adds to its complexity. Family businesses have been described as unique and challenging social organizations with unique characteristics that should be acknowledged by members, advisers, and researchers. These special characteristics will be discussed in the remainder of this chapter. Without a proper understanding of the special nature and characteristics of the family business sector, its potential to create economic growth and prosperity in local and regional communities cross-nationally cannot be realized.

The formation and growth of new firms is a complex process, and many factors associated with this process can only be identified by in-depth investigation at the micro-level of a new firm and its new founder(s). A wide range of models has been proposed to explain why businesses are formed. One model, presented by Gibb and Ritchie (1982), suggests that business start-ups can be understood in terms of the situations people encounter and the social groups to which the new business founders relate. This approach stresses the differential importance of various social influences at significant points in the individual's life cycle on the start-up process. This approach, like the trait approach, in which venture initiators are born, not made (McClelland, 1961; Brockhaus, 1980, 1982), the psychodynamic models (Kets de Vries, 1977) associated with social marginality (Stanworth and Curran, 1973; Scase and Goffee, 1980, 1982), and the person variable approach (Chell, 1985), which uses Mischel's (1973) cognitive social learning variable, are not without their limitations. A common thread throughout these models is the importance of the reasons leading to business start-ups.

There has been a tendency among researchers to develop universal theories. However, many researchers believe that they must break away from this framework, particularly in studying new business formation, because of the complexity of the venture initiation process. For example, researchers should consider differences in the characteristics of the individuals who start the ventures, the organizations that they create, the environment surrounding the new venture, and the process by which the new venture is started. Carsrud, Gaglio, and Olm (1986) suggested a model that examines the interaction between psychological, personal, demographic, organizational, and situation/environmental variables in the venture-creation process. Since the problems of studying business formation are exacerbated when one examines the reasons for new business formation across national boundaries, there is further reason to employ conditional explanations.

Problems Facing the Family Business

Although family businesses are the subject of considerable interest in the USA, comparatively few studies have explored the nature and scale of family business activity elsewhere. Research in the United Kingdom, for example, has been conducted principally by historians. Detailed company histories of family businesses have been conducted, as well as wider overviews of the role played by family businesses in Victorian Britain. The issues facing contemporary family businesses in the United Kingdom have usually attracted research attention from sociologists rather than academics in business-related disciplines. Research on the scale, nature, and economic contributions of contemporary family business activity remains surprisingly limited in Africa, Europe, and the United Kingdom. Yet policy makers worldwide need to know whether they should attempt to encourage the survival and development of family firms.

The business survival issue and the intergenerational transfer of businesses between family members are recognized by researchers as the most prominent areas of concern to family business survival. Smaller family businesses are especially vulnerable, as often the expectation is that they will survive only five to 10 years. The social cost of this high failure rate contributes to the negative social and economic growth in many countries. The liquidation of a family business constitutes a loss not only to the proprietary family, which often has most of its assets tied up in the business, but also to the employees and surrounding community, whose economic well-being may depend on the survival of the business. The fact that very few family businesses survive beyond the first generation is therefore a universal phenomenon, independent of cultural context or economic/business environment.

Many factors contribute to the high failure rate or lack of longevity of family businesses. Family businesses are the most complex form of business organization, because the dimension of "family" is added to the common governance role of a typical corporation, namely the owner, management/ employees, and the board of directors (if there is one). This duality significantly increases the complexity and the number of roles to be managed. The increased complexity in roles created by the added dimension of family in business is a perceptual source of conflict.

Important issues and the problems faced by a family business have been noted by researchers as follows:

- succession from one generation to the next and the associated change of leadership;

- leadership is seen as a drawback;

- the hardworking entrepreneur often does not have time to devote to his family;

- ineffective communication might be an important obstacle in family businesses operating effectively;

- external issues facing family businesses include increased international competition, the inability to adjust to market needs and wants, the negative impact of inheritance taxes, relationships with unions, and constantly changing governmental policies;

- the issue of internal conflict in family businesses. Decades of research has concurred that the successful management of conflict is important to the success of a family business.

The Developmental Nature of the Family Business

To ensure its long-term survival, a family business must prepare itself for the personal and organizational development tasks it will face in the future by considering people, families, and businesses as dynamic entities undergoing clinical processes of birth, growth, and decline. These life cycles were developed in the literature from individual physiology, organizational theory, and family business theory. The challenge remains to find ways of clearly describing the complex evolutionary patterns of human organizations in general, and family business in particular, because the governance of a family business should be guided by its position in the evolutionary life cycle.

Hershon (1975) was one of the first researchers to take a multigenerational perspective on the family business life cycle, rather than focusing on what transpires during the tenure of the founder or a single owner/manager. He proposed a two-dimensional graph that explicitly links the progress of a family through three generations (the management succession axis) and normatively suggests appropriate management styles or "patterns" (the organization development axis) for each stage in the evolution of the family business. A similar model was developed by Benson, Crego, and Drucker (1990). McGivern's model (1978, 1989), which was based on that of Kroeger (1974), proposed that there is a bridge between the organizational life cycle models and family business succession, and provides valuable insight into the management of succession in small family businesses. Other business developmental models have been proposed by Goldberg (1991), Handelsman (1996), Leach (1994), and Neubauer and Lank (1998).

Organizational life cycle models generally assume that the organization will outgrow the managerial capabilities of the founding entrepreneur, and evolve in such a manner that ownership and management become separated. Such models typically ignore issues of succession, and fail to consider the distinct nuances inherent in family-owned and family-managed businesses. Dyer (1986) developed a four-phase model that describes stages in the family business life cycle. The four phases are: creating the business (when market success and business survival are central); growth and development (when estate planning and the distribution of ownership and assets are major tasks); succession to the second generation (when conflict between business elements and family elements is characteristic); and public ownership and professional management (when the family business transitions into professional management and ceases to have the distinctive character of a family business). Researchers point out that the most useful models are those whose stage descriptions promote better understanding of the current state of the family, the ownership of the business, and the business itself. To make a useful contribution, models should predict both the transitional and the next-stage challenges that have to be faced, and should suggest steps that could be taken to minimize future disruptions.

The next two models to be described were developed by Ward (1988, 1991). The first conceptualization proposed by Ward (1988) specifies three different life cycles, namely the business life cycle, the organizational life cycle, and the business owner's life cycle. Ward (1988) believed that various "forces" influence the passage of the family business through various predictable patterns of growth and change. Among these forces are the following:

- the nature of the business (type of product, its stage in the life cycle, competitive and market conditions);

- the character of the organization (size, complexity, speed of change);

- the motivation of the owner/manager (their major focus);

- family financial expectations (the evolution of its needs);

- family goals (its major focus).

Ward's (1988) model (see Table 2.2) gives three stages of growth in the life cycle of a family business, namely

- Stage I: early;

- Stage II: middle;

- Stage III: late.

Table 2.2   Evolutionary stages of a family business

	Stage I	**Stage II**	**Stage III**
Age of business (or business renewal)	0–5 years	10–20 years	20–30 years
Age of parents	25–35 years	40–50 years	55–70 years
Age of children	0–10 years	15–25 years	30–45 years
Challenges:			
Nature of business	Rapidly growing and demanding of time and money	Maturing	Needing strategic "regeneration" and reinvestment
Character of organizations	Small, dynamic	Larger and more complex	Stagnant
Owner/Manager motivation	Committed to business success	Desires control and stability	Seeks new interests, or is semi-retired; next generation seeks growth and change
Family financial expectations	Limited to basic needs	More needs, including comfort education	Larger needs, including security and generosity
Family goals	Business success	Growth and development of children	Family harmony and unity

Embedded in the model are parts of the life cycles of the parents or owning generation and their children, thereby anticipating Ward's later ownership framework, which places greater emphasis on the generational perspective. While Ward (1991) claimed that his approach applies to both entrepreneurial and mature family enterprises, the underlying schema is most applicable to founder-owned and founder-managed enterprises. However, if subsequent generations achieve "regeneration", it is easily conceivable that the model could repeat itself several times in dynastic families. The challenges of each stage vary, and there are difficult transitions. Individual family businesses will stay for varying periods in each stage, and many will not continue to exist through the three stages. Management styles and strategy, among other things, must change over time if the enterprise is to prosper.

Ward (1991) also looked at the evolution of the family company through two different perspectives: ownership (Table 2.3) and management (Table 2.4). In Table 2.3, three stages are formulated, and the familiar evolutionary step approach is once again highlighted. However, in this instance a multigenerational model is presented, with which many family companies can be identified. Dominant shareholder issues are presented for each stage, and the inter-stage transitions can be extremely difficult. Ward (1991) does not posit that there is any automatic progression through the stages. Quite apart from the constant danger that the business may collapse or be sold out of the founding family at any time, family enterprises may stay in the same stage for generations. For example, the oldest child may inherit all the shares and behave like a founder, or in a Stage two company one sibling may buy out another. In this case, the dominant shareholder issues start to look very much like those of a founder-stage company. Likewise, Stage three companies can cycle back either to Stage two or to Stage one (a process sometimes labelled "pruning the family tree"). Thus, multiple combinations and permutations are possible in the ownership structure during the lives of family enterprises.

Table 2.3   Ownership issues in the evolving family business

Ownership stage	Dominant shareholder issues
Stage one: the founder(s)	Leadership transition Succession Spouse insurance Estate planning
Stage two: the sibling partnership	Maintaining teamwork and harmony Sustaining family ownership Succession
Stage three: the family dynasty (also called the cousins' confederation)	Allocation of corporate capital: dividends, debt, and profit levels Shareholder liquidity Family tradition and culture Family conflict resolution Family participation and role Family vision and mission Family linkage with the business

Source: Ward (1991).

Table 2.4 views the life cycle of the family business through a different lens, namely the evolution of management stages. This is in fact a hybrid of a business approach, management system, and organizational form (Ward, 1991). Dominant management issues vary with each predictable stage, and the transitions can be problematic. Further research is needed on the way in which these two models interact in the real world. One can hypothesize that, depending on which stage of the ownership model coexists with which stage of the management model, they could be mutually supportive or mutually antagonistic, with either beneficial or catastrophic consequences for the family enterprise. Based on these two models, Ward (1991) proceeded to describe his experience with the role, structuring, and managing of the board of directors of private (mostly family) enterprises.

Gersick et al. (1997) took a variation of the three-circle model and chose to focus on Family, Ownership, and Business, breaking down each one into an individual life cycle. The result is a three-dimensional matrix they call their "Dimensional model" of the family enterprise (Figure 2.2). The "Family" axis within the model comprises four stages, namely: young business family (older generation at work); entering the business (the next generation is employed in the firm); working together (of two generations); and passing the baton (succession). This has been strongly influenced by the work of other individual and family life cycle theorists. The "Ownership" axis is derived from Ward (1991) and the three stages are re-labelled, namely: controlling owner, the sibling partnership, and the cousin consortium. The descriptions of each and the intermediate transitions reflect Ward's (1991) fundamental views. The third axis is the "Business" one, which is also made up of three stages, namely the start-up, the expansion/formation, and the maturity.

Table 2.4   Management issues in the evolving family business

Management stage	Dominant management issues
Stage one: entrepreneurship	Survival Growth
Stage two: professionalization	Adopting professional management systems Revitalizing strategy
Stage three: the holding company	Allocation of resources Overseeing investment Corporate culture Succession and leadership Performance of investment Strategy Shareholder relations

Source: Ward (1991).

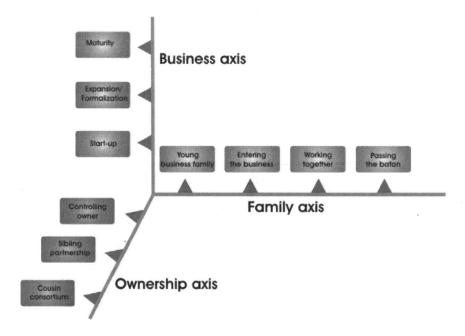

Figure 2.2   The dimensional model
Source: Gersick et al. (1997).

The value of Neubauer and Lank's (1998) developmental model is that it combines three of the major strands of the life cycle literature. The inevitable downside is the large number of possible combinations that can be derived from the "4 × 3 × 3 matrix" (Neuebauer and Lank, 1998). Furthermore, a given family enterprise (particularly a larger and older one) can be in more than one stage on any given axis. Gersick et al. (1997) were thus forced, to the advantage and relief of Neuebauer and Lank, to focus periodically on archetypes such as "controlling owner", "young business family", or "start-up businesses".

Conceptual Models and Approaches to the Study of Family Business

Relationships in family businesses are dynamic and interdependent because what occurs in the family may have effects on the business and vice versa. Furthermore, management is sometimes a concern in family businesses because ways of interacting among family members may interfere with financial business decisions. These ways of interacting can divert limited resources from targeted family members' goals. They may, in turn, lead to short-term decisions that are not conducive to long-term sustainability of the family business. The long-term health and sustainability of any family business depend on its ability to anticipate and respond to change. Whether responding to normative transitions or non-normative crises in either the family or the business component of the family business, new patterns of interaction are needed for a family business to remain healthy when these changes occur. Due to the interdependent yet integrated nature of family businesses, they are a unique group with a range of complexities that occur at the intersection of the two systems. Whether studying families that own businesses or businesses owned by families, the prevailing theoretical orientation is a systems paradigm.

Model development should begin with the premise that sustainable family-owned businesses require both minimally functional families and successful businesses. This premise is based on research of home-based businesses indicating that personal or family management practices affect the revenue of home-based businesses, and on the literature on family businesses that establishes that family conflict threatens business viability. Although the literature acknowledges the interaction of families and businesses, the dominant perspective is that family influences harm a business and keep it from being managed in a professional manner. According to the prevailing view, families and businesses are believed to be two "naturally separate" institutions or systems. From this perspective, a business is results-orientated and objective, basing decisions on contribution to output, whereas a family is emotion-orientated and irrational.

An alternative view is that businesses are motivated by the pursuit of profit, while families are motivated by biological imperatives and social norms. The most frequently recommended strategy for the successful coexistence of the two systems by both business management consultants and family therapists is what is sometimes called "separation" or "clear boundary definition". One of the advantages of a systems model that guides research design is that it provides a means of aggregating research results to provide a picture of the whole system. A system exists in an environment which is, itself, a set of systems. Consequently, in developing a conceptual model to guide empirical research, deciding whether to use a dual or single system paradigm is not as important as including both the family and the business in the model and selecting the key characteristics of the family and the business for inclusion. A theoretical model is built on the prevailing paradigm of overlapping systems. The key features of the overlapping family and business systems are different from the prevailing paradigms, however, in that it is not acceptable to sacrifice the family for the good of the business.

The Integration of Family Functionality and Business Success

Most models developed to explain family businesses reveal a preference for dual systems rather than a single system. Researchers argue in favour of viewing the family business as a single system – as a whole that is greater than the sum of its parts. They note that the dual systems approach focuses on characterizing the two systems, rather than characterizing the whole, and that it results from the interaction of the two. Tagiuri and Davis's (1982) model characterizes the whole that results from the overlap of systems. They propose a Venn diagram model of family businesses in which key attributes of the family businesses derive from overlapping membership in family, ownership, and management groups. The key attributes emerging from the overlap are simultaneous roles, shared identity, a life-long common history, emotional involvement, private language, mutual awareness, privacy, and the symbolic meaning of the family company. Each of these attributes is both a strength and a weakness, which explains the common description of their model as a "bivalent attribute" model.

Churchill and Hatten (1987), on the other hand, propose a research framework for studying family businesses with succession as their anchor. The framework is built on stages of the family business that derive from the biological reality of parent and child being separate in age and business experience, but joined by bloodline and family experience (Churchill and Hatten, 1987). They see themselves as adding a temporal dimension to Tagiuri and Davis's (1982) model of family business, much as family development theory emphasizes the temporal dimension of families. The stages of family businesses are identified as owner-manager, training and development of the new generation, partnership between the generations, and transfer of power. The order of the stages is fixed, but the duration of the stages is dependent on the characteristics of the two generations. Inclusion of the third generation, though not precluded, is not readily apparent according to Churchill and Hatten (1987).

Davis and Stern's (1988) model of family business adaptation, survival, and growth is considered important. In their model, the dimensions of family business that determine its success are the task structure and family organizational behaviour. The family interrelationship system, technology, and market demands are critical inputs from the business environment. Although this is a dual system, the family's interpersonal relationships and intergenerational "process" are aspects of the business environment rather than a full-fledged model of a family system. Davis and Stern (1988) improved previous models of the family business in three ways: first, by using adaptation, growth, and survival (in other words, success) as the criterion for determining key attributes rather than difference from non-family businesses; second, by referring to Churchill and Hatten's (1987) intergenerational process of families as well as interpersonal dynamics of families; and third, by allowing for the influence of market forces and technology. Wortman (1994) proposes a global conceptual paradigm for family business. He derives his attributes from a survey of the literature on family businesses. The form of this model is very similar to the family ecology models, with their emphasis on the focal system's interactions with particular aspects of the environment. It would be more appropriate to call this an ecological model than a single system model.

Paradigms of Family Functionality

Researchers note that there is a lack of unified theory about the family, along with a proliferation of measures of family functioning. Family ecology theory (Bubolz and Sontag, 1993), family development theory (Rogers and White, 1993), family systems theory (Whitchurch and Constantine, 1993), and family resource management theory (Deacon and Firebaugh, 1988) are potential sources of theoretical models to be used in enhancing our understanding of business-owning families. The first of these family functionality theories to be considered is family ecology theory.

FAMILY ECOLOGY THEORY

Family ecology theory differs from other theoretical orientations in that its focus is on families as they interact with their environment. Grounded in the heritage of home economics, family ecology theory is a synthesis of ecology and general systems theory, and underscores the importance of resource management in family adaptation and in creating environment sustainability. The focus is, on the whole, defined as the family and its interdependence with external systems. But the roles of the individuals who constitute the family can also be examined. Bubolz and Sontag (1993) proposed that, ideally, family ecological research (a) views individuals as physical-biological and social-biological entities who are organized in a family and interact with one another, and (b) studies the interdependence of the individuals and the family system and all the systems external to the family system.

A limitation of family ecology theory is its highly abstract theoretical concepts. Bubolz and Sontag (1993) noted that this abstraction creates an opportunity for defining concepts and identifying the links between concepts more concretely, although they acknowledged that this is not easy work. Notwithstanding the high level of abstraction, Roberts and Feetham (1982) used the theory to develop the Feetham Family Functioning Scale, one of the most well established self-report instruments for measuring family functioning (Sawin and Harrigan, 1995).

FAMILY DEVELOPMENT THEORY

The unique contribution of family development theory lies in its focus on explaining how families change (White, 1991). Early formulations of the theory suggested that families pass through a predetermined sequence of life cycle stages. According to Mattessich and Hill (1987), one criticism was that many families did not fit into the normative life cycle, and that the theory ignored the historical timing of significant life events. Another criticism was that the theory did not recognize the relationship between the family career and the development of other careers, such as education and work. In an effort to address these issues, White (1991) asserted that family development has no determined cycle; rather, it is a stochastic process. Stages are marked by events, such as marriage, birth, death, and divorce, which change the structure of the family. White (1991) also stressed that the timing and sequencing of the events determine how families function as they move into new stages. Additionally, societal norms, expectations, and sanctions, which are implicitly determined by the historical context, determine the order, prescribe the timing, and are influenced by several institutions, and each individual family is influenced by specific sets of expectations and norms depending on its institutional affiliations and family structure (White, 1991). Thus, those involved in family-owned businesses have a unique set of pressures and experiences that are different from either the family or the business realms, but which could be explored from either perspective.

GENERAL SYSTEMS THEORY AND FAMILY SYSTEMS THEORY

Psychiatry, not psychology, was the path by which general systems theory was introduced to the study of the family in social science. Thinking about families as systems laid the groundwork for family therapy. The key concepts of general systems theory as related to families are the mutual influence of system components, hierarchy, boundary, equifinality, and feedback. The family systems literature tends to fall into one of three main areas: (a) the understanding of the family processes, (b) the relationship between the family system and other systems, or (c) morphogenesis, the study of how the structure of the family systems changes. Research studies that take a systems approach to families are well developed in only a few areas. Marital interaction was the first area in which family systems theory was used. Systems approaches have also been used in the area of family dysfunction, where problems such as bulimia, anorexia, alcoholism, and family violence are seen as symptoms of a family problem, rather than as the problems of an individual. The most highly developed area in which systems theory has been used is the development of marital and family taxonomies. The leading family taxonomies – Olson's Circumplex Model (Olson, Sprenkle, and Russell, 1979) and the Beavers systems model (Beavers, 1982), are both based on family systems theory.

As could be expected, systems theory is not without its critics. Criticism of general systems theory includes the difficulty of operationalizing concepts because of the ambiguity of the theory; difficulty in specifying relationships among concepts, which then leads to a lack of explanatory power; and lack of parsimony in the theory. Its application to families, in the form of family systems theory, has been useful in applied research on family functioning and measures of family functionality.

FAMILY RESOURCE MANAGEMENT THEORY

Another theory to consider is the so-called "family resource management theory". Maloch and Deacon (1966) introduced the systems approach to the study of resource management in 1966. By 1975, Deacon and Firebaugh's (1975) systems model was the most widely used approach to the study of resource management. In the Deacon and Firebaugh (1988) model of family resource management, the family's system is described in terms of relationships rather than structure. According to this theory, the family is composed of two subsystems: personal and managerial. The purpose of the personal subsystem is procreation and the socialization of family members. The purpose of the managerial subsystem is to support the development of family members. Input from the family's external environment is filtered through the personal subsystem to the managerial subsystem. Inputs to the managerial subsystem are demands for action and resources. The managerial subsystem plans and implements the use of resources to meet demands. The outputs of both the managerial subsystem and family system are satisfaction and changed resources.

The systems framework emphasizes mechanisms by which the environment influences family resource-use behaviour. The first mechanism is through the family's supply of resources and the idea that societal norms and values heavily influence the standards used to assess those resources. The second mechanism is events (unexpected occurrences requiring action) about which information directly enters planned construction. The concept of events acknowledges uncertainty, and places control and feedback in a more prominent position. In addition, this system's framework introduced the dynamic concept of sequencing, defined as decisions related to the temporal and special ordering of activities to meet demands. Prior to that time, the spatial family resource management literature viewed the specification of goals and standards by which attainment of goals would be assessed as sufficient for goal achievement. The introduction of sequencing acknowledged the multiplicity of means by which a single goal could be met, and provided a means of coordinating multiple goals.

Paradigms of Family Business

"Success" is an ambiguous term commonly used by both lay and professional people to describe the achievements of a business or a person. Business owners are motivated by more than just extrinsic rewards, such as increasing personal income. They suggest that intrinsic rewards (e.g. meeting challenges), independence (e.g. maintaining personal freedom), and family security (e.g. building a business) are just as important as set goals that motivate sustained entrepreneurship. Business success, then, is about more than financial success. Two fundamentally different paradigms have been used to examine the determinants of success. One paradigm is the business in an economy. The other is an economically mobile entrepreneur. Leading examples of the former are Davidsson's (1991) model of entrepreneurship growth and Greenberger and Sexton's (1987) model of venture success. The leading example of the latter is human capital theory (Becker, 1993; Portes and Zhou, 1992). Schumpeter's (1934) constraint theory and Knight's (1921) choice theory also fall into this latter category, as does assimilation theory (Jiobu, 1988). Not surprisingly, the paradigms propose different determinants of success, although there may be as much variability within paradigm type as between types.

Davidsson's (1991) model of entrepreneurship growth views small business financial growth over time as the sum of ability, need, and opportunity. In Davidsson's (1991) model, education and entrepreneurship experience are positive determinants of ability. The manager's age or a business's age are determinants of need. The rate of innovation, market growth rate, customer structure, country characteristics, industry structure, geographic dispersion, and community characteristics are determinants of opportunity.

Greenberger and Sexton's (1987) model of venture success focuses on the role of the entrepreneur and how entrepreneurial behaviour changes as the company grows or succeeds. The model includes components that are important in new venture initiation (vision, personality, control desired, and salience of events, self-perceptions, social support, and control possessed) as well as two additional components, namely organization vision and empowerment of subordinates. Other models determine success by considering macro-level determinants, such as country or community characteristics and industry structure (Davidsson, 1991), or micro-level determinants, such as individual endowments of the entrepreneur (Greenberger and Sexton, 1987), with little consideration given to the owner's management capabilities and the impact such capabilities can have on success.

THE ECONOMICALLY MOBILE ENTREPRENEUR

Models of economic mobility and entrepreneurship, on the other hand, nominally focus on the individual, but they too emphasize either community characteristics and industry structure or the individual endowments of the entrepreneur. Human capital theory is the most frequently used theory among researchers taking this approach. Becker (1993) defined human capital as stocks of skills, knowledge, intelligence, and health that could be used to generate both monetary and non-monetary resources. Any increases in human capital stock results in higher future earnings, improved job satisfaction over the course of one's life, and greater appreciation for non-market activities and interests (Ehrenberg and Smith, 1997). Becker (1993) contended that human capital theory helps to explain such diverse phenomena as interpersonal and inter-area differences in earnings, the shape of age-earning profiles (the relation between age and earnings), and the effect of specialization on skills. Zuiker (1998) used human capital theory in her early analysis of Hispanic self-employment. She viewed assimilation as human capital, and incorporated aspects of the family, individual, and relationship capital into her human capital theory of Hispanic self-employment.

Sociologists examining economic mobility have proposed cultural and disadvantaged theories (Light, 1979), assimilation theory (Jiobu, 1988), and enclave theory (Portes and Zhou, 1992). These theories place more emphasis on community characteristics than human capital theory does. Cultural theory posits that both the cultural and psychological characteristics of groups predispose members to select business ownership as a means of achievement. According to disadvantage theory, those who are at a disadvantage in the labour market turn to self-employment to avoid low wages and unemployment. This theory has much in common with Schumpeter's (1934) constraint theory, with an ethnic twist.

"Assimilation" refers to the process by which groups adopt and are absorbed into the dominant culture. As groups become more assimilated, their members are less disadvantaged in the labour market and become more upwardly mobile. Ethnic enclaves now allow their members to compensate for their disadvantages in the labour market by trading with people like themselves and relying on informal group enforcement of informal contracts. Measure of assimilation and enclave membership can be viewed as human capital because, although the theories are stated in terms of groups, the measures are individual measures. The measures are also consistent with the productive feature of human capital.

The Family FIRO Model

The FIRO model (Schutz, 1958) and the Family FIRO model (Doherty and Colangelo, 1984; Doherty, Colangelo, and Hovander, 1991) offer a systemic view that integrates various typological depictions and provides for the setting of priorities across a full range of family business changes and dynamics. The models articulate three core dimensions of group and family interaction: inclusion, control, and affection/intimacy (see Figure 2.3). These dimensions constitute a developmental sequence in the formation and history of groups and families. That is, issues of inclusion (such as membership and boundaries) are the initial priorities for any group or family, followed by control and power, and then by issues of deep interpersonal connections. The main difference between the FIRO and Family FIRO models lies in the nuances of the groups with the related vs. non-related members. Because family businesses involve both personal family dynamics and more impersonal business dynamics, this study combines the original FIRO model and the Family FIRO model.

"Inclusion" refers to interactions that concern membership, organization, and bonding (Doherty, Colangelo, and Hovander, 1991). Inclusion within the family business defines the family business's core makeup. It defines who is in and who is out of the family business, how the family assigns roles to its members, how bonded its members are, and how it defines itself in relation to the outside world (Doherty, Colangelo, and Hovander, 1991). Inclusion has three categories: (a) structure, (b) connectedness, and (c) shared meaning (Doherty, Colangelo, and Hovander, 1991). Issues of inclusion often surface in family businesses when there are differing perceptions of who should be involved in running the business and making business decisions. One member may feel a sense of unfairness about being excluded from different aspects of the business. Doherty, Colangelo, and Hovander (1991) posited that financial arrangements lead to inclusion tension when either the spouse is dissatisfied with their own involvement in financial decisions that are considered critical or with the spouse's involvement in those decisions, and/or when financial values and beliefs clash.

"Control" refers to family interactions that concern influence and power exertion during family conflict. Control interactions usually take place in families when members experience competing needs and overtly or covertly attempt to address these conflicts. Applied to family businesses, control issues come to the forefront of a couple's daily interaction when frequent disagreements occur. An important distinction should be made between this control dimension and the concept of power, which is well represented in the family sociology literature. Research suggests a growing consensus about the separation of power structures, which concern hierarchy and role patterns, and power interaction, which deals with negotiations, influence strategies, and conflict management processes.

Integrating these concepts of power structures and interaction with the Family FIRO model, family issues and interactions concerning structural/role clarity (power structures) belong within the inclusion domain. The domain of control (Doherty, Colangelo, and Hovander, 1991) captures those issues related to working out tensions that develop, that is conflict management (power interactions). This dimension is composed of three major types of control interactions: dominating, reactive, and collaborative. The latter is considered the most constructive because parties aspire to a balance of influence rather than unilateral power imposition or reactive undermining of the others' power attempt (Doherty, Colangelo, and Hovander, 1991).

"Integration", rather than affection or intimacy as used in the original FIRO and Family FIRO models, applies to family business interactions. The change in terms is intended to capture dynamics specific to business rather than general family dynamics. Integration means to make a whole by bringing all the parts together. It brings together the interactions among family members and the financial decisions and goals of the business. It is characterized by individual and collective creativity used to solve problems and get work done. Researchers indicate that there should be a sense of change and a willingness to take risks. When these characteristics are present, they lead to the well-being of the whole system and the achievement of goals. Integrated family business connotes an environment of trust and creativity that brings a higher level of openness to interactions about both family and business issues that influence the achievement of goals. A healthy company is the foundation of family business continuity, and family and business goals are forces that steer each family business through predictable patterns of growth and change.

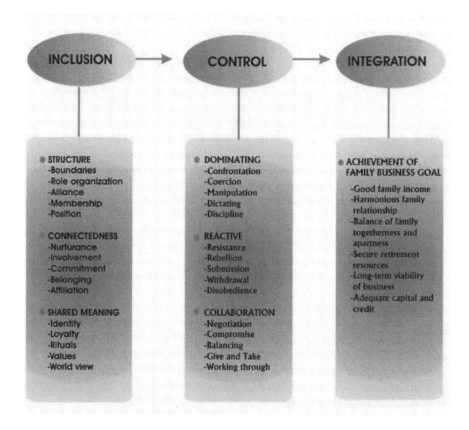

Figure 2.3   Family FIRO conceptual model of family business
Source: Danes et al. (2002).

There are two aspects postulated by the FIRO and Family FIRO models that make particular contributions to work on family business. Firstly, when a family business faces challenges stemming from major or ongoing stressful events, its patterns of inclusion, control, and integration will require reconstruction. Secondly, embedded in these models is an optimal sequence for managing major challenges. More successful adaptation will ensue, if family businesses address their issues in priority sequence. Doherty, Colangelo, and Hovander (1991) suggested that inclusion is the sine qua non for successful resolution in the control and integration areas. Without effectively addressing the inclusion issues, control dynamics cannot be adequately addressed, thereby precluding the desired side-effect of integration (Doherty, Colangelo, and Hovander, 1991).

When families and practitioners view the core problem only as one of control or power, they are likely to lose sight of the belonging, connectedness, and fairness issues that are often at the heart of business conflict. The developmental approach from the FIRO and Family FIRO models allows for structural issues such as identity, role, and justice to be viewed as more than merely a conflict to be addressed rationally and logically through usual conflict resolution approaches. They suggest, rather, that these structural issues can begin to be understood as the root of each spouse's sense of "couplehood", or the essence of what it means to be a family member working within a family business. It is about testing, questioning, and reaffirming one's sense of belonging, responsibility, and entitlement – namely inclusion – in the couple relationship, as embedded in the interrelated family-business system.

The Sustainable Family Business Research Model

This section describes a model of family business that, up to now, is sufficiently detailed to guide empirical research on all family business types and business-owning families, as well as sufficiently flexible to permit researchers to use more than one theory as they symmetrically analyse the parts of the whole. This model was developed to guide the design of data collection and analyses for the 1997 National Family Business Survey (NFBS) by Stafford et al. (1999). The systems model of family business pairs a model of family business success with a model of family functionality to yield a model of family business sustainability.

The focus of the model, depicted in Figure 2.4, is sustainability of the family business achievements. In this model, business achievements and transactions between the family and the business are a necessary prerequisite for a family business. Together at the same time, there are family resources and constraints (both broadly defined to include family processes) that can be viewed as occurring more or less independently of the business. By the same token, there are business resources, constraints, and processes that are more or less independent of the family. The general goal of research based on this model is to identify family and business resources and constraints, processes, and transactions that are most likely to lead to business and family achievement and sustainable family businesses. The model differs from previous models of family business in several ways.

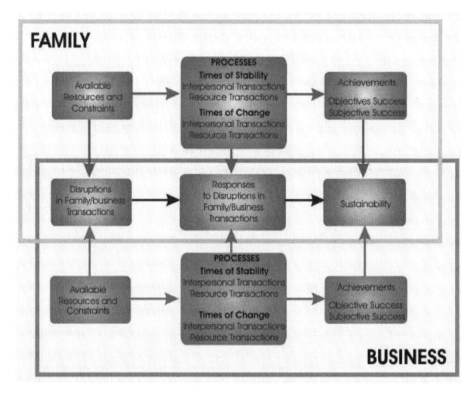

Figure 2.4   Sustainable family business models
Source: Stafford et al. (1999).

Perhaps the most noticeable difference is the inclusion of the family in the model at a comparable level of detail with the business. The most substantive difference from previous models is the inclusion of key features of the family and business systems. The family and business systems include resource use as well as interpersonal relationships, because as viable social systems, families are purposive and rational. According to both neoclassical economic theory of the family and Becker's (1965) household production theory, to survive, families must be efficient in the pursuit of profit. Times of change and times of stability are also included as a means of acknowledging the differences in processes that families and businesses engage in when their own structure and environment are relatively stable versus when they are dynamic (Stafford et al., 1999). Although the model includes analogous processes in the family and business systems, it separates them to call attention to the differences in purpose and specific content of the processes in the two different systems.

The family-supported system portrayed in Figure 2.3 is a purposive social system. As such, it takes available resources and constraints and transforms them via interpersonal and resource transactions into achievements. The achievements are both subjective and objective in nature. Interpersonal and resource transactions may change during times of environmental change, structural change, or both. This portrayal of a family is consistent with Becker's (1965) household production model of the family economics as well as family ecology, family systems, and family resource management models of families. According to the economic theory, the purpose of families is the pursuit of satisfaction (Stafford et al., 1999). According to family resource management theory, the purpose of families is procreation, socialization, and the support and development of family members.

Regardless of the purpose, the achievements that result from family transactions have a subjective component and an objective component. Satisfaction would be an example of a subjective achievement. Level of living would be an example of objective achievement. It would be appropriate to assess achievements using criteria consistent with the family's purpose. Available resources and constraints arise from the family's environment and from within the family itself. They include the family members' human capital as well as their assets and debts. Family goals can be thought of as a resource that motivates the use of other resources (Stafford et al., 1999). Societal norms and laws, technology, the economy, and the laws of nature are important constraints of family choice. The family combines market goods and services and its own labour to yield achievements. The transactions necessary to yield some achievements are relatively goods-intensive, while others are relatively labour-intensive.

For example, resource transactions are relatively goods-intensive; interpersonal transactions are relatively labour-intensive. It is more important for the family to select appropriate transactions for the desired achievement than it is to classify transactions as either interpersonal or resource. Most real transactions are both (Stafford et al., 1999). The model classifies transactions as interpersonal and resource in order to acknowledge explicitly both dimensions of family transactions, and to establish the relevance of both bodies of literature (Ward, 1997a). Families have distinctive styles of interpersonal interaction and conflict management. Whiteside and Herz-Brown (1991) also noted that families have tasks to accomplish and management styles and structures to accomplish them.

As previously stated, the business system in Figure 2.3 is also a purposive social system. It takes available resources and constraints, and converts them into achievements via resource and interpersonal transactions. According to neoclassical economic theory of the business, the purpose of the business is to maximize profit, which is defined as revenue in excess of cost (Ferguson, 1972). The purpose of the business should provide the criteria for assessing success, whether this is indicated by objective measures, such as adaptability, growth, and survival, or subjective measures, such as an owner's sense of achievement or pleasure in providing a way of life that is consistent with personal values (Stafford et al., 1999). Available resources include the human capital of employees, owners, and business culture, as well as assets and debts of the business. Goals and objectives that are consistent with the business's mission, and group commitment to the mission are also resources for the business. Technology is both a resource and a constraint.

Stafford et al. (1999) noted that the economy, culture, and laws of nature constrain the choice of transaction. Business managers choose transaction-appropriate processes to achieve the desired goals and objectives efficiently, resulting in objective success, subjective success, or both. Actual transactions are both interpersonal and resource transforming. These transactions for business are commonly referred to as "production for goods and services". The model classifies transactions as either interpersonal or resource-based, rather than as goods or services, in order to acknowledge explicitly the emotional orientation of businesses as well as their task of resource orientation.

Business organizations have distinctive styles of interpersonal interaction and conflict management. At the interface of the family and business systems, both the family and the business respond to disruptions in their regular transaction patterns. These disruptions may come from either outside the family and business or from within. Outside sources of disruption include public policy changes, economic upheavals, and technological innovation. Inside sources of disruption include marriage, birth, death, and divorce. The disruptions may be either good or bad and they require a response from both the family and the business. The extent of overlap between the family and the business systems will vary from family business to family business. In family businesses where the prevailing orientation is to keep family and business separate, there is little overlap. Conversely, in family businesses where the overlap is great, the area of interface between the family and business systems are considerable. Sustainability results from the confluence of family business, business success, and the appropriate responses to disruptions. In other words, sustainability requires the ability of the family and the business to cooperate in responding to disruptions in a way that does not impede the success of both.

Summary

It can be seen from the preceding literature review that family businesses are shaped internally, as described by these models. Externally, they are shaped by factors within the economic environment of the host country. Family businesses are the backbone of the global economy, and in many respects the free enterprise system is built on these enterprises. The main purpose of this chapter was to examine the nature and importance of family businesses globally. As the biggest component of the global economy, the family business should be a focus of discussion, analysis, and attention.

Family businesses should be kept healthy and well governed, as the well-being of our society depends on them to a large degree. Various unique characteristics of family businesses, as well as how they differ from non-family-owned businesses, were discussed in this chapter. The overall lack of longevity of family businesses is a major cause for concern, and a better understanding of their unique characteristics and problems would enhance efforts to protect their considerable contribution to national economies worldwide. This chapter makes a contribution in this respect, by synthesizing and integrating the current literature on family businesses.

Case Study:
A Family Restaurant Blends Cuisines across Cultures

Franco Vaccarino

Nestled in the Ruahine and Tararua mountain ranges is the city of Palmerston North in Aotearoa New Zealand. With around 80,000 inhabitants, it is the fourth largest city on New Zealand's North Island. Palmerston North is a culturally diverse city with more than 100 nationalities contributing to the multicultural mix. The city is reputed to have the highest number of restaurants, eateries, and café bars per capita in New Zealand. The 130 restaurants boast a vast selection of ethnic food options, including Chinese, Indian, Thai, Japanese, Korean, French, and Cambodian, to name a few.

One of these restaurants is owned by a Turkish family that migrated to New Zealand in 2007.

The Kökçü family members were born in Turkey. The mother moved to Germany when she was three years old. Later, she moved back to Turkey, got married, and had two children. During the children's first and second years of schooling, their grandmother became ill in Germany, so the family moved there to look after her. As would be expected, school was very difficult for the children in Germany as they now had to do all their studies in a foreign language.

After the grandmother passed away, the family decided to stay in Germany and not return to Turkey. The father opened a small Turkish Italian restaurant, more like a take-away rather than a sit-down restaurant. He managed the take-away restaurant and his wife helped him.

Once the children had completed their secondary schooling, they would have had to do further studies in order to be able to go to the local university. An uncle of the family who had been in New Zealand for 12 years, suggested that the daughter should come to New Zealand where she could start working in a café as most students do to earn some money and then go to university. After careful consideration, the parents felt that they did not want their daughter to go alone, so a decision was made for the whole family to move to New Zealand.

In 2007, the Kökçü family arrived in New Zealand. A difficult decision that faces most migrants when they move to a new country is where to settle. The Kökçü family wanted to find a city where they could set up a restaurant, similar to the one they had in Germany. The capital city, Wellington, which is a two-hour drive from Palmerston North, was an option; however, the competition was stiff as there were other kebab shops in the area. Although many migrants have to change their careers when they move to a new country, the Kökçü family was keen to continue in the food industry as they had had a restaurant in Germany for 10 years and, before that, a restaurant in Turkey.

Before arriving in New Zealand the parents had not done any research on the restaurant business there, but relied entirely on the uncle to guide them and assist them. The parents were used to the restaurant world so it was not new for them to set up a restaurant; however, the environment was different, and this was one of the difficulties. In Germany, the family had bought an established restaurant so it was merely a case of transferring ownership, whereas in New Zealand they wanted to start a new restaurant. New Zealand has different consents and licences that the family had to apply for. Different regulations added to the difficulties of setting up the family business. Once they had found a venue for their restaurant, they had to apply for permission to make internal modifications, and this took longer than anticipated. However, the family believes that these new difficulties did not create such an obstacle that they should abandon their dream of having a restaurant. They always felt that the people they dealt with in setting up their restaurant were very friendly and helpful, and this made it a lot easier.

Finally, the new Turkish Italian restaurant opened its doors to the public. The family business consisted of the father and the mother (who were the major shareholders), the daughter and the son, and two cousins from Turkey who were qualified chefs.

One of the fears of the family was how to grow the restaurant, especially in a city where people have so many options to choose from for eating out. People know about Turkish food as there is another Turkish restaurant as well as a kebab take-away in the city, but the Turkish Italian, or "kebab–pizza" combination, was new to the city. Initially, customers found this cultural blend of foods a bit strange, but they liked the idea that the parents could order kebabs and the children could have pizzas. Some first-time customers often enquire about this combination and expect the family to either be Italian or somehow related to Italians as there is the notion that only Italians can make pizzas! In fact, just after two years of opening the restaurant, there was a very positive write-up in the newspaper about their pizzas, stating that this restaurant provided the "best pizzas in town". This certainly boosted the family's confidence, as well as their commitment to continue providing top quality food.

In Germany, the family spoke Turkish at home and German when conducting business, but when they came to New Zealand they had to change to English. The children learnt English at school in Germany, so their English was good, although they point out that it has improved since they arrived in New Zealand as they have to use it every day with customers and suppliers. The parents have had to learn English in New Zealand as this is imperative when dealing with customers and suppliers. When they do not know the English word for something or when they struggle to explain a concept, they use gestures to communicate and thus manage to get the message across. As with most migrants moving to a country that speaks a different language to their own, it becomes an enormous challenge to learn the new language. As the Turkish community is small in Palmerston North, the family has had to learn English in order to socialize with local communities as well as with other migrant communities.

The family has settled in well and has not experienced major cultural difficulties as they did living as immigrants in Germany. A sensitive situation that has arisen is more from a religious perspective in that many customers are not aware that most Turkish people follow the Islamic faith. Part of the

Islamic faith is that food must be halal. Some customers enquire whether halal food can be eaten by everyone and whether it affects the taste of the food in any way, whilst others ask about the link between religion and food. This provides the opportunity for intercultural dialogue and helps people broaden their understanding of different cultures and religions.

As the food served at the family restaurant is halal, there are Muslim customers as well. Some other customers do not know why there may be so many Muslim women who are covered with scarves at this restaurant. As the women in the Kökçü family do not cover their heads, customers do not know they are Muslim, so they are always approached and asked about the Muslim customers. In addition, this restaurant provides a "bring your own" wine option for customers who want to enjoy a glass of wine with their meal. Some Muslim customers may get offended to see wine bottles on the tables as this is not appropriate according to their religious beliefs, and may wonder whether this is in fact a restaurant run by Muslims. The Kökçü family is therefore faced with some difficulties in trying to maintain a halal kitchen, but also allowing customers to bring their own wine. Were they to have a "no alcohol" policy, many customers would not choose their restaurant and would go somewhere else instead. It is difficult for them to try to accommodate all their customers, but usually through conversations, customers have a better understanding of cultural and religious issues. The family believes that when you move to a different culture you have to adapt to that culture and cannot expect the host culture to have to adapt to your culture.

This close-knit family works very hard in the restaurant, which is open seven days a week for 11 hours a day. Although each family member gets one day off per week, they work long hours. Both their daughter and son are studying at the local university and are supported by their parents. They do, however, continue to work at the restaurant in the evenings.

Chapter 3

The Impact of Culture on Immigrant Entrepreneurship

It is well accepted that people in particular localities share a number of common characteristics, such as religion, political views, lifestyle patterns, and approaches to work. People normally vary in the ways that they live their lives, but the variations are often reasonably predictable within and across groups of people. The variability is the descriptive dimension of what is termed "culture". The field of international management often neglects specific aspects of culture in favour of a more easily defined (and less theoretically precise) parameter denoted by geopolitical boundaries (Hofstede, 2001) when discussing managerial practices. Since a broad and complete overview of culture is beyond the scope of this chapter; however, the impact that culture exerts on how immigrants govern their families and their businesses will be explored in some detail.

Researchers have demonstrated an increasing interest in studying the development of business activity as a pattern of adjustment by some racial and ethnic groups. The major theoretical perspectives guiding this chapter are "middleman theory" (Bonachich, 1973) and "ethnic enclave theory" (Wilson and Martin, 1982). Although there is considerable overlap between these theories, they appear in the literature as unique perspectives that enhance our understanding of the development of business activity by racial and ethnic groups. This chapter also explores the degree to which one enterprise is more prevalent within certain ethnic groups than others. Most studies simply combine all "white" ethnic groups together into one category, which they then compare with certain "racial" ethnic groups (e.g. Asians/Africans versus Europeans/Americans). Given this narrow focus, one can expect that questions still persist about which ethnic groups, if any, are more likely to pursue entrepreneurship.

Defining Culture

The word culture is commonly spoken in everyday language to describe a host of different concepts. Traditionally, the word derives from the Latin word "colere", which translated means "to care for", "to build", or "to cultivate". Hence, culture usually refers to something that is derived from or created by the involvement of humans. Culture is often used to frame concepts such as "arts and culture" and "organizational culture". According to Dahl (2004), what all of these concepts have in common is the suggestion that culture is an intangible entity that involves a number of collective and shared artefacts, behavioural patterns, values taken together to form the culture as a whole. Furthermore, Soares, Farhangmehr, and Shoham (2007) noted that culture is a convenient universal for the many differences in market structure and behaviour that cannot easily be described in terms of more concrete factors. Culture probably impacts most – if not all – dimensions of human behaviour.

Triandis (2000) defined culture as a shared meaning or system, found among those who speak a particular language/dialect, during a specific historic period, and in a definable geographic region. It functions to improve the adaptation of members of a culture to a particular ecology, and it includes the knowledge that people need to have in order to function effectively in their social environment. Culture thus refers to the core values and beliefs of individuals within a society, which are formed in complex knowledge systems during childhood and reinforced throughout life. According to Samovar and Porter (1994), culture refers to the cumulative deposit of knowledge, experience, beliefs, values, attitudes, meanings, hierarchies, religion, notions of time, roles, spatial relations, concepts of the universe, and material objects and possessions acquired by a group of people in the course of generations, through individual and group striving.

Kluckhohn (1951) summarized the definition of culture as being transmitted mainly by symbols and comprised of the distinctive achievements of groups of individuals, and includes their embodiments in artefacts. Additionally, culture consists of traditional ideas and their attached values in particular. Other commonly applied definitions of culture include Herskovits' (1955) formulation that culture is the man-made part of the environment. Triandis (1972) and Osgood (1974) defined it as a perception of the man-made part of the environment. Sweder and Le Vine's (1984) view was that culture is a set of shared meaning systems, whereas Schein's (1985) view was that the core of culture is the untested assumptions of how and why to behave. Hofstede (1980) defined culture as a set of mental programmes that control an individual's responses in a given context, and Parsons and Shils (1951) viewed culture as a shared characteristic of a high-level social system.

There are several cultural influences on the institutional and organizational levels of human endeavour. Culture shapes the organizations that evolve and the nature of social structures as they grow and adapt (Hofstede, 2001). Societies shape their collectives and social aggregates according to the rules implied by culture. In collectivist cultures (comprising most traditional cultures) people are more likely (a) to think of themselves as interdependent within their groups (family, co-workers, tribe, co-religious, country, etc.) rather than the individual self (reflecting the independent self), and to see themselves as autonomous individuals who are independent of their groups; (b) to give priority to the goals of their in-group rather than to their personal goals; (c) to use in-group norms rather than personal attitudes to shape their behaviour; and, (d) to perceive social relationships as communal. That is, they pay attention to the needs of others and stay in relationships even when that is not maximally beneficial to them. There is evidence that these four aspects are interrelated.

Two broad cultural groupings have been identified in the cultural literature, namely the collectivistic and individualistic cultures. These two differ in that the individualistic culture places a low emphasis on broad, social networks of extended families and friends. The individualistic culture reflects on purely individual reward and action. Collectivist cultures have languages that do not require the use of "I" and "you" (Kashima and Kashima, 1997, 1998). They also have many culture-specific relational terms that are not found in individualist cultures, such as "philotimo" in Greek (Triandis, 1972), which expresses a feeling of compassion, regarded as a positive attribute of an individual who does what the in-group expects. "Amae" in Japanese reflects tolerance of deviation from norms by a dependent person (Yamaguchi, 1998). "Simpatia" among Latin Americans (Triandis et al., 1984), reflects the expectation that social relationships will include mostly positive and very few negative behaviours. Collectivists use action verbs (e.g. "offered to help") rather than state verbs (e.g. "he is helpful"). This difference exists because collectivists prefer to use context in their communications.

Culture also impacts on people's behaviour and organizations. A great deal of management research has been directed towards understanding corporate culture (also referred to as "organizational" culture), which refers to the peripheral or more easily influenced values and beliefs that an individual holds. An organization's culture has a relatively weak influence on an individual's core cultural beliefs and values. If these beliefs and values are threatened by organizational practices, one can expect dysfunctional work behaviour or maladjustment. Thus, an individual's behaviour in an organizational setting is a product of knowledge systems that are acquired both culturally and individually through unique life experiences. The potential for and frequency of entrepreneurship has been shown to be associated to a great extent with the occurrence of certain cultural values. Research has consistently shown that differences in organizational and work behaviour can be explained by cultural and religious factors (Thomas and Mueller, 2000), and cultural values, such as individualism and collectivism, can be linked to the level of entrepreneurship and innovation in a society.

Foundational Research on Culture

Several authors have pointed out the biased nature of culture-related research, with a large proportion of research originating in the West and America exporting the major theoretical frameworks, research design methods and analysis, and means of codifying and organizing scientific knowledge systems (Featherman, 1993).

It is thus important to stimulate the production of rigorous, culturally sensitive research in a variety of geographical settings to ensure that our knowledge base in research becomes less Americo-centric. The logic of collectivist social thought was used in the 1980s to argue that the achievement of relationship and harmony with others would be a major goal in collectivist systems valuing group stability. Since 1980, social scientists have relied on Hofstede's (1980) monumental work *Culture's Consequences* to compare the locations of 40 nations on four dimensions of cultural values. New dimensions have been added to his topology, and more comprehensive value measures have been developed. Others have researched ways to conceptualize and measure culture, such as the assessment of social axioms. In addition, eco-social indicators have been combined to provide a means for comparing cultural systems. These new approaches to making sense of culture variation are being utilized to explore ways in which a person's cultural background may be scientifically linked to their social and commercial behaviour. The growing appreciation of the role of culture in organizational behaviour will enhance our understanding of good governance of both the family and the business.

If one accepts that culture is a system of collective values that distinguishes the members of one group from another, then national culture acts as a common frame of reference according to which members of a group (society) view organizations, the environment, and their interpersonal relations (Geletkanycz, 1997). As mentioned above, one of the most commonly employed descriptions of national culture was developed by Hofstede (1980) who isolated four basic cultural dimensions: uncertainty avoidance, individualism, masculinity, and power distance. Uncertainty avoidance measures the ability of a society to deal with inherent ambiguities and complexities in life. Cultures that are high in uncertainty avoidance rely heavily on written rules and regulations, embrace formal structures as a way of coping with uncertainty, and have very little tolerance for ambiguity or changes. According to Kreiser, Marino, and Weaver (2001), individualism describes the relationship that exists between the individual and the collectivity in a culture. Societies high in individualism value freedom and autonomy, view results as coming from individual (and not group) achievements, and place the interests of the individual over the interests of the group.

Masculinity is primarily concerned with the level of aggression and assertiveness present in a culture. Highly masculine cultures place a high level of emphasis on assertive and ostentatious behaviour, and material goods and prestige are highly sought after. Individuals tend to exhibit a high need for achievement, and organizations are more willing to engage in industrial conflict. The fourth cultural dimension, power distance, is a measure of the interpersonal power or influence between the boss and the subordinate, as perceived by the least powerful of the two – i.e. the subordinate (Hofstede, 1980). According to Kreiser, Marino, and Weaver (2001), high power-distance cultures exhibit an unequal distribution of power, strong hierarchies, and control mechanisms. In power-distance cultures, there is less communication among organizational levels, and a heavy emphasis is placed on subordinates being deferential and obedient to those in positions of power.

Researchers have cited numerous reasons for utilizing the cultural dimensions posited by Hofstede (1980). These include the parsimony of the framework (McGrath et al., 1992), the reliability and validity of the measures (Shane, 1994, 1995), the capacity of the model to tie cultural orientation to institutional differences between countries (McGrath et al., 1992), and the ability of the framework to accurately predict individual behaviours (Mueller and Thomas, 2001). Hofstede's (1980) cultural dimensions have also been employed extensively in entrepreneurship research, having been utilized to examine entry mode (Kogut and Singh, 1988), rates of innovation (Morris et al., 1993; Mueller and Thomas, 2001; Shane, 1993), entrepreneurial differences between countries (McGrath et al., 1992; Takyi-Asiedu, 1993), and behavioural differences between entrepreneurs and non-entrepreneurs (McGrath et al., 1992; Morris and Peng, 1994).

Cultural and Structural Theories of Ethnic Groups

In an attempt to understand the relationship between culture and entrepreneurship, Butler and Herring (1991) suggested middleman theory and ethnic enclave theory as they can be thought of as cultural and structural patterns of entrepreneurship. Both frameworks identify cultural and structural patterns of various ethnic groups that facilitate or hinder success in the business world. Middleman theory has developed propositions relating to ethnic solidarity, societal hostility, and the development of business enterprises. This theory proposes that, for groups that adjust to society by developing enterprises, hostility is generated towards them from the larger society, and this increases ethnic solidarity, which in turn promotes the further development of business enterprises. As a result, an entrepreneurial culture develops that keeps the groups from falling to the bottom of the economic ladder in society. Over time, such groups begin to occupy the middle part of the economic system, hence the term "middleman".

Butler and Herring (1991) suggest that, because of the small amount of capital required, immigrant groups in this tradition are more likely to concentrate on small-service enterprises. In addition to a heightened sense of the importance of business, these groups develop a strong emphasis on the education of their offspring. As a result, immigrants' children are more likely to become professionals, especially in areas that are entrepreneurial in nature. They are often found in occupations such as law, education, and medicine. Those who are not professionals are more likely to develop enterprises in the middleman tradition.

Enclave theory also stresses the development of small business enterprises within ethnic communities, but adds the element of labour market theory. There are two theoretical constructs of this theory, primary and secondary. The primary sector is made up of jobs that are "good", as measured by excellent opportunities for promotion, remuneration, and company "perks" (e.g. health care plans, quality of workplace, and retirement plans). The secondary sector consists of "bad" jobs that do not provide the employee with opportunities for promotion, remuneration, and company perks. According to the enclave theory, ethnic groups can create the analogue of the primary and secondary jobs within their enterprise, showing how, within a particular ethnic enclave, there exist both "good" and "bad" jobs. One of the major differences between the two theories is that while middleman enterprises are found throughout the host population or city, ethnic enclaves are usually concentrated in one section of a city where an immigrant group has settled.

Another cultural explanation that attempts to account for differential rates of entrepreneurship among diverse ethnic groups is social learning theory. This perspective proposes that "role models" act as important environmental factors in forming career preferences. Observing, identifying with, and appreciating the behaviour of others make certain callings more noticeable than others. Through a process of various learning and emulation, people make cognitive evaluations of the overall attractiveness of specific career options. They are either encouraged or discouraged to enter a particular occupation. People are more likely to enter a particular career or profession if they have seen role models successfully performing the activities associated with that career. They are also less likely to pursue a path in which significant others have been unsuccessful. Research has established the relationship between social learning and entrepreneurial behaviour and consistently shows that over 70% of entrepreneurs come from homes where parents or close relatives owned a small enterprise or were independent professionals such as lawyers, farmers, or accountants. Therefore, members of certain ethnic groups are more likely to be exposed to entrepreneurial behaviour. Cultural and structural explanations pose some difficult challenges, however, for analysts who want to distinguish between the separate effects of cultural and structural elements on ethnic entrepreneurial behaviour. As both culture and structure are so extensive, it is advisable to allow ethnicity to act as a proxy for cultural elements.

Culture, Problem-Solving, and Negotiations Skills

It is unfortunately true that the cultural embeddedness of strategies and strategic knowledge in problem solving has not received a great deal of attention in the literature. Most of the cross-cultural research on thinking and problem solving belongs to what van de Vijver and Willemsen (1993) call the "formal tradition". In order to understand the interaction between problem-solving strategies and cultural context, we can, as a first step, look for appropriate metatheoretical frameworks. Berry (1993), for instance, in his "ecological approach", argues that behaviours are adapted to the ecological as well as the socio-political context in which they occur. This context emphasizes a functional perspective on thinking. It implies that problem-solving strategies are usually not developed for their own sake or because cognitive skills are valued *per se*, but in order to tackle specific adaptational problems. These strategies are used as long as they fulfil their specific purpose, no matter how awkward or suboptional they seem to be from the outside. The importance of practical activity for the development of problem-solving styles has been stressed by the so called sociohistorical school. According to this line of thought, the development of problem-solving skills is dependent on (among other factors) culture-specific tasks and goals, the typical ways of transmitting knowledge (e.g. abstract instruction vs. guided participation), and the available material and symbolic tools.

Empirical studies in the "cognition-in-action" tradition have clearly demonstrated that people develop and use highly sophisticated strategies in dealing with specific tasks that are important to them; in many cases, however, people are not able to generalize the strategies to other contexts. More importantly, within the complex problem-solving perspective, it is possible to develop a framework for the understanding of national cultural influences on the development of problem-solving patterns and strategic knowledge. Strohschneider and Gűss (1999) argued that, from a strictly functional position, there are basically five (probably inter-related) aspects of culture that contribute to the development of specific problem-solving patterns.

- *Predictability and "planability" of the environment.* It is obvious that the stability of the environment (taken here to include climatic as well as social or economic aspects) is influential in the development of problem-solving styles (Gardner and Rogoff, 1990). If an environment is completely unpredictable, there is not much problem solving required because there will be routine solutions available for all kinds of tasks. Only when the environment is dynamic does some sort of problem solving become necessary. Slow and predictable rates of change may allow for knowledge-based, analytic, and long-term strategies to develop (Agarwal et al., 1983; Sundberg et al., 1983). An environment in a constant state of flux (as in change) requires *ad hoc* and short-term strategies (Lindblom, 1959);

- *The degree to which a culture requires and promotes experiences in different areas of problem solving ("exposure").* Exposure may be related to the accountability of the environment, but may also be a function of dominant value systems or the availability of resources necessary to promote exposure. It has been shown in intercultural studies that the amount of problem-solving experience is a crucial factor in the development of strategic competencies. The greater the range of problems from different domains the individual has to tackle, the more likely they are to develop the strategic competence necessary to deal successfully with novel and complex problems. The amount of schooling and the methods of teaching are important in this context. In particular, if learning at school is equated to absorbing and repeating prefabricated solutions, there will be only limited development of problem-solving expertise;

- *Legitimacy of norms and value system.* Value systems and philosophies of life are means of reducing uncertainties and defining proper goals, as well as ways of reaching these goals. If value systems have a high degree of legitimacy and therefore assume the status of behavioural norms, value systems can again reduce the necessity of problem solving. In so-called post-modern societies, value systems often have lost their traditional, prescriptive power or have become fragmented. Different domains of life (like family, profession, and leisure time) may be only loosely integrated, and even if there is high accountability on a day-to-day basis, when it comes to important or critical events the individual has a choice of different strategic possibilities.

- *Power distance and social hierarchy.* Attempts to solve a problem make sense only when one is given sufficient leeway not only to find a solution but also to make it work. The notion of "control span" captures this idea. High power-distance cultures are more likely to limit the control span of individuals who are not at the top of the hierarchy, and thus hamper individual problem solving rather than promoting it. This is not to say that high power-distance necessarily results in poor strategies. However, problem-solving techniques will concentrate more on possibly adverse social implications of decisions, and will therefore be rather conservative or risk-avoidant.

- *Individualism versus collectivism.* This raises the question whether one type of culture requires more problem solving than another. However, there should be differences in the degree to which the social environment is taken into account. How individualistic cultures reinforce individualistic problem solving, aimed at increasing personal benefits even at the cost of others, is well documented. In collectivist cultures, personal benefits are less valued if other members of relevant groups suffer or if group-orientated values (group harmony) are endangered. Therefore, individualistic cultures should require short-term, problem-focused strategies as compared to collectivist cultures.

For all cultures, negotiation is a form of social interaction (Mantzaris, 2000). It is the process by which two or more parties try to resolve perceived incompatible goals (Carnevale and Pruitt, 1992). In order to understand the effect of culture on negotiation, it is useful to have a mental mode of negotiation. What is it that people mean when they say they negotiate? What is involved in negotiating? What is a good outcome in negotiation? What does it take to get a good outcome? What goes wrong in a negotiation that has a bad outcome? If culture has an effect on negotiation, the mental models of negotiators from one culture may not coordinate with those from another culture, making the specification of a single mental model problematic.

According to Brett (2000), there are two ways to approach this problem of specifying a mental model of negotiation. One is to specify the model in use in one culture and then compare and contrast its elements with the elements of models of negotiation from other cultures. Alternatively, researchers can specify the mental models of negotiation in many different cultures and aggregate their common and unique elements. The latter approach is less likely to overlook culturally unique aspects of negotiation, but requires the prior existence or current construction of many culturally "emic" (unique) models of negotiation.

In the latest empirical research on the new wave of e-negotiations, Harkiolakis, Halkias, and Abadir (2012) suggest that in terms of the negotiation process, culture can be seen as practices and values that frequently show up and uniquely characterize one of the parties. Practices mainly refer to organization style such as the degree of centralization of authority, formalization of communication, and depth of organizational hierarchy. Values refer to employee/negotiator preferences in undertaking task execution and making coordination decisions. Both categories influence micro-level behavioural patterns in individuals. The presence or absence of culture as a decisive factor in negotiation has been debated frequently and while there might not be sufficient scientific evidence to suggest a direct relationship of culture and outcome, it will be a parameter that no one can ignore. Given that traditionally in the past we followed formal etiquette and communication rules in negotiations, it is almost certain that the requirement to understand culture will be an absolute necessity for present day and near future negotiators. Understanding the cultural context in which emotions are displayed is important for knowing how to manage those in moving strategically through the negotiation process.

Harkiolakis et al. (2012) highlight that real problems in negotiations arise when opposing cultures meet. A low-context negotiator might believe they made their offer explicit in the textual message of the offer while their counterpart high-context negotiator might still be waiting on the non-textual aspects of the message before forming an opinion. In such situations, low-context negotiators should go the extra mile to enhance the communication with additional actions such as making a phone call to introduce themselves and engaging in social banter with the other party before addressing any issue. In an intra-cultural environment, communications with issues of conflict and negotiation are more predictable because negotiators do not have to contend with linguistic or cultural differences. In fact, negotiation behaviour is tactical. Individuals who have the same cultural background tend to think, feel, and react similarly in accordance with their shared cultural heritage.

The primary purpose of this chapter was to assess the nature and importance of cultural influences on immigrant entrepreneurship and family businesses. Besides defining the concept of culture in a family business context, this chapter also explored cultural theories about ethnic groupings. Not surprisingly, regional variations have been found in the levels of entrepreneurship between countries. In their repeated cross-national studies of entrepreneurship, researchers suggest that regional variations in the levels of entrepreneurship are influenced by the cultural values of the people. Cultural and economic-structural determinants of the new business formation rate are positively connected, thus suggesting that cultural differences in both values and beliefs help explain regional variances in the supply of entrepreneurship. Despite the cultural relationship, various other studies on migrant and ethnic entrepreneurs have found that cultural beliefs and values rarely suppress aspiring entrepreneurs.

Case Study:
An Immigrant Entrepreneurial Culture
is Born: The Greeks of South Africa

Christian Adendorff

Researchers have often conceptualized entrepreneurial organizations as possessing three main characteristics: innovation, risk-taking, and proactiveness. Recent research suggests that the three dimensions of entrepreneurial orientation may vary independently of one another (Dess, Lumpkin, and McGee, 1999; Kreiser, Marino and Weaver, 2001; Lumpkin and Dess, 1996). This suggests that aggregated measures of entrepreneurial orientation may provide misleading results during the research process, as the individual contributions of each of the three dimensions of entrepreneurial orientation may not be clearly stated. It has been argued in the literature that future research on entrepreneurial orientation may benefit from considering innovation, proactiveness, and risk-taking – separate and unique dimensions of entrepreneurial orientation.

Mueller and Thomas (2001) theorized that ethnic culture is responsible for causing individuals to engage in behaviours that are not as prevalent as in other cultures. The argument that national culture affects individual behaviour has often been linked to the formation of business-level entrepreneurial orientation. Various researchers have argued that key decision makers within a business determine the overall strategic orientation of the organization. If national culture affects the way that individuals behave within organizations, and individual behaviour affects the strategic orientation displayed by these organizations, then it stands to reason that ethnic culture may play a significant role in determining the overall level of a business's entrepreneurial orientation.

Those who have researched the process of assimilation of Greeks in South Africa have noted the emergence of a distinct culture as a cross-breeding between Greek and South African cultural configurations (Mantzaris, 2000; Koliopoulos and Veremis, 2002; Dicks, 1971). The Greek-South African cultural fusion has allowed many Greeks to assimilate into the general South African culture by a cushioning of the shock of transition. However, at the same time, the South African-Greek culture may have accentuated the dilemma of cultural identification with one or another culture (Mantzaris, 2000). Thus, the South African-Greek culture may have influenced assimilation of the various generations of Greeks, either by accelerating the process through the introduction and speedier acceptance of South African culture configurations, or by slowing the process through a perpetuation of Greek cultural configurations.

Assimilation refers to the process of culture change that takes place when a person is exposed, over a long period of time, to a culture different from their own. Such a process is more often reciprocal, since both groups contribute elements that eventually get combined into a new culture. Mantzaris (2000), Vlachos (1965), Pederson (1950), Hofstede (2001), and Koliopoulos and Veremis (2002) concur that there are three elements involved in the process of culture change. These are:

- the native culture of the group, or the culture of the larger society;
- the "foreign" culture, or the culture of the immigrant group;
- the emerging culture, or the culture "as it is becoming".

Such a reciprocal process and the emergence of a distinct culture have been going on for almost all ethnic groups in South Africa, as well as internationally. Koliopoulos and Veremis (2002) noted the formation of a new Polish-American society out of those fragments separated from Polish society and embedded in American society. This society, in structure and prevalent attitudes, is neither Polish nor American, but constitutes a specific new "product" whose "raw materials" have been partly drawn from Polish tradition, partly from the new conditions in which the immigrants live, and partly from American social values as the immigrant sees and interprets them (Koliopoulos and Veremis, 2002).

In similar vein, out of the contact of the American and Greek cultures, a new hybrid culture, the Greek-American culture has emerged (Vlachos, 1965). Mantzaris (2000) noted that the emerging South African-Greek culture acted primarily as an agency of adaptation to the culture of the larger society. It is the cushioning medium through which the immigrants and younger South African-Greeks were brought up in the ethnic culture, getting acquainted with the workings of the larger South African society, and/or through which members of the ethnic group familiarized themselves with the basic workings and procedures of South African society. At the same time, in a successful combination, the South African-Greek culture can contribute to the preservation of an ethnic subculture within the pluralistic framework of the South African social structure (Mantzaris, 2000). In short, the South African-Greek culture is a distinct culture form, differing from both the South African and Greek cultures.

Characteristics of Greek Culture

The South African-Greek culture is quite distinct from that of Greek culture proper. Whereas in Greece culture progressed and evolved with the passing of time (Koliopoulos and Veremis, 2002), the South African-Greek culture, as transplanted by the earlier immigrants, did not change, despite the time that passed. In the preservation of the original culture, there was an assertion of nationality and "Greekness" by the earlier immigrants. Especially for the older generations in South Africa, any concession to progress, any concession to change, or any deviation from the cultural patterns handed down by tradition would be a concession to "Africanism" (Mantzaris, 2000). In this way, it can be said that Greeks in South Africa represented a conservative element, by retaining aspects of rural culture, such as family organization, which, according to Koliopoulos and Veremis (2002), have changed in Greece itself.

This general idea can probably explain the perplexity of the (urban) Greek, who, coming from Greece to South Africa today, finds among the South African-Greeks a unique culture even against their own standards. By the same argument, the frustration of South African-Greeks visiting Greece, and especially the big cities, can be explained by their bewilderment at not recognizing in Greece a culture that they have been taught to expect while in South Africa (Mantzaris, 2000).

The South African-Greek culture is also distinct from the South African culture in that many of its basic elements are composed of Greek cultural configurations that are not part of the typical South African way of life. As has been indicated above, this South African-Greek culture is important in that it has successfully combined distinct elements of the two contributing ways of life. Typical Greek culturally influenced behaviours include hospitality, spontaneity, patterns of recreation, family discipline, and mutual interdependence (Koliopoulos and Veremis, 2002; Dicks, 1971). From the South African side, there is the contribution of various cultural elements such as order, business initiative, punctuality, and a certain political philosophy of the rainbow nation (Mantzaris, 2000). All these factors (and behaviours) contribute to form a unique South African-Greek culture.

There are several elements that combine to form what can be termed an "emerging South African-Greek culture". These are discussed below.

Linguistic Adjustments

A first example is the new South African-Greek language that is developing. This language is characterized by similar grammar and new words borrowed from onomatopoeia and English idiomatic expressions. A new language has developed, which has the characteristics of an almost completely new dialect (Spiro, 2003). It is fascinating to hear South African-Greeks converse in a dialect that, although unknown to listeners, sounds familiar to both South African and Greek ears.

Spiro (2003) pointed out that most of the words derived from English are rough "sound" translations with familiar morphological affixes, which characterize most of the Greek grammar. At the same time, it should be borne in mind that the early immigrants came mostly from rural regions, in which many of the things they found in the modernized South Africa did not exist in their country (Koliopoulos and Veremis, 2002; Mantzaris, 2000). They had to adopt a whole new vocabulary that would render familiar the many things that surrounded them in the new country, but at the same time would be Greek words in their basic linguistic structure (in phonology and morphology). Words like *farm, ginger-ale, radio,* and *sport* had to be phonologically adapted to Greek, and the easiest solution was to give them first Greek phonology and second Greek morphology (Spiro, 2003). The selected list of words of the South African-Greek dialect in Table 3.1 illustrates the linguistic adjustment to the larger society.

Table 3.1   A selected list of words of the South African-Greek dialect

English	South African-Greek	English	South African-Greek
Arrest	Arrestaro	Hospital	Spitali
Automobile	Atmobily	License	Lasintza
Bank	Bank	Machine	Mashini
Bar	Barra	Market	Marketta
Basement	Besimo	Meat	Meaty
Basket	Basketta	Meter	Metre
Beef-stew	Beefestoo	Mop	Mapa
Bill-of-fare	Billoferry	Move	Movaro
Boss	Bossis	Note	Nota
Box	Boxy	Park	Parki
Bum	Bammis	Peanuts	Peanotsa
Candy	Kantia	Picnic	Picniki
Car	Carro	Post-office	Postoffy
Carpet	Carpeto	Showcase	Sokessa
Cream	Creamy	Sidewalk	Salisvori
Dollar	Tallero	Sport	Sportis
Elevator	Eleveta	Stand	Standtza
Farm	Farma	Steak	Stecky
Ginger-ale	Gingerella	Stove	Stoffa
Grocery	Grossaria	Ticket	Ticketto
Hotel	Hoteli	Yard	Iarda
		Yes	Yes or ja

Source: Adapted from Spiro (2003).

Anglicization of Names

The linguistic transformation has also had ramifications for Greek proper names (Cassia and Bada, 1991). Since names are part of a language, they can change as the language is modified. Changes in names illustrate two aspects of the process of assimilation:

- those changes that are made chiefly in order to facilitate pronunciation and spelling, but which do not necessarily remove the evidence of ancestral origin;
- those changes of name that completely conceal the nationality of origin and are intended to do so. This is a form of "passing" (Cassia and Bada, 1991).

According to Vlachos (1965), the analysis of the name change in an immigrant group affords an additional measure of the assimilation process. A tremendous amount of name changing has taken place in South Africa, and as the immigrants became part of the nation, they sometimes dropped their old cognomen entirely and adopted a totally different South African one. This criterion of assimilation should be used with caution, however, since it can denote only a simple adaptation to the external reality of facilitating pronunciation rather than Africanization itself (Mantzaris, 2000). Families sometimes happened to have Greek names that were easily readable in the English language and thus they were not forced to change them, at least for reasons of spelling (Vlachos, 1965).

Dual Consequences of South African-Greek Culture

The following section deals with the "buffer effect" and conflict as experienced by South African-Greeks.

"Buffer Effect"

The existence of a distinct South African-Greek culture has had the effect of easing the transition to the general culture prevailing in South Africa (Spiro, 2003). Through the channels of the South African-Greek culture, the members of the Greek community become accustomed to many of the workings of the larger South African society within the context of their own familiar group. At the same time, this distinct culture helps cushion the shock of an immediate confrontation between the members of the ethnic group and other South African cultures (Mantzaris, 2000).

Conflict

The same South African-Greek culture, however, can work in a different direction. For many of the members of the Greek community, it contributes to the problems of a cultural conflict (Mantzaris, 2000), for there is always a "Greek tragedy" somewhere in their everyday way of life. The conceptual scheme of assimilation demonstrates that transition from one culture to another is not always harmonious, and calls for certain forms of adjustment (Cassia and Bada, 1991; Koliopoulos and Veremis, 2002; Mantzaris, 1995, 2000; Vlachos, 1965). According to Kolipoulos and Veremis (2002), transition can take two forms, either the form of a personal adjustment to the culture of the larger society, or the form of social integration. The latter implies the harmonization of the ethnic groupings with the structure of the larger (national) society. Both Koliopoulos and Veremis (2002) and Mantzaris (2000) pointed out that there is an important distinction between the first conflict of generations, that is, conflict between individuals in different "generations", and secondly, a conflict within the individual. The conflict of generations is a conflict that indicates lack of social integration. Conflict within the individual arises from a social situation as a result of incompatible cultural goals, which indicates personal maladjustment.

Conflict of generations   The problem of adjustment becomes more profound with the younger generations (Mantzaris, 1978, 1995). The existence of a unique South African-Greek culture indicates the conflict between earlier and later generations by the simple fact that the different generations belonged or strove towards different cultural configurations (Mantzaris, 1995). The South African-Greek culture could presumably satisfy neither the older (and more conservative) generation, nor the younger one, which strives and thinks more in the realm of the South African culture (Mantzaris, 1978).

Vlachos (1965) observed that, in America, the older generation of Greek-Americans seem to deal in three different ways with the cultural conflict exemplified by the hybrid Greek-American culture:

These are:

- resistance to change and outright condemnation of the American way of life;
- resigned toleration, which indicates the feeling of inability to cope with the assimilationistic forces of society;
- finally, there is a conscious effort to understand the culture of the larger society and to adjust to the changing outlook of the younger generation.

There is often outright rebellion against the traditional way of living, but an arrangement of mutual toleration with their parents seems to be more prevalent (Mantzaris, 2000).

It is interesting to note, however, that South African-Greek families, with the help of their church and the many formal organizations, have been able not only to provide adequate socialization, but also to create a certain pride in identification with the Greek group. Early habits formed in the family were continuously reinforced with the larger Greek group (Mantzaris, 2000; Spiro, 2003; Cassia and Bada, 1991; Koliopoulos and Veremis, 2002; Vlachos, 1965). The important contribution of the South African-Greek family rests in many cases on the fact that, in contrast to other ethnic groups, it offered a more or less systematic programme of education in Greek traditions in the context of African reality. Through the cumulative experience of the second generation, an accommodating South African culture was passed to the third and fourth generations (Mantzaris, 2000).

The decisive factor in conflict or integration of generational ideas seems to be the pattern of South African-Greek cohesion. Whenever there has been a well-organized Greek community to support the earlier Greek socialization of the family, the second or third generation South African-Greeks have been rather successful not only in achieving more or less stable equilibrium with their elders, but also in finding a larger intimate group for identification (Mantzaris, 2000; Spiro, 2003). Assimilation and transformation, as indicated above, have had numerous ramifications for South African-Greeks. Not only did they have to deal with conflict in their efforts at transition, but they also had to deal with conflict from within.

Conflict within the individual   The phenomenon of generational conflict due to poor social integration has already been discussed. There is, however, another kind of conflict, namely conflict within the individual, which, as noted before, is a manifestation of lack of personal adjustment. In an examination of the Greek communities in South Africa, the various members have been found to react differently to the conflict deriving from incompatible culture goals (Mantzaris, 2000).

An analysis of the third and fourth generations produced the following different manifestations of personal adjustment to conflict:

- The individual largely conforms to the dominant tendencies of the Greek community and remains a part of it. In this sense they are not considered "Africanized" despite many external identifications with the South African culture;
- Although assimilated into the larger community, this person still plays an important role in the organized Greek community life. They somehow balance both ways of life, with fluctuations in their intensity of participation in the life of the Greek community. It should be noted that such an individual, although absorbed by the larger society, still identifies themselves as "Greek" and does not hide their ethnic origin;

- Although in no way participating in the life of the Greek community, this person is considered by the other members of the Greek community (as they consider themselves) as a member of the ethnic community at large. They are viewed as transmitting "Greekness" between first and third/fourth generations – the "Greekness" being considered mostly in an abstract way of ethnic identification;

- In this case, the individual loses contact with the Greek community entirely, and in many ways becomes part of a hate group against the members of the Greek community. They blame the older people for their insistence on "Greek ways" and ridicule every effort of the Greek group to promote Hellenism or ethnic distinctiveness;

- Finally, there is the "cosmopolitan" South African-Greek, who appreciates the problems of the Greeks in South Africa and also the general importance of preservation of certain cultural patterns. At the same time, this individual makes a conscious effort to remove the barriers that separate the first generation from the larger South African community. They usually have higher education and intellectualize the problems of the ethnic stock and also idealize the ramifications of Greek cultural configurations. This person is one of the most important agents for the continuation of the Greek cultural tradition. In addition, through their idealization of the Greek culture and Hellenism, they contribute in a cumulative way to the various forms of a "return" trend or increasing identification with the Greek tradition at large.

In general, however, the majority of people in the second/third generations are, in one way or another, in an ambivalent position towards both the Greek and the South African communities. These feelings of ambivalence and the effort to find some form of adjustment result in conflicting attitudes and difficulty in creating clear-cut cultural identification (Mantzaris, 2000).

Hofstede (2001) pointed out that marginality can also exist for the third/fourth and successive generations, as long as some form of ethnic culture is perpetuated. The third/fourth generations, however, face the question of the co-existence of the ethnic culture and the culture of the larger society from a different perspective. They have not felt the immediate collision of two different ways of life, and, although in many cases the pressure of the Greek culture through the parents was strong, most of the youngest South African-Greeks have been reared in the same way as the rest of the South African population (Mantzaris, 1995, 2000).

For the third/fourth generations of South African-Greeks, separation from the larger South African community is inconceivable. At the same time, the younger South African-Greeks understand that there are elements of differentiation from the rest of the population; elements that in many instances, far from being sources of feelings of inferiority, are factors of proud identification with a historical and cultural past. There is often a growing feeling of willingness to accept the fact of ethnic origin and to provide oneself with elements of social location in an ever-growing, anonymous, mass society (Mantzaris, 2000; Spiro, 2003). Mantzaris (1995, 2000) opined that the third generation, in most cases, has achieved a more stable psychological identity that permits recognition of the diversified character of the South African society.

The South African Family

Despite many influences that could have reduced its effect, Mantzaris (1978) and Spiro (2003) noted that the family has remained the strongest institution of the South African-Greeks. It is not only the main agent of socialization, but also the chief educational preserver of Greek ideals and the Greek way of life. Examination of the South African-Greek family provides an opportunity to view more closely the moulding of personality of its younger members, the transmission of the South African-Greek culture, and the changing patterns through the generations (Mantzaris, 2000).

The Patriarchal Form of the Family

The patriarchal form of the Greek family has always been emphasized (Koliopoulos and Veremis, 2002). In immigrant families, the father has traditionally been the central figure of dignity and authority, whose decisions were the law of the house (Vlachos, 1965). In early immigration periods, a woman's place was in the home, despite the fact that many of them had to fight side-by-side with their husbands for their survival in the various countries (Koliopoulos and Veremis, 2002). Women were not expected to be interested in anything other than their children and their husbands. The father was the "benign survivor" in the home, and in his presence no joking or fooling around was permitted. His rule over the children was illustrated in the traditional Greek saying "fear breeds respect; respect breeds love" (Vlachos, 1965; Koliopoulos and Veremis, 2002).

The patriarchal form of the family, the close supervision and guidance of the children, and customs imported from the rural parts of Greece invariably caused conflict between the older (presumably more conservative) and younger (presumably more progressive) generations, especially in matters of courtship and marriage (Koliopoulos and Veremis, 2002). There was strong opposition to dating, and it is with great hesitation that the immigrant parents, or even later generations of South African-Greek parents, sometimes accede even to restricted dating among their children (Mantzaris, 2000). Special attention at this point should be given to the phenomenon of intermarriage among South African-Greeks, denoting "structural" assimilation, as contrasted to the intense desire of generally older South African-Greek parents to marry off their daughters and sons to persons of Greek background.

Intermarriage has been a very important indicator of the assimilation process. In most cases, it facilitates the acquaintance of the mates with a different cultural perspective, brings diversified backgrounds closer, and thus accelerates the process of assimilation (Vlachos, 1965). The general conclusion in the literature on ethnic and religious intermarriages seems to be that in South Africa (as compared with inter-religious marriages) inter-ethnic marriages seem to conform more to the conventionally assumed pattern, that is, heterogamy sets in after the first generation and continues with each succeeding generation without change (Mantzaris, 2000).

Information concerning the marriage patterns of the Greek ethnic group is rather sparse, because of the general lack of census data on South African-Greeks. The matter becomes more complicated with the confusion between religion and nationality. The fact that Greek Orthodoxy is not a separate category in religious breakdowns further compromises the availability and accuracy of information on religious intermarriage involving South African-Greeks.

Because of their central role in the life of South African Greeks, many cultural patterns associated with religion and family remain distinctly Greek and in many respects are more tenaciously conserved than in Greece proper. On the other hand, structural assimilation in the institutional areas of economic status-vocations, organizations and formal associations, commerce, and education, has been very rapid, with the South African-Greeks approximating the general population in these areas.

The Greek Language

Many researchers have emphasized that as long as non-English tongues persist, full assimilation has not taken place (Koliopoulos and Veremis, 2002).

The same findings are also reported by Mantzaris (2000), who found that the Greek language has become almost extinct among South African-Greeks in the third and fourth generation, because of the inevitable forces of assimilation. According to Mantzaris (2000), other Greek authors, who visited several Greek communities in South Africa, have found not only the absence of the Greek language (structural assimilation), but also a lack of desire for a continuation of Greek language learning (cultural assimilation).

Bilingualism is an acknowledged characteristic of the first and second generations of immigrants. Bilingualism creates a conflict situation that is usually resolved by assigning distinct social spheres to each language.

Most often, the South African-Greeks create a sharp dichotomy between "internal" Greek and "external" African. In such a language arrangement, the Greek speech is reserved for close intimate relations and the English for open or diffuse social relations. There is above all a core of Greek phrases, untranslatable in their exact meaning into English, which are used to describe situations or feelings of a more intimate nature (Spiro, 2003).

The questions of language learning and language use run deep in the South African-Greek community (Spiro, 2003). Greek language, ethnic identity, ethnic entrepreneurship, and the Greek Orthodox Church are linked in an indivisible cultural trait of South African-Greeks. The existence and continuation of one presupposes the others (Mantzaris, 2000). This trinity is fostered and encouraged by a feeling of cultural superiority and by the idea that South Africans, as well as the rest of mankind, love and admire Greece and anything Greek. Because of the central role of the Greek language in the ethnic culture, its absence signifies high structural and cultural assimilation (Spiro, 2003).

South African-Greeks and Religion

In attempt to preserve their traditional way of life, the Greek immigrants thought first of all of transplanting their churches (Spiro, 2003); thus, as soon as a few Greeks got together in some city or town in the country, one of the first things they thought of was to establish a place of worship. According to Mantzaris (2000), Greeks accomplished this through the organization of an orthodox community, something that is not usually pursued before the number of Greeks in a locality reaches 300–400. However, there have been cases where a group of 30–40 or of even 15 families managed to build their own church (Mantzaris, 2000). The Greek Church symbolizes for the South African-Greek their ethnic background and is their only visible link with the homeland, providing at the same time a clear group identity. The Greek is born into their religion, and church affiliation symbolizes for them the Greek way of life (Mantzaris, 2000).

Expressed in another way, religion and the Church are almost synonymous for the Greeks, and the Greek Orthodox religion is entirely synonymous with Greekness. When the Greek asks, "Is he a Christian?" they mean "Is he Greek?" The Greek Church is the main factor in Greek continuity among emigrants nowadays. According to Spiro (2003), the Church becomes the focal point from which clubs and organizations radiate. Many formal organizations in the community are established through the Church, and quite often the Church and its grounds are the gathering places for all kinds of activities. Many events, such as movies from Greece, meetings, dances, lectures, and picnics are sponsored and continuously encouraged by the Church. The Church then becomes a major moving force of Greek families, and by its structure and flexibility manages to balance spiritual duties with social functions (Spiro, 2003).

The many religious festivities, especially during Easter and Christmas, provide group participation in impressive rituals and ceremonies, which help in the reaffirmation of faith in Orthodoxy and Hellenism. The priest is ever-present at social functions to provide the needed eulogy, since most social events such as marriages, baptisms, and even divorces have to have the sanction of the Church in order to be valid according to the dogma. The priest thus becomes indispensable in the life of a Greek community (Spiro, 2003; Mantzaris, 2000; Koliopoulos and Veremis, 2002).

But the Church also plays a role as an educational institution in Greece (Spiro, 2003). From the historical past of Greece, the Orthodox Church has been by necessity the "school of the nation". In many Greek communities in South Africa, the churches have established independent schools with a curriculum that has among its primary aims the teaching of the Greek language and the Helleno-Orthodox tradition.

Since the establishment of Sunday schools, the younger generation is taught by the priest, specially hired Greek teachers, or other members of the Greek community the history and the role of Orthodoxy, Greek civilization, and accounts of the continuity of Hellenic history. In all Sunday schools the fact is constantly stressed that the history of the early Church and that of Byzantine Greece are synonymous. Children are expected to take pride in the role of the Greeks in the expansion of Christianity and in the fact that the records of the early Church were written by Greeks in Greek (Spiro, 2003). The supremacy of Orthodoxy is continuously emphasized, together with the underlying cultural superiority of the Hellenic tradition. The prevalent ethnocentrism about the role of the Greeks in the world and the general interpretation of history is exemplified in the continuity of Greece from Ancient Greece through Byzantine to modern Greece (Spiro, 2003).

The impressive ceremonies of the Church, its long tradition, flexibility, and adaptation to the larger society and the fact that South African-Greeks are born into their religion, are among the factors that account for its preservation and central role in the Greek community. As a repository of Greek values and one of the conservative agents, the Greek Church, with its continuous emphasis on Orthodoxy and Hellenism, has been one of the important resistance blocks to assimilation (Mantzaris, 2000). The general presentation of the central role of the Greek Orthodox Church should not, however, mean that assimilation has not taken place. In the institutional area of religion, researchers can see assimilation as a result of both positive and negative influences (Mantzaris, 2000; Spiro, 2003).

The South African-Greeks and Their Community Life

Because of the pattern of Greek immigration, that is, mostly "chain" migration and sometimes a "gravitational" one, distinct groupings in South Africa, based on Greek island or mainland regions, were soon formed (Mantzaris, 2000). As people from the same village usually emigrated together and helped each other to settle in the same place, it was inevitable that large groups of people from the same locality would gather in one place (Dicks, 1971; Vlachos, 1965; Mantzaris, 2000; Koliopoulos and Veremis, 2002).

According to Mantzaris (1978, 2000), these early groupings were held together by a strong sense of Hellenism, which was the product of centuries of struggle for national existence, by the identification of the Greek Orthodox Church with this struggle, and by the absence of profound differences of customs between the various regions and districts of Greece. The external unifying force has been the "accumulation" of problems, and the effort through a Greek community structure in South Africa to cushion the shock of transition from the native culture to the culture of the surrounding society (Mantzaris, 2000).

The concentration of Greeks in large urban centres and the "gravitational" pattern of settlement described above were also results of the social background of the Greek immigrants. The average Greek is a gregarious person who has lived their life surrounded by relatives and friends (Spiro, 2003). In South Africa, immigrants immediately felt the need to be surrounded by their countrymen, with whom they could use the same language, and with whom they could once again celebrate the traditional Greek holidays (Koliopoulos and Veremis, 2002). An isolated life on the farm, instead of the usual bustling village life, would be inconceivable to the Greek immigrant. Furthermore, given the communal character of Greek rural life, in case of need, the Greek immigrant who was living close to other Greeks would know whom to run to for help, or whom they could ask to be, for example, best-man at their wedding ceremony or godparent for their children (Vlachos, 1965; Mantzaris, 2000; Spiro, 2003).

The effects of the pattern of the migratory process have already been alluded to. The ever-growing circles of common background present a simplified version of the general "community" settlement patterns and interconnections of the Greek ethnic group. The first kinship concentrations (gatherings of close relatives at the same place) were followed by locality (village or town) aggregations. These were results of the "chain" letters and the recruitment of members of the ethnic community from the same place of origin in Greece. Such groupings were later reinforced by the selection of marriage partners, either by matched marriages (*proxeneio*) arranged through the relatives back in the homeland and preferably from the same village from which the early immigrant came, or by actual voyage by the prospective bridegrooms to their native locality and personal selection of their mates (Mantzaris, 2000; Dicks, 1971; Vlachos, 1965; Koliopoulos and Veremis, 2002; Spiro, 2003).

The larger societies (indicating broader regional delineations in Greece) must be understood not on a territorial basis in South Africa, but rather as divisions transcending such lines. These are societies of persons coming from a certain larger geographical region of Greece, such as Macedonians, or Arcadians, or Cretans. It is interesting to note, however, that even such regional and larger societies have major geographical areas of concentration in South Africa, necessitated once more by the pattern of immigration to the country (Mantzaris, 2000).

Mantzaris (2000) suggested that a bond connecting all these various Greeks in South Africa has been the national societies and organizations, which have made a valiant effort to rally the South African-Greek population in a manifestation of pride and identification with the Greek ethnic background. In general, it was South African reality that permitted the several immigrant groups to see themselves as a broader common group. South African experience taught the Greek people to disregard particular customs or *mores* of the various localities in the face of an attraction to a larger affiliation. Such an affiliation was achieved on the basis of a common language that permitted communication with each other (Mantzaris, 2000). Thus, the immigrants started thinking of themselves as a large united group on the basis mostly of a common language and religion, rather than a particular place of origin (Koliopoulos and Veremis, 2002). Instead of being identified as Roumelians or Peloponnesians, they became "South African-Greeks", although there are still intra-ethnic lines of division among this larger group. South Africans could more easily understand such identification on the basis of language. To the general South African public and to other immigrants, language meant culture, and very soon nationality as well (Mantzaris, 2000).

The community structure among Greeks in South Africa, described above, points to the overall pervasive factor of factionalism and regionalism that runs through the Greek communities in South Africa. These patterns of factionalism and regionalism (characteristics carried over from divisions in Greece) have extended to the South African-born generations, and determine much of the nature of social relationships among South African-Greeks. Social contracts and close friendships, Mantzaris (2000) observed, tend to be confined to the groups of the parents. Choices of godparents and marriage sponsors are usually kinsmen or fellow "villagers" of the parents. The South African-Greek community, therefore, can be understood not only as an overall cohesive totality, but also as a federation of diversified sub-groups, determined basically by place of origin in Greece (Mantzaris, 2000).

The difficulties of characterizing a "Greek community" are not only the result of definitional difficulties, but also part of a confusion that seems to run through the whole understanding of Greek aggregations in South Africa (Mantzaris, 2000). It may be advisable to describe a Greek community in an ecological sense as including all the persons of Greek cultural background residing within a given community territorially defined in South Africa. In the literature of ethnic relations, the existence of an ethnic community has been taken to denote lack of assimilation because of the strong group identification (Mantzaris, 2000). There is, however, considerable evidence refuting such a conclusion. It is not the existence or non-existence of a Greek community that can be used as an index of assimilation, but rather the extent to which the structure of an ethnic community is integrated into the total social structure.

Spiritual Kinship: Blood Brotherhood, Spiritual Brotherhood, Godparenthood

According to Cassia and Bada (1991), traditional Greek society, in the past and currently, possesses a number of institutions to turn non-kin (*kseni*) into fictional kinsmen. These include blood brotherhood, also called foster brotherhood (*adelfopiia*), spiritual or soul brotherhood (*psihoadelfosini*), adoption (*iothesia*), and Godparenthood (*koumbaria*). Most of these practices, especially those involving spiritual brothers, appear to be folk practices not officially sanctioned by the Church. Although there are significant variations between them, they possess a cluster of similar characteristics. For example, blood brotherhood and spiritual brotherhood are alike in the following ways: they are often collective, and link together two kinship groups rather than individuals; the relationships are transmitted across generations; and they are often used to prevent an outbreak of hostilities in situations where the vendetta and relations of hostility threaten to disrupt social and commercial life (Cassia and Bada, 1991).

Outside the blood relatives, another form of relation that brings people together is the Greek institution of "*Koumbaros*". A *koumbaros* is the person who acts as either the best man, Godparent, or mentor in social and commercial life. This is a very important relation among the Greeks, who consider the *koumbaros* a member of the extended family. In its original form, the *koumbaros*, either in marriage or baptism, was supposed to act as the spiritual mentor of the person under their guidance. The institution of *koumbaros* has permitted the Greeks in South Africa to create additional secondary relations with each other, especially among families who already have other blood ties, and to bring a partner into their family business (Mantzaris, 2000).

It is interesting to note that the Greek institution of *koumbaros* can be used as an indication of strong association with Greek culture. This means that the Greeks of South Africa who are engaged in the relationship of *koumbaros* are less assimilated than the persons who are not. This phenomenon can also be interpreted to imply that those South African-Greeks already peripheral to the Greek group do not enter into the relationship of *koumbaros* (Dicks, 1971). It should be noted that some family clans that do not have any *koumbaros* relationships are considered the most "Africanized". On the other hand, the clans with many *koumbaros* (and blood) relatives are considered the most "Greekish" in the community (Vlachos, 1965; Dicks, 1971; Koliopoulos and Veremis, 2002). Those persons not belonging to any of the family clans and being more or less isolated despite the expectation of high assimilation remain distinctly Greek. There are older persons, widows, widowers, and older unmarried Greeks who, despite their limited association with the various Greek communities, remain isolated from the larger South African community in a Greek world of their own (Mantzaris, 2000).

Types of South African-Greek Families

As has been indicated above, the family is the centre of life for South African-Greeks. The family embodied, and for many still embodies, the ideal Greek way of life and constitutes one of the last institutions to maintain ethnic culture. However, there have been many changes in Greek family organization in South Africa, which can be visualized in terms of a continuum ranging from the almost-Greek-peasant family to the highly assimilated South African type of family. Thus, in the context of the Greek communities in South Africa, three basic types of South African-Greek families can be distinguished.

The First Generation South African-Greek Family (the "Greekish")

By "Greekish" is meant an organization of parents and offspring in which both parents are of foreign birth and in which there is a conscious effort to perpetuate the Greek way of life. This family is characterized by the confusion of adapting to the highly industrialized society, since the majority of the parents came from rural areas of Greece. Such families in South Africa (what other members of the community have labelled "Greekish") tend to be isolated from the larger community and are the core of the various family clans (Mantzaris, 2000). They are typically older people who, having severed their ties with the Greek homeland, have found it particularly difficult to adapt to the new culture. More often, given the uncertain position in the larger South African community, the older members of these types of families have turned inwards, thus becoming more Greek than the Greeks back in Greece (Koliopoulos and Veremis, 2002). By tenaciously holding on to the peasant traditions, they try to avoid "Africanization", which is considered by many of them practically treason to what they consider the real essence of Hellenism (Mantzaris, 2000). Among the general characteristics of this type of family are patriarchal orientation, the sharing of common goals, a strong sense of obligation towards parents and children, strong in-group solidarity, and the many family celebrations (Vlachos, 1965).

The Second Generation South African-Greek Family (the "Greeks")

The category "Greeks" is characterized by parents and offspring in which one or both parents are South African-born, but are of Greek extraction. It is a transitional type of family organization, trying to bridge the gap between Greek and South African cultures. It is characterized mostly by a state of conflict between Greek and South African values and by many internal and external pressures, which often lead to confusion and disorganization (Mantzaris, 2000). Mantzaris (2000) offered that, in terms of its adjustment to the larger South African society, three forms prevail. First, there is marginality, with resulting continuous ambivalence to either Greek or African culture forms of family organization; second, there is complete abandonment of the Greek way of life; and third, there is increasing identification with the Greek culture as a compensatory scheme. Among the general characteristics of this type of family organization are weakening of patriarchal orientation, mobility, lack of participation in either the South African or Greek community, lack of common goals, less religiosity, weakened in-group solidarity, and rebelliousness towards parental supervision (Koliopoulos and Veremis, 2002).

The Third/Fourth Generations of South African-Greek Families (the "Notiafrikani")

Mantzaris (2000) described this type of Greek family as the organization of parents and offspring in which one or both parents are South African-born. In many respects, it is the type that can be considered typical of the rest of the families of the larger South African communities (Mantzaris, 2000). In this family there are, however, many remnants of the ethnic culture (Koliopoulos and Veremis, 2002).

The most important characteristic of this type of family organization are its egalitarian orientation and basic atomistic character (Dicks, 1971). The transformation of the extended family (first generation) to clusters of nuclear families (third/fourth generations) has been likened by Mantzaris (2000) to the general changing patterns of family structure in South Africa. In South Africa, the cohesiveness that derived from the older patriarchal forms of the extended families has been replaced since World War II by isolated South African-Greek households, especially of the third/fourth generations. Despite the increasing atomistic character of the various families, there is still a certain integrated network of mutual assistance within the larger clans, in the form of an independent kin/family system (Mantzaris, 2000; Koliopoulos and Veremis, 2002; Vlachos, 1965).

Greek Families and Social Rules

As late as 1980, an estimated two thirds of murders or attempted murders in Greece were inspired by the male's need to uphold family honour in the face of public humiliation caused by the victim. Although many of the superficial aspects of traditional social behaviour, relationships, and roles have changed, especially in the cities, modern South African-Greek society still retains elements of a much more traditional set of values, such as the protection of a family's reputation. Since the 19th century, upward mobility has been unusually common in Greece. Because the ideal of generational improvement has been widely distributed, Greek class systems have been much more flexible than those of other European countries (Da Vinci, 2003). This flexibility also applies to South Africa. The family is traditionally the most important institution in South African-Greek society. People think of themselves primarily as members of families, and rarely as individuals in the existential sense.

Other writers have noted that South African-Greeks traditionally identify themselves first as members of families, then according to their places of origin, and lastly as citizens of a nation (Mantzaris, 2000).

Traditionally, all Greek marriages were arranged, generally through the mediation of a matchmaker (Cassia and Bada, 1991). The latter, although unrelated to either family, knew them well enough to be confident that their children were well suited. Opportunities for the young people themselves to meet were rare and restricted to church, in the presence of their parents, and during the "Sunday afternoon walks", where girls and boys strolled separately. Love was not seen as a good reason for marriage, for romantic love was not highly esteemed in traditional Greek society. Divorce and separation were virtually unknown, because through the system of marriage and dowry, kinship and economic ties were so rigidly defined that neither partner could opt out of a marriage without devastating social consequences (Cassia and Bada, 1991).

Urbanization and modernization have altered the attitudes of South African-Greeks towards marriage. The expansion of school systems has meant that boys and girls meet from an early age and are exposed to modern ideas about social and sexual relations. The great increase in the number of women in the work force has also liberated them from strict parental control (Mantzaris, 2000). The family is still seen as the basic social unit of all strata of South African-Greek societies, whether rural or urban (Koliopoulos and Veremis, 2002). For an individual not to marry or to remain separate from their family is viewed as unusual behaviour. Sons and daughters still live with their families until they marry, bypassing the Western tradition of living independently between these two stages of life. Families play a large role in the selection of a mate, although the traditional arranged marriage is now less frequent than in previous generations (Spiro, 2003).

The basic household, or nuclear family, includes a husband, wife, and their unmarried children. This unit may also include a parent or another family relative, and in most regions a young married couple may live with the parents of the one spouse until they can gain financial independence. In rural tradition, the groom takes his bride to live with his parents at least for a short time; they may remain in that house or in one in the same area, creating an extended family (Mantzaris, 2000). In traditional Greek society, manhood was attained through marriage and becoming the main support for a family. Similarly, it was only through marriage that a woman could realize what was seen as her main purpose in life, becoming a mother and homemaker. Remaining single reduced a woman to the marginal role of looking after aged parents and being on the periphery of her married siblings' lives (Cassia and Bada, 1991).

Mantzaris (2000) highlighted the fact that a separate "dwelling unit" for the nuclear family has always been recognized as a prerequisite for the couple's economic independence. Accordingly, the head of the family has been seen as morally justified in pursuing the interests of his dependants in all circumstances. The principle of *"symferon"*, that is, self-interest, overrides every other consideration. Acting in accordance with the principle of *symferon*, Greek parents do everything in their power to equip their children for the future. In present-day South Africa, this involves providing the best possible education for sons, and securing a house as well as an acceptable education for daughters (Mantzaris, 2000).

In traditional Greek villages, houses were built close to one another, encouraging the close contact and cooperation that were necessary for survival in a context of general poverty. The close-knit community of families provided a sense of belonging and security, but also greatly restricted individuals within accepted norms and boundaries in all aspects of life (Dicks, 1971). Urbanization has had a liberating effect. As people became wage earners, the self-sufficiency of the nuclear family grew at the expense of community interdependence (Koliopoulos and Veremis, 2002), and despite changes in its structure, the family remains strong in the South African-Greek society (Mantzaris, 2000).

The Impact of Culture on Greek Immigrant Entrepreneurship in South Africa

Within the ethnic business literature, a pronounced association between the family and the business has been made, but there has been a parallel neglect of the dynamics of the family at work. The family has often been seen as critical to the success of minority enterprise (Mars and Ward, 1984; R. Ward, 1987). Phizacklea (1984) argues that ethnic solidarity would suggest that cultural features like the ideology of self-help, the operation of fraternal frameworks and the importance of the family unit are integral to the development of a minority enterprise. This could also be true of South African-Greeks. The intensive use of familial labour in key positions in the business have often been viewed as critical to the "success" of the business (Mars and Ward, 1984; R. Ward, 1987) and would therefore help to account for the success of South African-Greek family businesses. Two basic reasons have usually been put forward to explain its ascendancy in minority businesses. Firstly, family labour is cheap, and relatives are prepared to work for long hours (Blaschke et al., 1990). Secondly, family occupation of managerial roles is seen to ease the problem of managerial "control". In their study of minority clothing firms in London, Paris, and New York, Morokvasic, Waldinger, and Phizacklea (1990) made the point that running a business with relatives and co-ethnics as partners resolves the problems of trust and delegation, an integral part of good governance.

Watkins and Watkins (1984) argued that entrepreneurs are likely to be the progeny of entrepreneurial families, although this does not necessarily mean a continuation of the established family businesses. They add that the male entrepreneur is likely to have a traditional-style marriage with a wife who plays a subservient and supportive role, both in the home, by (single-handedly) bringing up a family, and working in the business during the early stages of its existence. This usually involves doing the books for the company or undertaking secretarial, cleaning, or packing work. In contrast, female entrepreneurs are far more likely to be single. But, as Watkins and Watkins (1984: 224) have discovered, even when the female entrepreneur was married, "in those few cases where the husband was involved with the business it was usually in an *ad hoc*, peripheral, 'expert' role rather than a supportive subservient one".

Wheelock (1991) justified the term "familial economic unit" by pointing out that many women facilitate the survival of their partner's businesses through their domestic labour, which is not explicitly financially rewarded. Thus, women play critical roles in the survival of family businesses, through both formal, but unacknowledged, roles within the business and through a number of "their" ways, and yet because their roles are not usually recognized, their input is frequently ignored by researchers of small businesses.

For Greeks with prevailing patriarchal, masculine-predominance ideology, weakening only among college-educated urban men and urban women with at least a high school education, husbands and wives may have incongruous perceptions of the decision-making process, regardless of the societal stage of development or cultural ideologies. The incongruence between husbands' and wives' perceptions of decision making may be due to one or both spouses' need to dominate the family power structure or to adhere to "egalitarian norms". Thus, a spouse for whom it is very important to be predominant in decision making may perceive only those cues that permit him or her to see himself or herself as the most powerful member of the family. An analysis of Greek literature (by Koliopoulos and Veremis (2002) and Mantzaris (2000)), for example, showed that when husbands or wives perceive that they prevail in decision making, they are satisfied with their marriage, while the opposite is true when they perceive decision making as being "egalitarian".

Summary

South African-Greeks see economic development as the permanent concern and constant preoccupation of every society. If something is judged to be non-profitable, it is considered of secondary importance, and those involved in non-profitable activities are regarded as dreamers or non-functional elements. To yield profit, values such as competition, influence, expansion, greed, and the like are nurtured (Boutaris, 2003).

Although cultural hostility towards entrepreneurship may stifle it in a particular region, migrant entrepreneurs frequently move to new areas in order to start their enterprises. Thus, cultural hostility may prevent entrepreneurship in a particular region, but some other regions will, in part, benefit from the migration of the ethnic entrepreneurs.

The primary purpose of this case study was to assess in detail the nature and importance of cultural influences on the South African-Greek family. Additionally, this research has added to the body of culturally conscious research about the South African-Greek family, and how culture impacts on the way South African-Greeks will govern their family businesses. Cultural diversity and its effects on management challenges provided a framework and an in-depth understanding of South African-Greeks, their characteristics, religion, lifestyle patterns, communication, values, "norms", and approaches to work that affect their way of governing their families and businesses.

Chapter 4
The Immigrant Family Business: Defining Concepts

The type of business that an immigrant entrepreneur starts, how it is operated, and its success is shaped by the opportunity structure of the community, region, and country the immigrant is in as well as by the immigrant's group characteristics. Despite the importance of cultural factors, traditional theories of entrepreneurship pay scant attention to these factors in the rise of entrepreneurship and subsequent business strategies. The dominant economic and psychological factors that are conventionally referenced in the literature are limited to explaining entrepreneurship and business strategies among groups that are organized along ethnic lines. Perhaps the primary defining characteristic of immigrant entrepreneurs is the notion that they are quite intricately connected to family and ethnic community sources of support. This is in contrast to the rugged, individualistic, and self-made entrepreneur who is the paragon in Western business literature.

Cultural ties and specific cultural factors, of which identity is one, define the immigrant entrepreneur's view of business conduct and strategies rather differently from those emphasized by the "mainstream" entrepreneur. The immigrant entrepreneurs' strategy is driven by business cash flow and turnover rather than margins. These and other culture-based observations suggest several implications of ethnic competition in the economy. One highlight in these new defining concepts of immigrant entrepreneurship is that the spread of such entrepreneurship across national borders may be a characteristic of the next phase of globalization – one that merges and extends the historical nexus of cultural identity and trade in interesting new ways.

Data about the incidence, profile, and propensity of immigrants to engage in business start-up are limited. Industry Canada has reported that new immigrants (owners with less than five years of Canadian residency) account for 3% of Canadian small and medium-sized enterprises (SMEs). The United States Small Business Administration reports 1,500,000 immigrant business owners in the

USA (representing 12.5% of all business owners) and those immigrants are 30% more likely to start a business than non-immigrants. The UK's Department of Trade and Innovation reports causality between entrepreneurial intentions and London's concentrated immigrant (ethnic minority) population. It has also been suggested that the propensity for firm start-up among immigrants in developed countries, including Australia, Canada, the UK, and the USA, is significantly higher than that among immigrants in less-developed nations.

For many immigrants, business start-up is born out of "necessity entrepreneurship", due to unfavourable employment markets in the host countries. Despite differences in age and education, immigrant business owners are thought to bring to business start-up unique and valuable social capital derived from diverse and international networks. New immigrants have also been described as particularly industrious and willing to engage in self-exploitation in order to gain competitive advantages over businesses owned by non-immigrants. Drawing on a sample of ethnic (versus new immigrants) entrepreneurs, scholars have reported that ethnic entrepreneurs from recently established communities were more likely to engage in transnational networking activities compared to entrepreneurs from well-established ethnic communities.

Apart from these direct ties to well established ethnic communities, ethnic members are embedded in several other networks that have a common ethnicity. Ethnicity implies clusters of relationships that embed members in a culture. They not only have associates in common, they are also joined together indirectly through third parties. People who know the same people often share the same perspectives and resources, and feel that they are similar. These networks may be rooted in social ties back home and may be created anew in a foreign land by those who have been excluded from mainstream entrepreneurial networks. By banding together, they create ties that are useful for future entrepreneurs. Hence, new immigrants/entrepreneurs are most likely to locate suppliers, clients, workers, and capital for enclave firms through multiplex, embedded relationships. These social factors are part of the institutional framework behind entrepreneurial migration.

Factors that Determine Entrepreneurial Migration

To understand the factors that influence entrepreneurial migration, n'Doen et al. (1997) introduced the profit-seeking model, which is based on an integrated social-economic framework and which can be applied to the study of entrepreneurial migration in developing countries (see Figure 4.1).

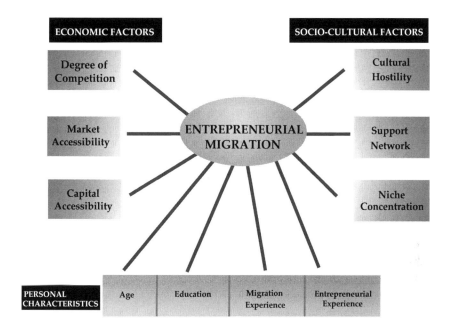

Figure 4.1   Factors that determine entrepreneurial migration
Source: n'Doen et al. (1997).

Migrants who engage in entrepreneurial activity consider such factors as market competition, market accessibility, niche concentration, capital accessibility, cultural hospitality, and support networks before deciding to move. These are factors related to geographic characteristics, but there are also personal characteristics, such as education, age, entrepreneurial experience, and migration experience, which affect the intention to stay. All these factors are the underlying determinants, and the migration variable of interest, the "intention to stay" in a particular region, refers to the number of years a migrant lives in a region. The decision to stay at a particular place is dependent upon migrants' perceptions of the security of their entrepreneurial activities. When a place offers very little security, the migrants will consider other potential locations (n'Doen et al., 1997). The model is presented in Figure 4.1.

According to n'Doen et al. (1997), 10 factors constitute the model. The first factor that determines entrepreneurial migration is the "degree of competition". Degree of competition refers to migrants' perceptions of the ratio of entrepreneurs to consumers in a given product line. Competition may occur within or outside the product niche. Entrepreneurs typically avoid higher degrees of competition and choose markets with lower competition. When a market is saturated, the possibility of realizing a profit is very low, and migrants therefore turn to other places to conduct their business activities. It could be expected that the relation between degree of competition and intention to stay is negative. In other words, the lower the degree of competition at a particular place, the higher the intention to stay.

A second factor to consider is "market accessibility". Market accessibility refers to the migrants' perceptions of the degree of access to the market or to consumers. The degree of accessibility is dependent on the prevailing local government regulation of access to strategic locations. As could be expected, a market with easy access is preferable to one with problematic access. In many instances, access to a particular location is sealed off by earlier migrants as a strategy to maintain business security. The recent migrants are then forced to consider other markets. Market accessibility is positively related to the intention to stay. In other words, the higher the degree of access to a particular market, the higher the intention to stay.

The third entrepreneurial migration factor to consider is "niche concentration". Niche concentration refers to the line of product controlled by a particular group at the current location. The concentration is measured by the concentration of people from a particular ethnic group in a given product line. The more people from a particular group who engage in selling a certain product, the stronger the concentration of the niche. A majority of migrant small and medium entrepreneurs are engaged in the distribution rather than the production sector. The variable niche concentration is thought to be positively related to intention to stay. In other words, the higher the degree of concentration of a certain product line in a particular market, the higher the intention to stay and the longer the length of stay.

The fourth factor determining entrepreneurial migration is "capital accessibility". Capital accessibility refers to migrants' perceptions of the chances to acquire credit at the current destination. Access to credit institutions is essential for business expansion in the future. Access is different from one region to another because of different bureaucratic and social settings prevailing at the time. There are also places where access to credit is very costly because of corruption. The variable capital accessibility exerts a positive impact on the intention to stay. In other words, the higher the access to a capital institution, the higher the intention to stay at the current place, and the longer the length of stay of entrepreneurial migrants.

The fifth factor determining entrepreneurial migration is "cultural hospitality". Cultural hospitality refers to the social response to migrants in a receiving society. Local hostility can be expressed in various forms, from a subtle response such as boycotting to harsh responses such as physical assault. Physical assault is very rare, but when it occurs it is the expression of a long period of mounting frustration among the local people. Soft hostile response can occur in an everyday form of resistance such as the exclusion of migrants from social activities among the local societies.

A sixth factor to consider is "support network". This describes a support network as migrants' relations with relatives, family, kin group, or friends in the receiving region. These people provide information or facilities during the process of settlement. Migrants who have family members or kin in a receiving region may reduce the probability of moving from the current place. Since migrants prefer to stay close to other family members or kin group, the larger the concentration of family and kin in a particular place, the greater the likelihood that the new migrants will remain there. The variable support network has a positive impact on the length of stay in the receiving region.

The seventh factor to consider is "education". The effect of education depends on the transferability of skills acquired during school years. For instance, migrants with a commerce vocational background may have an enhanced ability to assess preferable locations and have less of a tendency to repeat migration. Less-educated migrants are more prone to repeat migrations than are educated ones. Educated migrants prefer to remain at a certain place for a period of time before moving again. Education has a positive impact on the intention to stay. It is thought that the higher the level of education, the higher the propensity of the migrant to stay, and the longer they want to stay in a particular region.

The eighth variable is "age". Migration research consistently demonstrates a strong correlation between age and migration. In other words, younger individuals are more likely to undergo repeat migrations if they discover that the current place is unsuitable for entrepreneurial activities. They are also more likely to travel and experience more of the world before settling in a particular destination. In addition, older migrants usually have family with them, which decreases the possibility of repeat migrations. Thus, the older the age, the stronger the propensity to stay and the longer the length of stay.

The ninth factor is "entrepreneurial experience". Migrants with more experience demonstrate a better understanding of the type of location required for their businesses. Experienced migrants prefer to stay in a particular country and are compelled to leave only when extreme crises occur, such as ethnic disorder or riots. People with entrepreneurial experience are typically more aware of socioeconomic circumstances than those with less entrepreneurial experience. Those with greater experience are less likely to conduct a repeat migration, so they can reduce transportation costs. Entrepreneurial experience exerts a positive impact on the intention to stay. In other words, the more the experience in entrepreneurial activities, the stronger the intention to settle in a particular place, and the more the experience, the longer the length of stay of entrepreneurial migrants in the receiving region.

The tenth variable is "migration experience". Migration experience refers to the frequency of moves before the migrants finally settle at the current location. The total number of trips made by migrants from one place to another after the age of 18 can be used as an indicator of migration experience. Migrants with multiple moves are expected to move more than those with less migration experience. People from families with migration experience may also be more likely to move than those from families with no migration experience. Migration experience has a negative impact on the intention to stay. In other words, the more the migration experience is drawn on, the lower the intention to settle in a particular place and the shorter the length of stay.

Entrepreneurial Migration and Assimilation

The long and complex process of assimilation has as its starting point migration, which can be defined as the physical transition of an individual group from one society to another. According to Eisenstadt (1955), migration itself is accomplished, or can be seen to develop, through three basic stages:

- motivation to migrate, which includes all the feelings that give rise to the urge for emigration from the old cultural environment, and the circumstances facilitating this motivation;

- the social structure of the migratory process, that is, the general character of the migration, whether temporary or not, the kinds of immigrants involved, and so on;

- absorption or non-absorption of the immigrant into the social and cultural framework of the new society.

The basic fact of the migratory process (i.e. the physical transplantation of individuals) creates a whole new process of chain reactions and adjustments, which usually culminate in the assimilation of the immigrant into the new host society. Migration, in general, necessitates social and economic adjustments on the part of the community from which the immigrant originates, the one to which they move, and personal and social adjustments to the culture of the host society. It is important to note that migration is a demographic process that calls for assimilation.

Among the explanations offered towards understanding the assimilation effort of migrants (the effort to adjust to the larger culture) was one proposed by Hofstede (2001). They refer to the "melting pot" concept, which exemplifies the belief that foreigners will fuse with native stock with great rapidity and that a new type of composite will result. Mantzaris (2000), in his work on immigrants in South Africa, is a supporter of the "Africanization" concept, by advocating obliteration of any "foreign" attitude and cultural trait. Mantzaris (2000) regarded the goal of assimilation as a complete adoption of the cultural patterns of an African society. Opposed to the above concept, at the other end of the spectrum, are proponents of "ethnic federation", or "cultural pluralism", or "cultural democracy", based on the right of each group to maintain its particular life without interference, and which therefore describes assimilation as an accommodating scheme of mutual toleration. There have been many ways of proceeding in the analysis of the assimilation process of the several ethnic groups. Three basic questions, however, indicate the interest of the bulk of the literature on the subject:

- What is the meaning of assimilation, or what is the definition of the process of assimilation?

- What are the factors or variables involved in, or influencing, assimilation?

- How do we measure assimilation, or what indices can the researcher use as manifestations of a successful or unsuccessful assimilation of the culture into a larger society?

Assimilation is a process, and as a process one of its first characteristics is its time dimension. There is thus a continual emphasis on the slow character of the process, the gradual acquaintance with the new culture, and at the same time the still slower discarding of old cultural elements. Assimilation often takes a long time to be achieved; in some cases it may never be completed. There are many instances where, despite long periods of time, assimilation has been at a bare minimum, and where fusion of cultures would take a very long time. Assimilation, as a process, can be seen as operating on the individual as well as on the collective level. Such a distinction emphasizes the additional difference in time span for assimilation between the particular individual and the total ethnic group. Researchers have also observed that the individual may become "invisible" in all sorts of social contexts (e.g. work situation, church, cultural associations) but still retain contact with a group (ethnic club, language society), which may be visible as a group. Action and interaction may take place, but generally in the sense of "visibility", group assimilation may be a much longer process than individual assimilation.

The various levels of analysis involved in the discussion of the concept of assimilation and the importance of the above distinctions in the literature can be illustrated by the theoretical schemes of some of the previous research. Among the useful theoretical schemes of the assimilation process is a three-fold distinction by Vlachos (1965), who examined the assimilation of Greeks in America.

In Vlachos's scheme a distinction is drawn between:

1.   the *economic* and *technical assimilation*, which is an outward adjustment and conformity to the general modes of living;

2.   *cultural assimilation*, which includes new cultural traits, modification of the old, and psychological re-adjustment;

3.   *ethnic assimilation* is the ultimate test of assimilation and which Vlachos (1965) describes as a biological amalgamation, especially through intermarriage. The three-fold process of assimilation usually requires at least three generations and is strengthened with the accumulation of successive generations.

Koliopoulos and Veremis (2002) proposed a parallel three-stage assimilation process model consisting of:

1.   *external assimilation*, which is the deliberate and conscious adoption of more outward elements in the culture of the receiving group;

2.   *internal assimilation*, which is a gradual process affected by closer contacts being made with life in the host country, and the immigrant

beginning to appreciate the meanings of the cultural material appropriated; and,

3.   *creative assimilation*, which occurs when the member of the ethnic group views the host culture in a more objective and rational manner than one who is racially minded.

Hofstede (2001) offered an alternative exhaustive list of interacting factors that must be taken into account in order to understand the process of assimilation. He referred to the attitude of the dominant host group, attitudes of the minority group, cultural kinship, race, relative number of groups involved in the contract situation, rate of entrance of the minority group, manner of settlement (whether urban or rural, and the extent of isolation), the age and gender composition of the group, and the influence of certain personalities either in opposing or encouraging assimilation.

Mantzaris (2000) also discussed the elements affecting the nature and extent of the group's assimilation, such as tradition, visibility, real or imagined competition, cultural components of the immigrants, and the social pliability of immigrants. Other researchers have offered similar classifications of factors or variables involved in the process of assimilation, such as cultural kinship, language, religion, home life, flow of immigrants, legal obstacles, age opportunities, and segregation. All these factors involved in, or influencing assimilation involve a multiplicity of manifestations of social and cultural participation (Koliopoulos and Veremis, 2002; Vlachos, 1965; Hofstede, 2001).

Koliopoulos and Veremis (2002) who, as stated above, distinguished three stages of the assimilation process, offered some indices that can be used to assess the success of assimilation. Their indicators are particularly suitable to the second generation, such as:

- change in externals, that is, personal appearance, food habits;

- change of names;

- occupational adjustment, that is, moving away from the parental occupational specialization, increasing white-collar jobs;

- marriage, that is, postponement or avoidance of marriage and therefore greater independence;

- intermarriage;

- the birth rate and decreasing fertility;

- racial gestures, or fewer gesticulations;

- crime patterns, which denote the crossing of ethnic lines in delinquent acts and not "idiosyncratic" ethnic crimes.

Mantzaris (2000) proposed the following indicators of successful assimilation:

- economic integration, that is, jobs in factories, participation in unions, and increasing class and economic status;

- education, especially knowledge of English and more generally exposure to host country values through school;

- political activity and identification with host region's ideology;

- recreation, that is, mass participation, influence of movies, entertainment, and mass culture;

- above all, intermarriage, which transcends ethnic, religious, and racial boundaries.

There appears to be at least some convergence among the various authors on assimilation, which can be summarized as follows:

- despite the definitional subtitles, there is, more or less, agreement that assimilation is a process of adjustment to the cultural elements of a surrounding larger group;

- assimilation, being a process, involves a time dimension and therefore gradual acquaintance with the new culture over successive generations;

- there is recognition of individual and group assimilation;

- there is recognition of an underlying distinction between assimilation as denoting the position in the social order and as expressing the internalization of values and cultural standards of a larger society;

- in the various theoretical approaches, there are common elements with regard to the factors or variables involved in the process of assimilation. These common elements tend to emphasize:

  – the predisposition and cultural background of the immigrant;
  – the structure of the migratory process;
  – the predisposition of the receiving society and the sociocultural structure of the receiving area.

- the measurement of assimilation involves certain indices of participation in the host culture. These indices refer mostly to occupational or economic status, marriage, education, citizenship, and English language competence, among others.

The Foundation of Ethnic Entrepreneurship

One of the most important challenges that many necessity immigrant entrepreneurs face at the beginning of their entrepreneurial activities is a lack of capital. Many of them do not have access to formal financial sources and have to rely on their ethnic community to find the start-up capital. In fact, the ethnic community is of critical importance to the necessity-driven immigrant entrepreneur. Lack of access to financial capital can be counterbalanced by, for instance, an extensive use of social capital. In such cases, immigrants may take refuge in ethnic resources, meaning the sociocultural and demographic features of the whole group, which co-ethnic entrepreneurs utilize in business. Ethnic resources characterize a whole group, not just its isolated members. These resources may include kinship and marriage systems, relationships of trust, cultural assumptions, and a pool of underemployed co-ethnic workers. "Ethnicity" is a resource that is instrumental in many economic activities. Ethnic entrepreneurs can and do use this resource. However, ethnic resources are not always an advantage for the immigrant entrepreneur. Ethnic bonding can, at a certain point, become ethnic bondage.

Yet, these immigrant resource networks provide the co-ethnic employees that the immigrant entrepreneur needs for relief from the long work hours spent on the business and to overcome the "cumbersome" regulations imposed on employers to protect employees. The particularity of the co-ethnic employees is that they are flexible and do not expect to be paid like employees of the mainstream society. The relationship between the necessity immigrant entrepreneur and co-ethnic employees is one of solidarity.

The co-ethnic employees provide their flexible labour to help the necessity immigrant entrepreneur and in return get the status of worker, a social status that is very difficult to acquire in the mainstream job market. In many cases, these co-ethnic employees are family members of the necessity immigrant entrepreneur.

The ethnic community also represents the ethnic market niche that is targeted by the necessity immigrant entrepreneurs. Niche formation is a common phenomenon, and a process by which entrepreneurs who share a religious or other common background cluster together in an economic sector. Niche formation is the logical outcome of migration. Initially, newcomers have a restricted number of contacts, mostly with people from the same regional background. The exchange of information and recruiting of personnel takes place through these networks and results in a concentration of economic activity in certain sectors. Niche formation may result from a preference amongst migrants for working with people who hopefully will understand them better or are willing to honour their wishes regarding work, for example during the Sabbath or Ramadan. Within a niche market, ethnic groups can act as economic interest groups because group solidarity leads to the availability of all manner of resources at a relatively low cost. Solidarity results from trust within an ethnic niche market, which is maintained through the criss-cross network of personal ties. Trust can lead to low-interest rate loans and easy-to-obtain credit. The high degree of organization amongst immigrants enables them to generate and distribute resources – such as money, information, training, jobs, labour, and even interfamily ties.

Sometimes the product offered is an ethnic product that is well known and sought after by the ethnic community. The necessity immigrant entrepreneur maintains strong ties with the ethnic community. Despite the recent trend of immigrant entrepreneurship that includes women, the vast majority of necessity immigrant entrepreneurs in many developed countries are middle-aged male immigrants. They are, in general, involved in an endogamous marriage, and for many of them the spouse provides help in the business. Migrants can monopolize a sector when a link is made between pre-migratory skills on the one hand and an association between the specializations of the group on the other. Ideas in the host society about the qualities of the newcomers can lead to their exclusion, but can also reserve an economic sector for them in a more positive sense.

Niche formation need not occur only in a new field. The established population may also withdraw from a field that is no longer considered profitable, and be replaced by newcomers willing, forced, or able to work with lesser margins. Migrants may fill a gap in the market left vacant by others.

The nature of niche formation is determined, amongst other things, by the possibilities it offers for family members to get involved in it. When both men and women can work within the niche, a much closer relationship develops between the group and the economic sector. The possibilities for family members to become involved depend not only on the nature of the sector, but also on work options outside of it. When there are many possibilities within the niche, and only a few outside it, ethnic entrepreneurs can profit from the existence of a large reservoir of cheap labour. This will strengthen the success and continuity of the niche. The long-term development of a niche is constrained by the principle of competitive exclusion. A niche can support only a restricted number of entrepreneurs.

There is a downside to the ethnic enclave immigrant business. Critics retort that cultural arrangements relegate similarly poorly placed people without bargaining power to a narrow competitive arena. Drawing on ethnic enclave members often means exploiting them. Faultfinders assert that culture disguises economic power. Invoking culture and non-standard rules may be exploitative. The concept of the "eth-class" critiques the ethnic enclave concept positing that culture is classless. Hiring employees outside the labour code gives workers a short-term advantage, but not necessarily legal protection.

The New Wave of Immigrant Entrepreneurs

A new wave of immigrant entrepreneurs that has been steadily on the rise in the past two decades covers so-called opportunity immigrant entrepreneurs. These immigrants freely decide to start a business in a country other than their native land in order to take advantage of a business opportunity. Some of the goals have been cited in literature as follows: make money by earning from their business more than they would have earned if they were immigrant workers, enjoy their independence, or accomplish a dream. For some immigrant entrepreneurs, seeking business opportunities is part of their culture, so it is almost normal for them to seek business opportunities, start a business when they are settling down in the host country, and even go beyond borders through e-commerce. Groups within the wave of opportunity immigrant entrepreneurs can be identified as those who moved to their host country with the purpose of undertaking entrepreneurial activities; immigrants who came to the host country for academic or professional training and decided to stay on afterwards; immigrants who came temporarily for job opportunities and later decided to exploit a business opportunity; and the second-generation immigrants born in the host country.

Research has cited in the past decade the characteristics of a new generation of immigrant entrepreneurs. This new generation of immigrant entrepreneurs is highly educated and many hold a host-country university degree. This clearly distinguishes them from necessity immigrant entrepreneurs who, in general, are not highly educated; both groups tend to be natives of developing countries. Differences among necessity and opportunity immigrant entrepreneurs include: proficiency levels in English or other host-country languages, integration in their host country business community, stronger business relationships with the mainstream economy of the host country, and easier access to start-up capital from financial institutions of the host country. Scholars have defined several types of opportunity immigrant entrepreneurs – namely, traditional opportunity immigrant entrepreneurs, diaspora entrepreneurs, global immigrant entrepreneurs, and the ever-growing group of transnational immigrant entrepreneurs.

The contemporary literature on immigrant transnationalism points to an alternative form of economic adaptation of foreign minorities in advanced societies, based on the mobilization of their cross-border social networks. The phenomenon has been examined mainly on the basis of case studies that note its potential significance for immigrant integration into the receiving countries, and for economic development in the countries of origin. Although immigrant transnationalism has received little attention in the mainstream literature so far, scholars point to this group as the one with the greatest potential to alter the character of the new ethnic communities spawned by contemporary immigration.

The term "transnational fields" was coined in the immigration literature, and refers to the web of contacts created by immigrants and their home-country counterparts, who engage in a pattern of repeated back-and-forth movements across national borders in search of economic advantage and political voice. Initially, such contacts may be purely economic, and involve just the country of origin and that of the destination country. The literature on European immigration to the rest of the world at the turn of the 20th century features numerous examples of sustained cross-border contacts of an economic and political character. What is novel at present is defined by three influences on the growth potential of transnational immigrant entrepreneurship.

Firstly, revolutionary innovations in transportation technology and electronic communications facilitate easy, cheap, and fast contacts across long distances for the growth of the transnational immigrant enterprise. No matter how motivated, transnational political activists or transnational entrepreneurs of the early 20th century could not sustain the volume of or engage in the near-instantaneous exchanges made possible by new communication technologies. Secondly, the intense level of contact is made possible by these communication technologies incorporating the seemingly growing number of immigrants and their home-country counterparts involved in them. As they cease to be exceptional, transnational activities may become common and even normative, at least in some communities described in the modern literature. The third feature is the increasing involvement of sending-country governments seeking to promote and guide the transnational initiatives and investments of their respective diasporas. This growing official attention reflects the weight acquired by transnational fields and, in turn, their support and promotion by the global marketplace. The once improbable spectacle of people of modest means criss-crossing the globe and making use of technologies that were formerly the preserve of powerful corporates defies conventional expectations as to the role of labour immigrants in the world economy. The unconventional character of these practices has also led to scholarly scepticism about their scope and their real significance. Researchers have not been at the forefront of studies of transnationalism, and some have voiced fears that they represent just one more addition to the faddish rhetoric of globalization – stronger in grand pronouncements than in hard facts.

Furthermore, some scholarly attention has been paid to intergenerational transmissions of self-employment among immigrants. Intergenerational links to self-employment can act through different channels. An individual with self-employed parents can acquire specific human capital while helping their ancestors run their business. In addition, an individual with self-employed parents can also take over the family business and inherit the business contact network built by their parents. Thus, self-employment might be correlated across generations since the offspring acquire informal business experience from their parents; the immediate social environment provides social support through the transmission of practical skills and experience for a specific occupation that is typically not taught at school. If the offspring acquire informal business experience and managerial skills from their parents, they will most likely become self-employed individuals. Besides this, previous studies provide evidence that greater personal wealth of the first generation of immigrant entrepreneurs increases the probability for the second generation to enter self-employment.

Case Study:
An Entrepreneurial Immigrant
Family in Colombia

Melquicedec Lozano

The case herein considered is about Vladimir and his family. Vladimir was the fourth son of Mijaíl, a European Emigrant who left his country as a result of the economic hardship he had endured since before World War I started. Mijaíl fathered four sons and one daughter, all born in Colombia.

Departure from Europe and Immigration to Colombia

Mijaíl, Vladimir's father, comes from a region called, at that time, Besarabia, part of the kingdom of Rumania in the southeast area of central Europe. That area housed a very large Jewish population and belonged to Russia by 1915, when famine was prevalent as a consequence of the economic situation. The arrival of World War I could be felt, and the persecution of Jews had already started. People there believed that North America was the ideal place to work and prosper. This motivated Mijaíl to leave Besarabia and head to New York to look for a job. First, he arrived in Calais, France and when he attempted to board a ship to the United States, he was told that the border was closed and the only ship available was going to Cartagena, Colombia. That was the only option for Mijaíl, and he took it, because he could not go back. Eighteen years old, speaking Russian, his mother tongue, he arrived in Cartagena in 1918, with no knowledge of Spanish. Although he was a Jew, he started selling framed pictures of the sacred heart of Jesus, very popular among Colombian Catholics at the time. He then became a tailor, a trade that allowed him to get some income. Still in Cartagena, he soon filed the necessary applications to bring his wife from Russia.

Jaime, his eldest son, was born while Mijaíl was in Cartagena. They later moved to Barranquilla and then to Medellin where Adolfo, his second son, was born. They then moved on to the city of Bucaramanga where Ramon, the third son, was born. Vladimir was born after they returned to Medellin. They then moved to the city of Buga, where a daughter, the youngest of the children, was born.

They stayed for some time in Buga and started a fabrics and dressmaking business that gradually grew into a large store. Just as they were becoming prosperous, a fire destroyed everything they had. The perseverance and strength of the family carried them to the city of Palmira where Mijaíl began to produce trousers and travel with his son Ramon – who was more inclined towards commerce than the other children – to sell fabrics and garments in different towns.

After some time, the family moved to Cali, one of the three main cities in Colombia. The four sons and the daughter enrolled in school here. All of Mijaíl's children shared the entrepreneurial spirit, and years later Jaime moved to Barranquilla, after traveling around the world, and established a store and a movie rental business. Adolfo bought and sold emeralds and later started a company of chemical products, which he still has. Ramon set up a store with Mijaíl, near Barranquilla. Very early on, Vladimir began selling garments at school and then established his own company. The daughter, the youngest of the children, married when she was very young and became a housewife.

Mijaíl grew up in a hierarchical society, totally dominated by males. This is why he demanded so much from his sons. He always had his own business, and was bent towards commercial activities. This is one of the reasons why all his sons were so independent and none of them ever worked as someone else's employee. Mijaíl, by his example, always gave them the idea of being independent. It was clear to the family what it meant to be Jewish. Religion was important in their lives, because in a Jewish family, it permeates the daily activities at home, at dinner time, at work. Mijaíl, however, was not a religious person, although his wife certainly was because her father was a rabbi. Mijaíl always thanked Colombia, the country that welcomed him, where he didn't experience persecution; it was the country where he learned to speak Spanish, even though he never lost his foreign accent, nor did he lose the various languages he spoke, as his wife did, Russian and Romanian among them.

Vladimir, the Entrepreneurial Chemist

Vladimir was born in Cali. As a teenager, he used to sell garments in the market place. After high school graduation, he bought and sold sulphuric acid. He ran his experiments in a small room he rented at the Universidad del Valle, where he was studying chemical engineering. He paid rent by repairing university equipment and doing shopping errands for the necessary components. In this manner, the University also benefited. Thus his company was born, in the chemical engineering laboratory.

Upon graduation, he began as a tradesman, selling and renting equipment (mills and reactants, among others). He met his wife while in high school and they then studied together at the University. Later, he went to Israel for eight months, on sabbatical leave. Upon returning, he had the opportunity to buy a company that belonged to an Italian who was moving to another city. Vladimir persuaded Mijaíl to lend him money so he could start operating a milling factory. This was 38 years ago. Luis Hernando, his eldest son, was only a year old at that time. Luis Hernando joyfully recollects:

I remember that the company's facilities were small and our home was continuously turning into a warehouse. I went there many times. On the weekends, my father would tell me, "Come along, let's go for a spin." One of my sisters would not go because she has a condition of severe mental retardation, while my little sister was not interested, as she was bent on gynaecology from the time she was a child. As I grew up, I observed how things were run, how my father did business, how he led the company.

Luis Hernando also vaguely remembers that there were difficult times at first. However, the good times were to come, as Vladimir recalls with enthusiasm: "We started out very well producing the phosphoric acid for Quala's Fresco Royal, a production supported by President Belisario Betancourt because it substituted imports, and national products were favoured over foreign ones." With a thoughtful countenance, as if returning to the past, he continues: "Mijaíl, my father, always had a business, he was never an employee, and that led me to start a business." His wife nods and says: "I think that everyone's method of doing business had its roots in Mijaíl; everyone learned to work independently and did not inherit a fear of doing business."

Cultural Transference

Vladimir, with calm intonation and with the peace of mind obtained by one who has achieved his goals, says, with plenty of conviction:

Responsibility is learned by example at home and it is complemented by studying. It is in this manner that one develops the responsibility to get up early and go to work. Our daughter Marcela, the gynaecologist, tells us that she cannot imagine us doing nothing; and she is the same: she works non-stop.

His wife intervenes again, to back up his words:

I always liked the European education, and this is why we chose a German school for the children, because a European is more of a builder; he is more resourceful when starting from scratch. Europeans manufacture, Americans buy. European culture teaches how to do things, how to build. This has influenced this family a lot.

Vladimir and his wife transferred different customs to their children, which had been inherited from Mijaíl, his father. Not to owe anything to anybody was one of them. He was never inclined to get loans from banks. To be honest all the way and faithful to his word was another relevant policy, which amounts to saying, "your word is worth a lot; if you give your word you have to comply with it, even if you haven't signed anything". Another policy was "don't do anything for the love of it", as he said, to mean that you should do business as long as you profit or benefit. Vladimir also taught his children to be coherent and austere, even if this meant giving themselves few pleasures. Vladimir tends to be naturally rigid, while his wife is more spiritual, at the other end of the scale. His son Luis Hernando recalls how Vladimir had twice been close to bankruptcy, and that his mother had played a pivotal role in getting the company and the home ahead again. "One of my mother's conditions was that the house should never be mortgaged in order to save the company, from which experience I learned that the roof comes first", he asserts with conviction.

Luis Hernando identifies himself with a given country, perhaps due to the fact that his ancestors come from Europe; this does not mean, however, that he is nationalistic or that he clings to a given region. If he had to move to another country, he would do it with his family, which is most important. He notes confidently, with the joviality proper of someone who is currently 36 years old:

I would take my children and my belongings and move on somewhere else if necessary, but my family comes first. Other than that, I would not worry. I may think that way, perhaps because of the persecution endured by the Jewish people, which is there, latent. Perhaps I would not be able to say the same had I had ancestors from somewhere else.

And in reference to some of the good customs inherited from his grandfather Mijaíl, he adds:

There is this discipline that obviously comes from family history which I will also instil in my two boys. I want them to be world citizens, so that they don't feel tied to anything just because they are from here. There is a know-how originated from living together as a family, which does not depend on where you are; a way of thinking and behaving that will always let you set up a factory, which is complemented by a technical know-how concerning those things that you have learned to do.

Vladimir's Successor

Luis Hernando finished his high school and university studies in Cali. He graduated as a chemical engineer and worked for two multinational companies. He then traveled to Holland, where he obtained a master's degree in food engineering, and worked with his father upon returning to Colombia.

When he returned, he and his father began modernizing the company, to further open their business to the world, to travel out of Colombia more frequently, to update the technical standards. From the start, his father gave him a lot of freedom and this created some uncomfortable situations, because said freedom led to changes that sparked frictions between father and son. This resulted in Luis Hernando looking for a job somewhere else, because he could no longer stand the differences. Coincidentally, the opportunity came up to get a doctorate in chemical engineering in Holland, and he took it. For Vladimir, this was "like the end of the world". He tried to persuade Luis Hernando to desist, but the latter stayed away for five years, while maintaining contact to keep abreast of developments in the company.

This absence made his mother become more involved. The business grew very little during this time, just enough to carry on for those five years. The company was doing fine when Luis Hernando returned and his father made him a better offer to start working together again. Friction arose once more, but to a lesser degree, as a result of the cognitive loss that Vladimir suffered from, which forced him to delegate more. The business improved in areas such as legal issues, corporate government, statutes, and management strategies. Free from legal problems or marital conflicts, issues concerning the family company are handled properly. Today, it is a dynamic, entrepreneurial, and very innovative company with steady growth. There are 300 different products being manufactured, with know-how relative to many things because through the years, the family business continuously changes its core business and reinvents itself. It also has a versatile plant that facilitates innovating capacity. Accounting is well organized and this lets management know where money goes. Besides, there are no debts; dividends have never been paid, and company figures have always been clearly visible to all stockholders. All of the above makes management easier.

Case Study:
Domenico Napoli: An Italian Immigrant Entrepreneur in America

Leann Mischel

Upon meeting Domenico Napoli for the first time, one gets the impression of an energetic, social man with a strong Italian accent. In fact, he came to the United States (US) in 1987, when he was 18 years old – not yet a man, but no longer a boy. In the mid-1980s, the economy in Italy started to deteriorate. Domenico's family had always been successful in Italy, but the changing economic conditions caused some concern for everyone. His father did not want to lose the lifestyle he had worked so hard for his family to enjoy, and saw better opportunities in the US. Since he had friends already living in central Pennsylvania, Domenico's family moved to that area. However, the home they owned in Italy was not sold, the business Domenico's father ran was only leased to someone else, and cars were left behind with every intention of returning a couple years later when the economy, hopefully, turned around.

The move to the US in the summer of 1987 was not easy. Domenico and his three sisters spoke no English but would be starting school a few months later. A tutor was hired to teach them the English language so they could get through their education. Thanks to a friend in the school district, the tutoring continued during school hours even after school began.

Domenico's father was trying to introduce a car painting technology in the area that was very successful in Italy, but had not yet taken off in the US. So, when he relocated to the US he had the challenge of establishing his market – which he did successfully. A few years later, though, Domenico's father was injured could no longer run his car painting business. The family recognized that an alternative had to be found.

Entering the Restaurant Business

Domenico liked pizza. In fact, he had some relatives who owned a pizza shop in the area, and he would spend much of his free time helping at the restaurant. When his father could no longer run his business, Domenico persuaded him to open a pizza shop. In 1991, after many months of searching the classified ads for businesses for sale, they found a location about an hour from their home and opened their first pizza shop. In 1992, a second restaurant was opened closer to home, near the state capital. This shop was mostly delivery for local businesses. A year later, a third restaurant was opened in the cafeteria area of a local hospital. Thus, in a very short period of time, the family had opened three restaurants.

Traveling an hour each way between the restaurants became a challenge for Domenico and his family. They were not able to dedicate what they wanted to each of the locations, so, in 1993, Domenico and his father found a restaurant that had gone out of business that was located close to the first restaurant they had opened. This new location was outstanding. Not only would local traffic see the restaurant, but it was located on a busy thru-way that attracted a large number of travellers. The business was a great success, but Domenico's father wanted more. He noticed that since there were a large number of travellers passing by the store, a recognizable franchise might be more successful in the store's location. After much research, he turned the restaurant into a Dairy Queen and continues to run it as such to this day.

Expansion

As Domenico got older, he became more engaged in the business. He had taken over one of the restaurants that was located near an amusement park about 30 minutes from his home. Because of the restaurant's location, business was cyclical. He was very busy during the warmer months when the amusement park was active and less busy in the colder months.

By 2005, Domenico was married with two children and was anxious to expand his business. The question of how to expand was an issue. He was restricted, to some extent, by geography since both his parents and his wife's parents were now living close by and he already had a successful business located about 30 minutes away. Determined to make the restaurant more successful and to learn more about the catering business, he took a job at one of the local universities as a Catering Coordinator for about two years while running his restaurant.

Adding to the expansion challenge were limitations in the local demographics. The area where Domenico lives is very rural. The population in 2011 was 5,774 with a median household income of around USD 32,000 – well below the Pennsylvania average of just over USD 49,000. In 2009, the median house value was just over USD 125,000, again below the Pennsylvania average at that time, which was almost USD 165,000. The ethnic background of individuals living in the area was 88.8% white, 6% Hispanic, and 2.7% black. It was not uncommon to see Amish horses and buggies parked at the grocery store or even at the local Walmart. Where he lived was not exactly a thriving metropolis showing opportunities for tremendous growth. The location of his restaurant, about 30 minutes away, was similar, if not more remote.

But, Domenico knew pizza and he had the urge to do more than he was currently doing. So, in 2007, he opened his second pizza restaurant, nearby the first one.

Three years later, he found a location closer to home. Although located off the beaten path, he recognized that the only pizza alternatives close to home were the well-known franchises. Domenico was confident that people wanted something different. There were also opportunities to take advantage of the local university, which during the school year boasted approximately 2,400 students who consumed a large amount of pizza. He bought the restaurant and started selling and delivering pizza in the immediate area. He started the business believing that, given the local demographics, it would not be a huge success. He persuaded his wife to quit her banking job and work there as something more leisurely to do. She could run the business while their kids were at school and be home in plenty of time to spend the after-school hours with them while he focused on the other two restaurants about 30 minutes away.

Perhaps due to people's desire for more than the usual franchises, and Domenico's ability to market in the local area, this third restaurant became more successful than they had imagined. Around the same time, Domenico started to realize he wanted to spend more time with his family. Since he was spending so much time in the other restaurants, he rarely saw his children. Shortly after he opened the third restaurant, the economy started to turn. The financial crisis hit, some large factories in the area closed, and a large percentage of the local population near his first two restaurants lost their jobs.

Domenico recognized that the restaurants would not be able to do the same business, but, partially because of the attraction of the amusement park in the area, there was still a lot of potential. This was a great opportunity for him to focus less on that location and more on the store closer to home. He changed the first restaurant to be more banquet- and catering-focused, closed the second restaurant, and turned his attention to the third store located near his home.

The opening of two other restaurants followed soon after, both located closer to home and in walking distance from the local university. The first one, opened in 2011, is an upscale Italian restaurant, and the second, opened a year later, right next door, caters directly to the college crowd with pizza and sandwiches. Domenico now has three restaurants where he spends the majority of his time and which are located within a three-mile radius of his home, and a fourth pizza restaurant about 30 minutes away. He also continues to run the first restaurant, but since it focuses more on catering and banquets, less of his attention is needed there.

Looking Back and to the Future

Domenico admits that his biggest challenge was learning the English language. His father has been his buffer in helping him to learn how to run a business well and continues to be his financial advisor, financial planner, and overall mentor. While he never expected to stay in the US as long as he has, he did so because the economy back home was not good. The family never sold their home in Italy and still goes there on a regular basis. The business in Italy was eventually sold.

Domenico has no current plans for additional expansion and is not training his children to take over. His plan for succession is that, as he gets older and wants to be less involved with the restaurants, he will continue to oversee them while hiring others to be more engaged in their management. His children are now very involved in school and after-school activities and do not have a lot of time to even spend helping in the restaurants. It is Domenico's desire to let them choose whatever interests them and to allow those interests to evolve over time.

Chapter 5

Family Dynamics Impacting Governance and Sustainability of Immigrant Family Businesses

Ethnicity lies at the heart of culture, created through interactions among family members and their respective communities, and influences the way in which people view their world. Each particular culture, therefore, is a result of the norms and values that characterize and pattern these interactions. With regards to community resilience, the extant literature sees the family unit, influenced by its values, as a resource on which to draw in times of change and, in combination with its cultural past, is vital for the healthy functioning of communities. Although sustainable family business theory highlights several variables of family business functions that interface, this section conceptually develops a rationale for how the variable of good governance impacts long-term sustainability of the immigrant family business by focusing on how family dynamics impact good governance sustainability of the immigrant family business.

Immigrant Family Harmony and Communication

Within an immigrant family and business agreement, it is essential for the interests of the family to be known and communicated to all concerned. A viable immigrant family governance process cannot survive in an atmosphere of ignorance and distrust. Key areas of family life will flourish in an open communication culture or process. The literature on the topic advocates a continuous communication system between the immigrant family and the business in order to maintain family and business matters in harmony. Here, it is postulated that a culture of open family communication, reinforced by structured processes, is an integral precondition to creating a successful immigrant family governance process.

Immigrant Family Communication and Good Governance

A culture of open family communication, reinforced by structured processes, is an important precondition to creating a successful (immigrant family) governance process. Key areas of immigrant family life must also have an open communication culture or process, as a viable family governance process cannot survive in an atmosphere of ignorance and distrust. Researchers are of the opinion that the first principle of fairness in decision-making processes consists of giving those concerned a voice, and ensuring that their views are heard and represented. This voice gives stakeholders a way of shaping the decisions under consideration. Engaging in communication, by all concerned, is the first step for building fairness in the process.

The place to start is with the communication between the immigrant family members themselves, regarding family matters. In smaller first- and second-generation families, this communication can be facilitated through regular family meetings, guided by good communication processes for both family and family business matters. Families that have grown to a multi-generational stage may require a formal structure, such as an immigrant family council. The council can meet several times a year to discuss immigrant family issues, including the performance of the immigrant family business or immigrant family investments. Such meetings provide an open forum for immigrant family members to discuss outstanding matters with each other. The council may have key functional responsibilities, such as the nomination of family members to the company board of directors. The immigrant family council can also serve as an educational and mentoring facility for the younger generation. Most importantly, communication channels such as these help to create and sustain a culture of mutual trust within the immigrant family. A final requirement for open communication is the sharing of financial information. The practice of keeping key financial data from all but a small circle of family members should be avoided.

The maintenance of open communication processes among the immigrant family members and between the family and its business creates the knowledge and competency required by family members who will have responsible roles in the family governance model. Together with the accumulated experience of being exposed to financial results and discussing them with other family members, some of the understanding required for good governance can be developed in this way. Business and investment performance results become more familiar subjects for all the family members rather than unknown, distant data. What is really at the heart of this entire communication process is the creation of trust among immigrant family members.

Immigrant Family Harmony and Profitability

The immigrant family is said to be the predominant controller of businesses, contributor to job creation, the largest single source of start-up capital, and the most enduring institution for entrepreneurial activity in emerging economies. What distinguishes great entrepreneurial businesses from others is not only the ability to earn a living for themselves and others, but also the ability to create value – value that can result in capital gains. The recycling of entrepreneurial talent, business value, profit, and capital from immigrant family businesses is at the very heart of good governance systems of responsibility for economic renewal and individual initiative. Therefore, a goal of profitability is the long-term goal to create value added in a business. Here, "profitability" refers to the enforcing of a goal of profitability and crafting a strategy to achieve it.

Immigrant family governance is often highlighted by various authors as making the difference in firm performance and success. However, these authors all argue that the agency benefits accrued by immigrant business are a function of unified governance – the owners are also the firm's managers. What these studies fail to demonstrate is the unique impact of family governance on firm performance. There are many divergent conclusions on whether immigrant family firms have a bigger impact on firm performance than non-immigrant family firms. Other researchers concur by noting that noticeably absent from the immigrant family business literature are wealth creation topics such as entrepreneurial orientation and performance, high-growth companies, strategic experimentation, and finding supernormal returns.

Immigrant Family Harmony and Relationship Commitment

The literature focusing on relationships concentrates on the environment of a Western-country culture, and not on the international, immigrant, or cross-cultural scenario. The issue of commitment in cultural exchange is undeniable when expanding to foreign markets. Here, commitment is defined as the degree to which the immigrant family values the business and its future, as well as the commitment of the family members to operating the business within the family.

Needs, Cultural Values Alignment, and Good Governance

The immigrant family dynamic cannot be ignored in the entrepreneurship process of entrepreneurial immigrant family businesses. The immigrant family monitors and reviews business activities to determine whether they put at risk family traditions, culture, values, and assets in the core family business. Among organizational theorists, the tactic of ideological commitment to the notion that efficiency considerations and bureaucratic rationality should prevail in the work setting often leads researchers to ignore how the family dynamics of the founder/current owner(s) influence managerial behaviour. In immigrant family business, the family, ownership, and management are inextricably intertwined.

The more that personal needs and career interests/needs are aligned with opportunities offered by the immigrant family business, the better the chance will be that good governance and long-term sustainability will prevail in the context of the immigrant family business. Immigrant family business members who put family needs ahead of business needs are more likely to remain involved with the family business than those who put the business's needs first. Needs alignment in the immigrant family business context is the alignment of personal needs with career interest in relation to opportunities offered through and by the family business.

Case Study:
Transfield and Tenix: Endurance and Weakness in Two Migrant Family Businesses in Australia

Mary Barrett

Transfield is one of Australia's most prominent construction companies. The name itself: "trans" meaning across and "field", which suggests open spaces, reflects the firm's origins as a venture founded by two Italian emigrants, Carlo Salteri and Franco Belgiorni-Nettis, who crossed huge distances to Australia before establishing their own firm.

Carlo Salteri came from a well-to-do Italian family and began engineering studies before being called up in 1941. After the War he completed his engineering degree at the University of Turin, and then found employment in a large Italian electrical company. Franco Belgiorni-Nettis, by contrast, was born in a poor village. He was 24 when World War II began and joined the Italian army as a volunteer; but he was captured and spent three years at an allied prisoner-of-war camp in India. After the war, he too completed his engineering studies and began working for the same firm as Carlo.

In 1951, the firm contracted Carlo and Franco to build an electricity transmission line running from near Port Kembla on the south coast of New South Wales, Australia, to Homebush Bay in Sydney, Australia's largest city. The line would span about 100 miles. Carlo brought his wife and young family to Australia with him. Franco, scarred by his period of internment, had become estranged from Italy and his community there. Eventually, however, Franco was married in Australia by proxy to Amina, who emigrated to Australia in 1952 to join him.

The two men and their families were part of the wave of post- World War II European migrants to Australia, which allowed many war-weary Europeans to make a new life, and a new country to develop. When the contract ended in 1956, Carlo and Franco both chose to stay in Australia. Together they formed Transfield, a partnership that became one of Australia's largest companies, constructing the Gateway Bridge in Brisbane, the Sydney Harbour Tunnel, and many other large infrastructure projects. By the late 1980s, Transfield was the largest engineering firm in south-east Asia. It acquired the Williamstown Dockyard in Melbourne and, after winning an AUD 6 billion contract in 1989 to build 10 ANZAC class frigates for the Australian and New Zealand governments, it was also the largest defence company in Australia. Pope John Paul II's visit to Australia in 1986 included a tour of the Transfield factory at Seven Hills.

Transfield's founders were not a conventional business family: they were not related and they did not come to Australia to start a business. However, Transfield was a family business in less obvious ways. Carlo and Franco had vastly different temperaments but their shared experiences of starting Transfield in a new, rather alien land, made them as close as brothers. Franco, in an interview when he was an old man, recalled that freedom within his Italian family group "did not exist" and that as a member of the Italian army under Mussolini he had been "completely brainwashed". At the age of 16 he already wanted "release" from his family, something he achieved on his arrival in Australia. Release, though, was accompanied by alarming challenges: Australia appeared as "a total wilderness". Transfield welcomed many Italian immigrants to their first place of employment. Many arrived alone and Transfield offered family-like friendship and support.

In 1989, Carlo and Franco stood down from active management roles in Transfield Holdings (as the company was then named) in favour of their eldest sons, Paul Salteri and Marco Belgiorno-Zegna. (Marco's surname, Belgiorno-Zegna, incorporating his mother's maiden name, designated him as the family's eldest son and heir, in keeping with Italian tradition.) From then until about 1996, the company grew rapidly, changing from a construction business into a continuously diversifying entity, entering new fields such as defence, shipbuilding, power technology, services, investment, and partnering with government instrumentalities in major public sector projects. But Transfield's expansion also led to new problems, including the need to properly finance its activities. Transfield was finally refinanced in 1992/93, bringing stability to its operations. The founders also successfully addressed the need for a structure that gave authority to senior management, and created an expanded advisory board with external directors. These changes transformed Transfield into a modern industrial organization.

Despite this success, Transfield was not immune to the financial and psychological costs of disputes that regularly occur between business partners, family members, and friends. In 1994, when the founders were in their 70s, they decided to retire and hand over control to their eldest sons, Paul Saltieri and Marco Belgiorno-Zegna. The founders moved to board roles where they could remain involved in major policy decisions. Paul and Marco, the two new CEOs, could not have been more different from each other. Like their fathers they brought contrasting skills, outlooks, and expectations to the company. Marco was widely acknowledged as the risk-taker of the two, while Paul was prudent, cautious, and not prone to rushed decisions. The differences created tension that spread beyond the CEOs. It finally found an outlet in an apparently trivial dispute between the founders. Franco claimed he was the sole founder of Transfield Holdings and that Carlo had only joined later as a partner. Mutual accusations of lies were made, damaging the partners' relationship irretrievably and aggravating the tensions created by their sons' conflicting management styles. The impetus to split the company became irreversible.

The families kept a façade of amicability and remained silent about the details of the split until April 1996, when Transfield announced the break-up of its defence, construction, and technology empire into two organizations, with the Belgiorno-Nettis family retaining the name Transfield. Under the terms of the split, the Salteris took the Williamstown Shipyard and defence contracts, renaming their new enterprise Tenix, from the Latin "tenere", meaning tenacity. The Belgiorno-Nettis family retained property development, engineering, infrastructure, maintenance, and construction. Compared to the original giant organization, Transfield, the result was two much more modest concerns, both of which had to re-establish themselves.

The Salteri family, through various acquisitions and partnerships, built Tenix into its current position as a major player in the utility and infrastructure services industry throughout Australia, New Zealand, and the Asia-Pacific. Only one major branch of the company, Tenix Defence, has ever been sold. Its buyer, BAE Systems Australia, a subsidiary of BAE Systems plc, acquired

Tenix Defence in June 2008, making BAE Systems Australia the largest defence contractor in Australia.

Soon after the split with the Salteris, during which Franco had resumed more active involvement with the company, Franco again became a director on Transfield's board, and Marco resumed his position as managing director. But a further problem arose. In ensuring Marco's position at the head of the company, Franco failed to make a succession plan that took into account the interests of his younger sons, Guido and Luca. That mistake led to clashes between Marco and his two brothers. They particularly argued about risky projects, including the Bakun Hydro-electric Scheme in the Philippines, which was finalized without Marco's approval. Guido negotiated the AUD 150 million project, but by 2001 it had registered AUD 50 million in losses, an outcome that Marco blamed his brothers for. Guido and Luca asked Franco, who had voting control, for help.

Asking Franco to intervene did not lead to a peaceful solution. Marco sought unsuccessfully to buy out his brothers in 2001, but the family united against him, trying to freeze him out of Transfield's operations. Marco sued his family on the grounds of oppression of minority interests, lost the case, and lodged an appeal. Finally, in March 2001, Marco abandoned the appeal in return for a settlement in which the family would acquire his 30% interest in Exben, Transfield Services' holding company. He received an estimated AUD 70 million for his shareholding in Exben and remained on the board until he was fully paid out. Later that year, Transfield Services was listed on the Australian Stock Exchange with Guido as managing director and Luca as associate managing director. Both remained non-executive directors of Transfield Services. Marco eventually established his own investment firm. He is currently managing director of Avesta Corporation, a building company, and executive chairman of Lidco Corporation Pty Ltd, which supplies commercial and high-end residential aluminium window and door systems.

The founding partners reflected on events in their old age. They had been successful beyond their wildest dreams but by 1996 their joint creation had grown beyond their capacity to effectively control it. Moreover, while their shared experiences as migrants had helped them to manage their personality differences, they failed to combine the interests of their respective families. Later, the Belgiorno-Nettis family struggled to merge the interests of just one family's members. Nevertheless Transfield in its early years served Australia by creating jobs for the many Italian immigrants who arrived in their new country not speaking English and without pre-arranged employment. After the break-up of the original Transfield Pty Ltd and, later, the dispute between Marco and his family, Transfield and Tenix both contributed enormously to developing Australia's infrastructure and utilities. As entrepreneurs, Carlo and Franco created a bigger family than either of them could have imagined.

Case Study:
It's a Sweet Life: An Indian Daughter Successfully Manages an Immigrant Family Business in the United States

Meenakshi Rishi

The traditions of Indian immigrants in the USA are an affirmation of their ethnic identity, which is a critical psychological aspect of the minority individual in society (Dasgupta, 1998). Ethnic identity not only sheds light on attitudes and behaviours of the post-1965 Asian Indian immigrant community in the US, but also explains intragroup variations. The Asian Indian community in the US is an ethnically diverse one, with subgroups that follow distinct customs and religious beliefs. Of all the Asian Indian religious communities, the Sikhs are the oldest, originating from the Indian state of Punjab, and tend to be the best organized in terms of religious activity.

Sikhism is a monistic religion founded in 15th-century Punjab on the teachings of Guru Nanak Dev and 10 successive Sikh Gurus. Sikhism teaches its followers to embrace compassion, truth, contentment, humility, and love. In addition, it is every Sikh's duty to control and subdue lust, anger, greed, attachment, and ego. Sikhism unequivocally recognizes equality for all human beings and specifically for both men and women. Consequently, Sikhism advocates active and equal participation in congregation, academics, healthcare, and military among other aspects of society. Female subordination, including practising rituals that imply dependence, is shunned within Sikhism (Mann, 2004).

Census data show that 81.8% of Indian immigrants arrived in the US after 1980. They received no special treatment or support and faced the same discrimination and hardship that any immigrant group does. Yet, they learned to thrive in American society. In a *Business Week* article, Wadhwa (2006) compiled a list of Indian cultural values to illustrate the successful marrying of Indian-American entrepreneurial success and Indian cultural values: education, upbringing, hard work, determination to overcome obstacles, an entrepreneurial spirit, recognizing diversity, humility, family support/values, careful financial management, and forming and leveraging networks.

Scholars claim that Asian Indian immigrants have transplanted old-world gender ideologies and clearly dichotomized gender roles in their adopted country of residence (Dasgupta, 1998; Kar et al., 1995/1996). In her study of immigrants and their children, Agarwal (1991) states that although "several [first generation] women said their immigration to the United States brought them independence and liberation from the institutional repression of women in India ... the second generation Indian woman feels that old-world gender roles are still rigidly being upheld for her" (p. 52). This phenomenon can perhaps be explained by examining the gender-specific role that daughters of immigrants are given in the preservation of Indian ethnic/cultural identity.

Punjab Sweets is a family owned vegetarian Indian café in Kent, Washington, that has been in operation since 2001. In its early years, Punjab Sweets was a small bakery/snack shop that prided itself on selling fresh and appetizing Indian snacks and desserts. This family business was the original brain child of Iqbal Dha, Gurmit Dha, and Jasbir Rai. Iqbal and her husband Gurmit Dha immigrated to the US in 1980. Iqbal was a skilled cook and wanted to share her passion and excitement for experimenting with food and creating new recipes with the community. She initially catered small events but began to dream big as people complimented her on her culinary skills. In 2001, Iqbal Dha and Gurmit Dha founded Punjab Sweets in a joint effort with Iqbal's brother, Jasbir Rai.

In 2006, Harpreet Gill, the daughter of Iqbal and Gurmit, became co-owner of the family business and since then Punjab Sweets has come a long way from its small, dusty beginnings. Harpreet has used her considerable artistic talents to completely redesign the restaurant. The menu has been expanded to accommodate vegan preferences and "eggless" cakes that appeal to the large Indian immigrant community. Punjab Sweets has a Facebook page and a loyal fan following. It receives glowing reviews in the local press and boasts a growing clientele of customers. *Seattle Weekly*, a widely read source of information on restaurants in Seattle, featured Punjab Sweets on their 2006 Dining Guide cover and a 2007 review in the *Seattle Magazine* called the homemade fare at Punjab Sweets "hard to resist". Under the daughter successor's guidance, it is clear that the restaurant has indeed "arrived".

Harpreet's own entry into the family business was as dramatic as the success of Punjab Sweets has been. In 2004, while helping her parents manage Punjab Sweets, Harpreet decided to study for an MBA. Her original plan was to work part-time at the business, get her degree, and then seek a career as a business consultant. Her life changed with the cover story on Punjab Sweets that was featured in *Seattle Weekly*. She interpreted this as a sign from God and decided to stay in the family business and help it grow.

Harpreet's transition from worker/helper to family business co-owner was gradual; in her own words: "The lines were muddled at first, but eventually and over time the decisions, trust, and facets of running the business were my responsibility." The smooth path of the transition process was enabled by the fact that Harpreet's parents leave for India every year for several months and this has required them to handover large chunks of responsibility to Harpreet. Today, Harpreet is very comfortable in her new role and manages the overall operations of the company. She handles marketing, the presentation of the dishes and maintains regular contact with distributors and several local restaurants that Punjab Sweets caters to. Harpreet works as the cashier, serves guests and spends up to 80 hours a week working for her business. Harpreet thinks it's her MBA that challenged her to be a leader and constantly adapt to changing circumstances. As she comments in Seattle University's alumni magazine, "It is a blessing to be able to come into work and not know exactly what is to be expected."

Harpreet's deft handling of the business has certainly taken a load of responsibility off her father's shoulders and enabled her mother to retire. Harpreet beams when her father comes into the restaurant to ask her opinion. "My dad's proud of me – little things I do matter to him a great deal."

The success enjoyed by Punjab Sweets has spawned the opening of a second restaurant on the Eastside of Seattle. This new restaurant, called Preet's is managed by Harpreet's brother, Manpreet Dha. While Harpreet's parents wanted the ownership of Preet's to be split equally between the two siblings, Harpreet declined. She wanted to concentrate on running Punjab Sweets and, as she states, "I didn't want to lose a relationship with my brother over money and ownership". Family and relationships are very important to Harpreet and she is content helping her brother out occasionally and without acrimony over finances and responsibilities. She feels it is important to model harmonious family relationships to her daughter, Jasneet, who is 10 years old and at "an impressionable age".

But, Where's the Husband?

Dunemann and Barett (2004) note that, "Family values and other social considerations have a demonstrable influence over the conduct of family business" (p. 24). Harpreet's case is illustrative. While some may view her as an immigrant success story, people in her own community look down upon her choice of occupation. "The cultural mindset of Indians is very narrow and they do not consider serving customers in a restaurant as an appropriate occupation for someone with an MBA", said Harpreet. For Indians in general, and in particular Punjabis who hail from villages in North India, having an office and a secretary is the mark of success and picking up someone's dirty dishes after a meal is considered almost a menial task. Harpreet has tried to stand up for herself but it does not help that she is also a divorced single mother. People in the community still ask her mother when she will get re-married!

Traditional cultural values also permeate Harpreet's relationship with her parents. While her parents talked over the steps of running the business with her, they left some responsibilities unclear. This frustrated Harpreet in the beginning because she did not want to assume that she was "completely in charge" and question her parents' authority. In the Indian culture, the male is the head of the household and often makes decisions on behalf of the family. As Harpreet puts it: "Sometimes my dad would make a decision and not inform anyone as he thought it was his decision to make." Or, Harpreet's father would not give her the contact numbers of the suppliers leaving Harpreet aggravated and annoyed at his lack of trust. However, Harpreet's father soon had to relent on this score as his annual trips to India necessitated the sharing of information with Harpreet.

Harpreet has had to encounter cultural barriers and power distance issues at the supplier level too. As most of her Indian distributors are known to her family and several years older than her, Harpreet has to call them "uncle" because, "in our culture we have to call anybody older than us uncle or auntie". However, this cultural upbringing and respect for elders also sets the stage for cultural power distance. Harpreet gets the impression that her Indian distributors don't like to deal with a woman in charge and that conversations often seem to be going on at different wavelengths. It is at such moments that Harpreet has to solicit her father's help and experience in dealing with suppliers and distributors. She does not mind asking for assistance as she sees the business as a family business that is predicated on cultural values and interpersonal relationships.

The complexities of Indian management culture are also magnified when it comes to employee–employer relations. As Harpreet notes, "My textbooks may talk about keeping my employees at a distance; but my culture renders this impossible." Punjab Sweets has 10 employees, all women, who live in the surrounding communities. Some of her employees do not have reliable modes of transportation so Harpreet's family has to pick up and drop off the ladies at home. While this may seem awkward to Harpreet, she recognizes that her business is not a textbook business and that treating her employees with the respect she reserves for her own family members imbues them with a sense of pride in working for her. Hugs are commonplace in the kitchens of Punjab Sweets and Harpreet's mother visits the employees' families in India whenever she can.

While it is tough to operate a family business, Harpreet would have it no other way. She is interested in taking Punjab Sweets to a whole new plane of operations. Harpreet hopes to market her store's salted vegan snacks, which are currently available online (www.punjabsweetsonline.com). She has recently redesigned the snack's labels and envisions the healthy snacks being sold at local health food stores.

Harpreet also feels frustrated in her present location – a tiny ethnic enclave in the community of Kent that is a good half an hour's drive from downtown Seattle. She says that she is well-accustomed to the "penny-pinching immigrant mindset", and would like to deal with a younger, hipper, more business-like crowd that is closer to her in age and tastes. Her vision involves moving the restaurant out of its strip mall location to a downtown Seattle address. As a matter of fact, several of her clientele have been urging her to do so for a long time. While her parents do not object to this plan, Harpreet does not think she is in a financial position to make the transition. Plus, she does gain a lot from living in the tiny enclave of Kent. Her mom is available to take care of her daughter and her daughter is able to waltz into the restaurant and "help out" the staff on occasions. Moving further away from such a support network is not easy for anyone – least of all a single mother/entrepreneur like Harpreet.

The community is clearly important to Harpreet and despite the hectic demands on her time, she still manages to do good in the community. On a monthly basis, Punjab Sweets donates food and clothing to the Union Gospel Mission and Harpreet provides gift certificates for auctions and school fundraisers. Harpreet serves as an ambassador with the Kent Chamber of Commerce and is an active volunteer for Chaya, an organization committed to raising awareness about domestic violence issues in South Asia.

Harpreet is not sure of a plan of succession. She does not know if her daughter would like to follow in her footsteps. Meanwhile, Harpreet has come to realize that her management skills are a hodge-podge of her cultural values combining respect for her parents as well as a top-notch management education. While her parents may disagree on the "right" way of doing things sometimes, there is no debate on the core principle behind the daily operations of Punjab Sweets: Harpreet's parents and Harpreet are in total agreement that, "each and every person that steps through our door should feel as if they are very special and the guest of honour".

Additional Reading

Ferguson, A. 2001. A Family Feud's Last Episode? *Business Review Weekly*, 23(19), 58(1).

Film Australia. (n.d.) *Franco Belgiorno-Nettis: Teachers Notes*. Australian Biography Series 2. Available at: http://australianbiography.s3.amazonaws.com/study/4591_ausbiobelgiorno.pdf [accessed 19 February 2013].

The Sydney Morning Herald. 2010. Transfield Co-founder Carlo Salteri Dies. 13 October. Available at: http://news.smh.com.au/breaking-news-business/transfield-cofounder-carlo-salteri-dies-20101013-16jvq.html [accessed 19 February 2013].

TransfieldServ. 2012. *Transfield Services Corporate Video 2012*. Available at: https://www.youtube.com/watch?v=er8x8Oe5K-4 [accessed 19 February 2013].

Chapter 6

Entrepreneurship Issues Impacting Good Governance within the Immigrant Family Business

Entrepreneurship and Culture

Culture can be thought of as a group or community's set of shared beliefs, values, and norms. Extending this, culture can be seen as a collective phenomenon shaped by a person's social environment rather than their genes. It then follows that cultural differences arise from, among other things, regional, social class, religious, language, and gender variations. Further distinguishing such variations are values, deemed a critical aspect of cultural differences. Although corresponding relevant research sheds light on how a national culture can affect workplace values across different countries, it does not consider the existence of various cultural groups within one region or country.

Understanding how obstacles and challenges were overcome by long-term immigrant entrepreneurship in receiving countries that were popular destinations 30 and 40 years ago can add to our understanding of the process and guidance needed for the development of favourable policy frameworks for the new wave of immigration the world has seen on such a large scale in the past 15 years. The immigrants of 40 years ago faced similar hardships and barriers as do many new, present-day immigrants: flight from poverty and/or political unrest; very little formal education, and language and religious barriers; and, starting out on their migrant journey in late adolescence or early adulthood with little or no financial resources.

Vision and Good Governance

Strategic decisions are often complex and usually demand the analysis of large amounts of data to enforce good governance. As part of the strategic domain, the immigrant family business is managed and governed with the intention of shaping and pursuing the vision of the business that is shared by members of the family business in a manner that is potentially sustainable across generations of the business. A shared vision provides a common framework with which to assess available information and focus on relevant issues, thereby providing richer information for strategic decisions to ensure good governance.

Shared vision promotes coherence in stakeholders' expectations and opinions of an immigrant family business's goals. Established role interactions and a shared vision reduce the threat of opportunistic behaviour and help establish a social norm of reciprocity, which reinforces good governance commitments or faintly agreed decisions and directives. In an immigrant family business, a shared vision involves family members' collective ideas about the future of the business, including designed business domains, desired growth rates, and financial performance.

Niche ethnic entrepreneurial concentration provides jobs for immigrant family members and other relatives. As the immigrant family becomes established economically, it invites other immigrant family members to join. Entrepreneurial survivors face the challenge of ensuring the development of both the family business and the general business system, to sustain survival and growth of the family business into the next generations.

The main strategic concern of immigrant family business growth is to ensure that the process of growth is both supported and controlled by the structures and processes of the business. Growth can take a variety of forms: exploitation of scale economics by plant expansion, modernization of the technological base, diversification, and consolidation via merger or other less formal modes of strategic alliance. A central stimulus factor for a successful growth strategy is acceptance of the need for professionalization of commercial practice as the business develops from its previous family-oriented culture.

As a family business grows and matures, changes come about in ownership and governance, an identifiable business structure in family firms. Ownership eventually disperses and private investors may be sought out or the business opened up to attract capital. As such changes start to enter the family business environment, advisory councils or boards of directors may be established to facilitate the necessary strategic planning and other important business matters. Immigrant entrepreneurs can be seen as people who identify and utilize opportunities to the benefit of themselves and the environment. The literature suggests that the nature of immigrant entrepreneurship is aligned (sometimes) with growth; and that the opposite must also be true: growth is (sometimes) entrepreneurship. Immigrant family businesses that exhibit organic growth have the ability to detect emerging expansion opportunities and to align existing resources in new ways so as to take advantage of opportunities afforded by the new economic activities. Ethnic entrepreneurial growth can be seen as fostering the entrepreneurial spirit by following innovative growth strategies, thereby ensuring organic growth for the immigrant family businesses concerned.

Stakeholder Harmony and Good Governance

An immigrant family might influence the governance practices of a business, its basic characteristics, the quality of its management and possibly even an industry. In this study, family harmony refers to the mutual respect, trust, support, and appreciation that family members have for each other, having concern for each other's welfare, and having equitable conflict-resolution and problem-resolving measures in place. Earlier research into immigrant family business has failed to recognize family harmony as an important variable influencing perceived good governance. Yet, the idea of the "immigrant family" is so powerful in the immigrant family business context, that the immigrant family ideology will often define what is "correct and proper" in governing their businesses and what is "wrong".

Researchers have pointed out that the immigrant family can play a supportive role for the entrepreneur by providing money, contacts, labour, and other resources. The immigrant family can also be supportive of entrepreneurial endeavours and provide a safe haven from the vicissitudes of starting a new business. On the other hand, the immigrant family can prove to be an obstacle to starting and managing a new business, by providing few material resources and little or no social support. While much of the research on start-ups has suggested that resources such as capital, raw materials, and labour are critical for the success of a new enterprise, the role of the immigrant family as one of the "success factors" needs to be studied more scientifically. Researchers could find that the role of the immigrant family is a much more important determinant in business success than many of the other, more traditional, factors such as planning.

In contrast to the view that immigrant family businesses are more efficient due to reduced agency costs through relationships that align the goals and incentives of immigrant family owners and managers, is the alternative perspective that immigrant family firms are breeding grounds for relationships fraught with conflict. In the context of an immigrant family business, differing views within an immigrant family about the distribution of ownership, compensation, risk, roles, and responsibilities may make the family business a battleground where family members compete with one another.

Profitability and Good Governance

Having a goal of profitability and crafting a strategy to achieve it are what separates successful entrepreneurs from the less successful ones. Many entrepreneurs seek only to create a living for themselves. It is quite another thing to grow a business that creates a living for many others, including employees and investors, by creating value – value that can result in capital profitability gain.

Agency and stewardship theory have often been used to argue that immigrant family firm governance is more efficient than non-immigrant family enterprises and those immigrant family firms are likely to incur fewer agency and monitoring costs because the goals of a firm's principals (owners) are aligned with its agents (managers) since they are typically one and the same.

Trust and Good Governance

Trust plays an important role in business survival and success, and a significant body of literature emphasizes the positive influence of trust on organizational governance. Used effectively, trust represents a major source of competitive advantage for a business. As a governance control mechanism, trust provides some clear advantages. Being able to rely on the words and actions of others facilitates the smooth functioning of a social system.

Researchers recognize that trust potentially contributes to lower transaction costs, while contributing to more effective managerial coordination and collaboration within the business. Within the immigrant family business context, clear and transparent rules can clarify roles, responsibilities, and expectations of actors, enhancing the potential for trust in the working of the immigrant family business system. Consistent application of transparent, clear guidelines on key issues governing immigrant family and non-immigrant family members provides the foundation for process-based justice or procedural justice.

More specifically, openness to outside influence, transparency, and formalization of organizational activities and strong communication is argued to engender a reinforcing positive cycle of trust by fostering task-based or competence trust, instilling system trust, and continually renewing interpersonal trust. Additionally, a fair process is an essential part of establishing trust, commitment, and harmony in immigrant family businesses. A lack of fairness in the decision and managerial processes governing immigrant family businesses and their associated families is a source of conflict. An environment of fairness, according to fair process theory, improves both the performance of the immigrant family business and the members' satisfaction with it.

Research has repeatedly confirmed that internal trust is a competitive edge for family businesses. Immigrant family businesses represent unique organizational forms, with dimensions that go beyond the bottom line; consequently, business transactions are rarely purely economic. In other words, the immigrant family adds an additional dimension to these transactions. Trusting relationships among family members is used in governance as a vehicle to reduce risk. A mistrust of strangers and preference to hire family members may be especially likely for immigrant entrepreneurs originating from countries with weak legal structures, where "trust between family members can be a substitute for missing governance and contractual enforcement" (Bertrand and Schoar, 2006: 7).

Within the immigrant family business scenario, commitment is defined as the wish to have relationships at work continue as a means to ensuring the continuance of the business. As such, it can be seen in the light of an implicit or explicit promise between the members involved. The literature highlights three distinct types of commitment based on underlying motives – affective commitment, cost-induced commitment, and obligation-based commitment. Commitment based on affective motives, such as emotional attachment, belonging, and interpersonal respect, evolves as the relationship with another person or group develops and strengthens. Affective commitment is explained by some in terms of the congruence of valuing goals among participants. This means that relationship participants have common beliefs regarding behaviour, goals, and policies.

Case Study:
Good Governance within the Immigrant
Family Business: Y.K.Crystal Ltd

Ioannis Violaris, Nina Gorovaia-Zeniou, Athanasia Tziortzi

Introduction

The current case study is concerned with entrepreneurship issues affecting good governance in a small immigrant family business of Jordanian origin in Cyprus. Special emphasis is placed on variables of good governance, like family harmony, trust, communication, and business strategy.

Cyprus has transformed into an immigrant recipient country over the past 20 years. The starting point for this transformation was the radical changes in government policies regarding labour immigration in 1989 and the liberalization of labour markets (Gregoriou, Kontolemis, and Matsi, 2010; Trimikliniotis, 2008). The government, following pressures from employers, decided to allow the entrance of migrant labourers in order to meet labour shortages in Cyprus (Trimikliniotis, 2008). According to Trimikliniotis (2008) a number of international trends also contributed to the enforcement of this policy, including "geopolitical regional changes, such as the collapse of Beirut as centre of the Middle East, the collapse of the regimes of eastern Europe (with the resulting 'release' of investment in financial services), and the Gulf war; a world-wide growth in tourism and migration flows" (p. 13). The next wave of inward migration came after Cyprus' accession to the EU (Gregoriou, Kontolemis, and Matsi, 2010). It is estimated that the immigrant community consists of about 160,000 third-country migrants and 60,000 EU citizens (Trimikliniotis, 2008). This community is integrated within the local population and its members are either employed in local companies or operate their own businesses.

The Case: Y.K.Crystal Ltd

As mentioned above, the case study at hand deals with a small business owned by a Jordanian immigrant family in Cyprus and looks into entrepreneurship issues affecting good governance within this business. The company Y.K.Crystal Ltd (hereafter referred to as "the company") was established in 2009 by a couple of Jordanian origin. The company is a small supermarket, located in a suburb, Kaimakli, of Nicosia, the capital of Cyprus. In agreement with the traditional views of family businesses, the wife and husband are the ones who perform the business's daily activities. The wife's brother, who is a successful building contractor, is also informally involved in the family business as an advisor. He is the one who advised them to go into this business when they were considering different business opportunities. An interesting point to raise, which contrasts current minority ethnic enterprise theory, is the fact that the business was not set up in the context of an ethnic minority community but rather it was created to blend in with the local Cypriot community. According to the couple, this was due to the fact that the Jordanian community in Cyprus is scattered across cities.

The wife was born in Cyprus and she is now in her late 30s while the husband was born in Jordan and immigrated to Cyprus in 2000. The wife is a graduate in computer science, while the husband is a secondary school graduate. Their occupations prior to establishing the company were totally different. The wife was working at a clothing factory, while the husband was a house painter. Their parents did not have entrepreneurial backgrounds either.

In 2010 the couple decided to enter into this business following the passing away of the previous owner. Neither of them had any previous experience in this kind of business, but they decided to invest most of their savings in it as they hoped it would help them build a better future for them and their two children, seven and four years old. The amount invested reached 70,000 Euros.

Attempting such a business move without prior knowledge or experience said a lot about the way that this immigrant family operated and draws our attention to important variables of good governance impacting the sustainability of immigrant family businesses, those of family harmony, communication, and trust. The couple admitted that mutual support and trust between them is an essential part of the way they run their business and that this practice is what assisted the company to survive so far, especially in light of the economic crisis. Of course, the economic crisis did not leave the couple untouched. The business in the first two years was doing much better than it is now. The economic recession has affected their turnover, which is presently at 45,000 Euros per month.

The couple however, persists in their effort to keep their business "alive", having their children's welfare as a major driver. Their efforts concentrate on capitalizing on the benefits of owning the business as a family but at the same time they recognize that the fact that the company is run by a couple may have a negative side. The positive side has to do with mutual trust and dedication, which contribute to the development of the business. This is in agreement with theories supporting that trust in family businesses may be a source of competitive advantage (Steier, 2001). The downside they identify relates mostly to the day-to-day clashes and differences of opinion in running the business, which may unavoidably affect an otherwise amicable relationship.

Part of the reason for this "failure", in an otherwise harmonious family relationship, may be the fact that there is no formal boss–employee structure, although it seems the husband is "the boss". This is probably because the males traditionally take leadership roles in Islamic cultures. There is also no formal written contract of their employment terms, nor does any formal business plan exist.

In the absence of a formal business plan and the absence of support from their minority community, the immigrant family seems to be responding well to business transactions with their local customers and suppliers. The suppliers give them credit on the same terms as other Cypriot customers. Their customers are mainly families residing near their business. As an additional service, they provide home delivery and they aim at establishing friendly relations with their customers. They also offer some Arabic foodstuffs in an effort to serve other Arabs living in Nicosia. This emphasis on the development of social capital and informal capital in networks has contributed to the family business's survival in an otherwise "foreign" environment and has been a focal point of their business governance.

As far as regular contacts are concerned, the couple meets with the owner of the house (from whom they rent premises) once a month, daily they have to make a visit to the bank, weekly they contact their suppliers, and every day they see their customers.

Besides the elements of trust, communication, and commitment, the owners believe that the competitive advantage of their business is in the low prices of their products/services. This is due to reduced agency costs, which make the immigrant family business more efficient, and the overall focus of the particular business on following a low-cost strategy. This kind of orientation is especially important in light of the current economic situation and the fierce competition located near them – there are five or six supermarkets in the neighbourhood. An additional competitive advantage they see in their business relates to their emphasis on building networks and creating value for their customers. The couple specifically pointed out that their most important know-how relates to customer service. This knowledge is of tacit nature and can only be learned doing the job.

Looking at the story of this immigrant family business we can see that their governance relies a lot on elements having to do with trust, commitment, and informal networks. They do not follow any formal strategic planning and when pointed towards that direction for the future they showed resistance emphasizing the current economic situation. They mentioned that due to the economic recession they are not able to draft any plans. They seemed to be puzzled as to how the business will be able to survive during the recession and at least at present they do not seem to plan that their children will enter and succeed them in the business. The couple also pointed out that they were much more optimistic as far as their business prospects are concerned before the crisis.

Overall, it seems that the business as it is will face many difficulties in surviving the crisis, unless it adds some added value to it, such as a small coffee shop, an amusement corner for young people, or a dining area to offer perhaps Arabic food to locals and Arabs. It is also essential that the family business keeps capitalizing on important governance issues and that they incorporate some aspects of strategic planning that will allow them to strive for profitability and not just making a living.

Chapter 7

Cultural and Family Dynamics in the Governance of Immigrant Businesses

Researchers have suggested that ethnic groups can achieve upward economic and social mobility through business ownership. Various researchers opine that the governance of an immigrant family business is more complicated than that for non-immigrant family-owned businesses because of the central role played by the immigrant family. The same school of thought also points out that in immigrant family businesses (where ownership is controlled by a single immigrant family) the lack of effective governance is a major cause of organizational problems. One of the most formidable obstacles to the stability, growth, and success of the immigrant family business is the issue of governance. To build upon and to remain an immigrant family business, the ultimate management challenge is to enforce good governance. Because of the important role that immigrant family businesses play in the international economy, ensuring perceived good governance is of the utmost importance for the growth and sustainability of this component of the world economy.

Ethnicity

Ethnic networks, based on family and friendship ties, impact the immigrant family business with regard to their cultural, practical, and psychological functions in that they help immigrants in a strange land form their identity. These informal groups do not, however, have a homogenizing effect on the ethnic community. Entrepreneurship literature has traditionally used mainstream, Euro-American samples and theories portraying entrepreneurship as a series of individual decisions. However, when business operations call for aligning with the environment, one which may include group values such as collectivism, duty, and loyalty, this dynamic influences an immigrant family business more so than in the mainstream culture.

An exhaustive review of the entrepreneurship and ethnic business literature sheds light on the characteristics that create variations within ethnic groups: the ethnic group composition is composed of immigrants or natives, length of residence in the host country, and prior business experience and opportunities prior to entry or within the host country. These findings support conclusions in previous studies on ethnic entrepreneurship, including that immigrant business success is a function of the social networks and organizing capacity of the group. Finally, researchers as far back as three decades point to ethnic entrepreneurial success being linked to how residentially segregated the group is or has been, and how ethnic group assimilation and ethnic niche networks influence businesses' operating and financial patterns. On the other hand, research has pointed to ethnic entrepreneurial failure being an outcome of family problems. As such, immigrant enterprises have the challenge of overcoming two sets of pressures and, as immigrant entrepreneurs, must act as culture brokers working to also learn the techniques and meet the needs of the formal (host) economy.

Finally, little attention has been paid to how family dynamics affect the ethnic entrepreneurial process. Given that family can be a major influence on culture and core cultural values, deeper insight into family structure and relationships is critical to understanding how management processes in ethnic family businesses differ to mainstream businesses. As such, research emphasis must be placed on the role of the family, as well as marketplace conditions, in thwarting or facilitating the expansion of entrepreneurial opportunities for ethnic groups. Pointing out the nuances of various types of family structure (for example, hierarchical versus diffusely organized), recent research also lends to the significance of gaining this insight.

Culture

As culture-bearing units, the common values of ethnic groups contribute significantly to identity and particular ways of feeling, thinking, perceiving, and behaving – which in turn influence everyday actions and decision making. Compared to ethnicity, culture is more complex than ethnicity or race and so it is through family interactions, among its members as well as in relation to the community, that cultural behaviour patterns and values are embedded. As such, a business takes on the culture of the family that owns it.

When considering culture as a relational phenomenon, it is necessary to keep in mind the following two assumptions: during personal interaction the other individual's verbally and non-verbally communicated stance(s) define the roles; and, the informational world of perception and language is also distinguished in a relational sense. Regarding the latter, distinguishing between the role of one person as a father and as a boss is a relational act. In the case of immigrant or ethnic family business, this act must be considered in a cultural context.

Family Dynamics

Different "family patterns" and "governance patterns" have been identified as associated with the culture of a business. Expanding on earlier research and definitions of family patterns, family firm cultures, and governance patterns, research has offered a description of family firms as paternalistic (the most prevalent), laissez-faire, participative, or professional. However, the lack of focus on the family as creator and transmitter of culture detracts from this research, especially with regard to entrepreneurial emergence. In fact, many researchers following such a line have underestimated the critical function of the family in the development of practices, beliefs, values, and norms. This is also particularly true in the case of business creation.

The degree and nature of the interaction of members of a family and business with the community is influenced by the meaning that these individuals assign to the interaction. The business-owning family acts as a go-between for community–firm interactions and thus attitudes, beliefs, and values of the first influence the extent and nature of such interaction. Such an approach is supported in the literature, which notes that the success of a family business also depends on how aligned its management is with local community culture.

Variables of Good Governance in the Immigrant Family Business

STRATEGIC PLANNING AND GOOD GOVERNANCE

As is the case with any other business entity, strategic planning is critical for immigrant family business success. Research has shown, however, that immigrant family businesses are often reluctant to engage in formal planning. Research has noted that immigrant family firms often do not plan if the founder is focused on a previously successful strategy, and as a result they may become inflexible and inadvertently stifle growth. Immigrant family firms jealously protect their privacy and, as a result, planning may be neglected because it requires sharing what might be considered confidential information. Thus, the insistence on privacy often inhibits the success of many immigrant family businesses as it stifles proper business and strategic planning. The flipside is that proper planning, and strategic planning in particular, will enhance good governance and thus the survival and growth prospects of immigrant family businesses.

OUTSIDE ADVICE AND GOOD GOVERNANCE

Several researchers have suggested that the use of external advisers and governance structures, such as immigrant family retreats, immigrant family councils, or boards of directors, could generally play an important role in good governance. However, it is well documented that few small business owners see any benefit in soliciting the expertise of outsiders and, as a result, the use of outsiders is minimal. There is, therefore, a need for greater empirical evidence-based clarity of the role of outside advice in immigrant family businesses.

GOVERNANCE STRUCTURES AND GOOD GOVERNANCE

Here, the term "governance structures" refers to the overall existence of formal structures and their documentation. Immigrant family businesses are more likely to undertake strategic planning when they have effective governance structures for their businesses in place. The establishment and control of governance structures are strongly influenced by the board of directors, immigrant family council or assembly, or shareholders' assembly.

The long-term interest of the immigrant family shareholders must be maintained through the effective design of the governance structures in immigrant family business, such that the growth and continuity of the business can be ensured, and that the immigrant family's harmony and welfare are preserved. In short, if the proper structures are in place, the probability of the actual implementation of good governance is enhanced.

MANAGEMENT SUCCESSION PLANNING AND GOOD GOVERNANCE

The extant literature strongly supports the argument that succession planning in general and management succession planning in particular influence the continuity of the immigrant family business from one generation to the next. Despite the obvious necessity of proper succession planning in order to safeguard the continuity and vitality of the business, few entrepreneurs and small businesses take any steps to plan and carry out succession planning.

OUTSIDE ADVICE AND MANAGEMENT SUCCESSION PLANNING

The problem of both ownership and management succession has largely been the focus of research on immigrant family-owned businesses, as family dynamics come to the forefront during succession. Psychosocial dynamics that make it difficult for the immigrant entrepreneur to contemplate transferring ownership and management to the next generation has also been examined in research. Succession planning is in direct conflict with the entrepreneur's needs for control, power, and meaning. It has been suggested that the immigrant family, managers, suppliers, and customers may play a significant role in colluding against succession planning. The founder's family members may not want to accept the founder's mortality and may see the founder as the only person able to manage family conflicts and keep the family together. They are therefore reluctant to see the founder relinquish the leadership role.

The immigrant family may also be unwilling to upset the founder with discussions regarding retirement, because family members can be seen as being disloyal by suggesting retirement. Suppliers and customers who are used to dealing with the founder may resist forming relationships with the next generation of family members who are gaining in power. Thus, it is not at all surprising to learn that few immigrant entrepreneurs proactively engage in succession planning, often to the detriment of the family and the business.

The degree of mutual respect and understanding between the next-generation successor and the founder is a key factor affecting succession. Other critical factors are the degree to which next-generation career interests, psychosocial needs, and lifestyle needs are met through the business. Also, the degree of sibling accommodation rather than rivalry, and the immigrant family's commitment to perpetuate the family business are important to the succession process. It is important to look at succession not only from the perspective of the entrepreneur, but also from that of their relationship to the heir. Considering the heir's role and including them in the planning process is critical to effective succession management. There is general agreement that succession is more a process than an event.

A positive relationship has been found between management succession planning and the satisfaction of both owner-managers and successors with the succession process/event. Researchers found that immigrant family business owners often resist succession planning and that this, in turn, diminishes the probability that the business will survive beyond the first generation. Various other studies support the view held by many researchers that most owners do not plan adequately for succession.

Other researchers have suggested that the importance of management succession planning to business continuity has been overstated. While boards of directors, strategic planning, and frequent family meetings have been correlated with business longevity over multiple generations, research has found that this is not necessarily true for management succession planning. Similarly, other findings point to management succession planning not being critical to the survival of immigrant family businesses.

OUTSIDE ADVICE AND GOVERNANCE STRUCTURES

Several researchers have suggested that the use of external advisers and governance structures, such as immigrant family retreats, immigrant family councils, boards of directors, to name but a few, could generally play an important role in governance planning. One such body of work reported a positive correlation between the percentage of outsiders on the board of directors and the level of strategic governance in the business. The principle of the use of external consultants such as therapists, psychologists, estate-planning specialists, business economists, jurists, and fiscal experts has been advocated.

On the other hand, it has been found that relatively few immigrant family business owners believe it to be important to establish an advisory council, and not because they are unaware of the complexity of the succession process. Respondents in one study noted that they would consider bringing in an outside consultant at a suitable time, while another study highlighted that a very small percentage reported that the board of directors of their business had any function or contribution to make towards succession planning. The general lack of a board of directors or immigrant family council has been indicated in numerous studies. One study indicated that no positive correlation was found between the existence of both a formal or informal advisory board and the degree of management succession undertaken. The above discussion underlines the conflicting views on the nature of the relationship between the use of external advisers/ consultants and governance structures and management succession planning, calling for further investigation into the issue of management succession planning.

Case Study:
Governing the Asian Family Business:
Entrepreneurship and Aspiration

Claire Seaman

The case study presented here considers two key factors in the strategic governance of a family business within the Scottish Asian community, namely the family strategy and the strategy for the family business. Whilst the family strategy is often overlooked in discussions on the governance of small business, it is argued here that the two interwoven strands of strategy are integral to an understanding of governance challenges.

Defining the Scottish Asian community has been a subject of some debate, but based upon self-definition their importance to the vitality and diversity of entrepreneurial activity in Scotland has been highlighted (Deakins et al., 2005) and estimates indicate that their contribution to Scottish GDP in 2005 was between GBP 500 and 700 million (Deakins et al., 2005). The Scottish Asian community is estimated to account for 3% of self-employment in Scotland as a whole, but these figures are much higher in the major population centres (Deakins et al., 2005). Importantly, while businesses owned by Scotland's Asian community are well established, they tend to be the result of post-1950 migration and are less likely than other forms of family business to have been passed on to a second or subsequent generation (Scottish Government, 2011). To some extent, this group of businesses was typically created as a response to individuals being pushed towards entrepreneurship. This may play a key part in their future development. Therefore, the strategic approach to governance is considered here in the context of intertwined strategies relevant to the family and the business. These exist to some extent within all family businesses but become increasingly important where the family has been pushed into running a family business by circumstance rather than personal intent.

The family behind the business in this case study consists of a mother, father, and three children ranging in age from 15 to 20. The family forms part of an established Sikh community, which has an established track record in the development and management of small retail outlets that typically sell either clothing or food. The business is a small clothes shop that was developed within the context of the local community networks, conforming here to both minority ethnic enterprise theory, which highlights the importance of social capital and informal capital in networks (Deakins et al., 2005), and with traditional models of family enterprise. There are, for example, several members of the family involved with the day-to-day operation and governance of the business in either a full- or part-time capacity. Similar conformance with family enterprise theory can be seen in the generational shift from first to second generation, but with one important difference: aspiration. Whilst two generations currently work in the business, there is no immediate intent to cede control of the business to the second generation.

In part, this can be traced back to the intent of the founders of the business. When the family first moved to Scotland, the driving factors for the business start-up were "push" factors. The educational level attained by the parents included university-level education and this remains an aspiration on their part. As such, while the family is financially dependent upon the business, the aspiration for their children in career terms is very different. The view expressed regarding the business can be encapsulated by the quote: "We're in … business because we had to be … (we want) to provide something better for the children … we wouldn't want them to be trapped here …" (Mother).

This sense of being pushed into business, having been "successful enough" but hoping for something different for the next generation, is compatible with classic entrepreneurship theory that considers both "push" and "pull" factors within the context of the move into entrepreneurial small business. The notion that family succession must be a desired outcome is very far from the minds of this family and anecdotal evidence within the community suggests this is not atypical. What is less clear, however, is whether a business family may develop whereby the children branch out into different businesses on their own account. While there is little push for the current family business to continue – and, indeed, given the changing nature of retailing in the UK this may be a very sensible decision – there is no evident prejudice against the children going into business on their own account. This observation offers an interesting adjunct to work by Deakins et al. (2005), who highlighted the role that networks can play in restricting business development, suggesting that this effect may not be a passive "failure" to develop the business further but rather an active prioritizing of family strategy over business strategy.

The prioritizing of family strategy over the governance of the business is also apparent in the broader attitude of the parents towards their children's education. Highlighting the desire for their children to follow what are perceived to be traditional pathways towards success, the father commented: "We would want them to work as professionals … That is the route forward for them and for our family …."

This desire for professional-level education and a more secure future may also be influenced by ongoing changes in retailing in the UK. The drive towards larger stores and out-of-town retailing has adversely affected many of the small businesses traditionally run by minority ethnic groups in Scotland, and it seems likely that this trend will continue. What is less clear – though probably vital – is the role that pensions may play in the future strategies employed for both the family and their business. Commenting on the future, the father highlighted: "We thought we would go back (to the country of origin), but the children have grown up here ... they are British. The business has to be our pension. That is what we have."

This dilemma, for a family where the older members are educated and hope for an educated, professional future for their children whilst also acknowledging that their financial future is intrinsically linked to a fading retail format, forms a challenge for families, businesses, and communities alike. How such aspirations on the part of parents influence the aspirations of their children is a subtle and complex area of investigation (Gutman and Akerman, 2008), which sits alongside the dilemmas of funding educational provision for the family. However, the clarity of the strategic vision identified for the family and its impact on the potential future governance of this family business merits consideration. In part, the dilemmas highlighted here reflect the broader challenges of family business as a distinct area of study. The changing and highly variable nature of families is a constant challenge that to some extent precludes a unified view of family businesses (Fletcher, 2002). This does not alter the broad view that families are groups of people linked by ties of blood and marriage (Muncie and Sapsford, 1997), but adds the observation that within these broad boundaries individual circumstances vary and therefore present different contexts for research. A further question that merits research is the balance between entrepreneurial behaviour and small business start-up operations within the original family context.

Pushed into a business start-up by circumstances, the first generation adopted a business format relatively familiar within their community. Whilst this has been effective for the running of a small business and has certainly offered a platform for entrepreneurial behaviours in the introduction of new products and services, the distinction between small business and entrepreneurial behaviours is pertinent.

Chapter 8

The Sustainable Immigrant Family Business Model of Good Governance

As a significant component of the international economy, one would expect there to be extensive debate, analysis, and attention centred on immigrant family businesses. The incongruous reality is that this sector has been largely overlooked and ignored by academics and economic commentators alike. A review of relevant research on how good governance can assure long-term sustainability for immigrant family businesses has identified the following mediating variables as critical in this process:

- strategic planning;

- outside advice;

- governance structures;

- management succession planning;

- outside advice for management succession planning;

- outside advice for government structures;

- family harmony;

- family communication;

- profitability;

- relationship commitment;

- trust;

- commitment;

- vision;

- ethnic entrepreneurial growth;

- needs;

- cultural values alignment.

After taking the above points into consideration and critically reviewing the literature on this topic, a theoretical model was constructed as a visual benchmark for what the researchers conclude to be a flow of variables needed for and leading to sustainability of immigrant family businesses in the host society. This visual benchmark, as seen in Figure 8.1, along with the study benchmark variables listed above will be used in a follow-up study to develop a new theoretical model of sustainability in immigrant family business.

Figure 8.1, of good governance leading to a sustainable immigrant business, also illustrates the broad categories in the conceptual approach to defining variables of entrepreneurship, ethnicity, culture, and family dynamics as playing a "foundation" role in the building of immigrant family business sustainability.

Families, essentially mini-cultures that transmit the environment of larger cultures, assign meaning to ethnicity, which shapes cultural niches across national borders on a global scale. The ethnic groups and cultures of established nations may enter foreign countries as major populations. These include immigrant workers, voluntary migrants, historically "enslaved populations" or "indentured servants". Ethnicity and culture, regardless of place of birth or current residence, can be generalized to the broader, global context and are still transmitted by families. As such, extending theories of family business sustainability can be applied in any culture anywhere.

Extending this theoretical model of how immigrant family-related factors can be applied cross-culturally for good governance and immigrant family business sustainability, a more detailed model (see Figure 8.2) follows that specifies variables within each general category studied in this research. This theoretical model provides a foundation for and introduction to

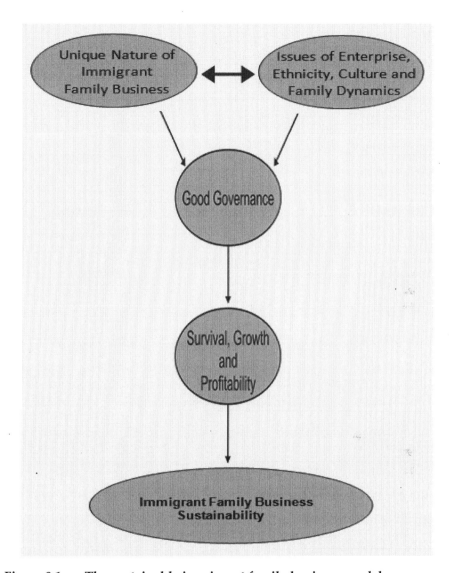

Figure 8.1   The sustainable immigrant family business model
Source: Researcher's own construction.

developing a new sustainable immigrant family business theory. Furthermore, this theoretical model acts as a basis of comparison for future research into how good governance impacts sustainability in immigrant family businesses. In doing so, this conceptual study offers entrance into an entire new area of research – that of sustainability factors in the immigrant family business. The model has been developed as a path diagram so that each theoretically proposed relationship can be described in future research by means of a hypothesis.

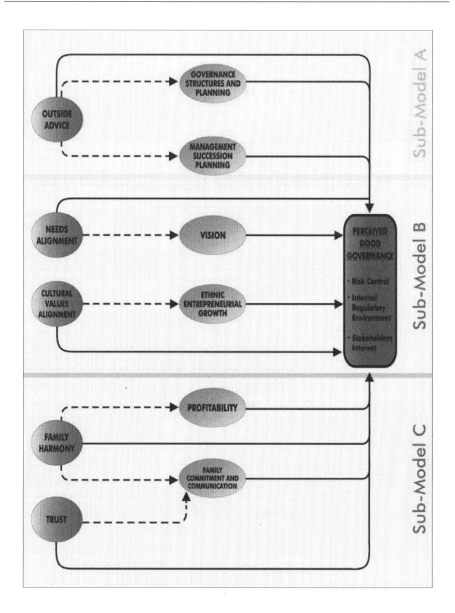

Figure 8.2   Path diagram of causal relationships: revised theoretical model
Source: Researcher's own construction.

It is worth noting that the literature has stipulated that family businesses with effective governance structures are more likely to undertake strategic planning. The findings of the present theoretical research would suggest that for immigrant family businesses, more focus should be placed on the underlying factors of strategic planning, as this should have a significant influence on risk control, the internal regulatory environment, and stakeholders' interests. Strategic planning and governance structures are important for immigrant family business success, growth, performance, control, and survival, and to promote continuity and family unity. More importantly, immigrant family businesses are more likely to prefer entrepreneurial opportunities with potential for long-term generation outcomes rather than dynamic growth risk strategies. Governance structures and planning within the immigrant family business context do provide for two components, namely governance of the business and governance within the family. These governance structures and planning should also help develop fair procedures and rules of conduct, to ensure that the emotion-based family system does not impede a professionally oriented family business approach, and that potential conflicts between the business goals and values and those of the family are appropriately addressed.

The use of outside advice in assisting immigrant family business is an important factor that influences both the governance structures and the planning of the management succession process. Important elements of this factor include the involvement of outsiders' expertise (i.e. lawyers, accountants, and the use of advising consultants) to assist with its governance. Outside advice for the immigrant family business should be considered for the right reasons. Since family members may lack objectivity in certain business decisions and have emotional attachments to the core business, family businesses need outside advice in addition to that of family board members to obtain more varied and objective advice.

Adopting initiatives for outside advice will help to reduce what is theorized as the immigrant family's greatest stumbling block to business sustainability and the area of greatest resistance – that is, emotional attachment to the business. With outside advice, entrepreneurial activities are more likely to be evaluated on merit, rather than emotion. As a result, links between the entrepreneurial driving forces are strengthened to ensure good governance. In order to make informed decisions on governance matters, supporters of the use of outside advice have argued that these members bring with them fresh perspectives and new directions, monitor and assist progress, act as catalysts for change, assist with the succession planning and processes, assist the governance structures and planning to increase risk control, facilitate adherence to the internal regulatory environment, and look after the stakeholders' interests to ensure good governance.

The use of other outside advice in immigrant family businesses can be found, but it is used only in very rare instances. A way for the immigrant family business to overcome the resistance to outside advice is to find common ground with outside advisors from within their ethnic and religious group. The significance of culture cannot be overlooked within these processes towards immigrant family business sustainability. Outside intervention will be more readily accepted by governance structures of immigrant family businesses if it comes from within their own ethnic enclave.

As previously stated, the significance of culture and the specific variables of ethnicity and religion have a considerable influence on many characteristics of family businesses, and may also directly influence the succession process such as the patterns, communication, modes of conflict resolution, education, divorce or separation rate, and the position of women in the family business. With improved education among the younger generations, traditional roles have been adversely affected, with direct consequences for immigrant family business succession. However, for the immigrant family business, succession planning is still traditionally a planned effort from within the family, to educate the prospective successor from an early age to be involved in the particular business. This involvement starts from grassroots level, and as the prospective successors grow older, they are only as involved as their first levels of education allow them to be, until successful succession has been accomplished. They are then prepared for their position and educated into their family business, normally after school, during their school holidays, around the family table, and through social gatherings from other support group projects within the ethnic enclave. This process allows for the prospective successor to be fully equipped and prepared for the tasks of an ethnic entrepreneur as an assimilated member within a social and ethnic enclave. In this way, the transfer process becomes culturally institutionalized and the rules of succession are clear to all the family members concerned, long before the actual succession takeover takes place, to ensure good governance.

The literature has also revealed that the quality of a family business member's personal life experience is in part a function of their ability to meet the developmental needs of the business. The immigrant family business member may see the personal needs alignment in general as the degree to which an individual's needs are properly aligned with opportunities available in the context of the family business. In other words, if there is a need for a specific skill within the family business the individual will be required to train/study in order to fulfil that particular need. This may require time, but, most often depending on the business needs, training to become, for instance, a chartered accountant, a lawyer or a marketer is undertaken on a part-time basis. In order to make informed choices about their future, the potential heirs need to assess their career goals, their family relationships, and their possible shareholding in the family business.

One approach suggests that a positive succession experience can be realized if the next generation family member has achieved fulfilment of three types of needs: career interest, psychosocial, and life-stage. Immigrants from patriarchal societies tend to believe that if the interests or competencies of their daughters do not fit the needs of the business, the family should provide them with a fair share of support to pursue other career opportunities. Failing this, they would have to fulfil a role in the prospective spouse's family business. It has become apparent from the literature that the more personal needs and career interests are aligned with opportunities offered by the family business, the better the chances that good governance will prevail in the context of the family business. Thus, as established in this research, needs alignment has a direct influence on perceived good governance in immigrant family businesses.

Aligning Needs of Good Governance with the Immigrant Family Business Model

VISION

It is the vision of almost all immigrant family business founders/current owners to provide jobs for family members or other relatives, and to financially support those family members in need, either locally or back in the home country. Once the family business becomes economically established, it will invite other family members to come from the home country to join the business or start up new ventures. This move, of course, can only be achieved by creating entrepreneurial growth.

Family business decisions are often complex, and usually demand the analysis of large amounts of data to ensure the process of good governance. A shared vision provides a common framework with which to assess available information and to focus on relevant family business issues. The literature makes it clear that when all the constituents in the family business share a common vision, opportunism is reduced and the sharing of information increases, thereby providing for richer information with which to make daily family business decisions. An understanding of roles and related tasks created by a shared vision promotes internal role specialization. This in turn improves the quality of information that the stakeholders have at their disposal for making decisions.

According to the literature, a shared vision promotes coherence in the stakeholders' expectations and opinions regarding organizational goals. This in turn promotes cooperative behaviour through clarified role interactions. A family council can provide the structure to implement and direct the shared vision through a "code of understanding" as part of their business plan. In a family business, a shared vision is said to involve the family members' collective idea about the future of the business, including desired business domains, desired growth rates, and financial performance. Frequent interactions enable family business members to forge a shared view of the goals of the family; family gatherings and meetings contribute towards the expression of shared beliefs.

CULTURAL VALUES ALIGNMENT

Generally speaking, a value is one mode of behaviour preferred over another mode of behaviour. Not only are these modes influenced by culture, but they are very diverse when different cultures are compared. Interestingly enough, research has noted immigrant family business owners often believe that alignment of cultural values (i.e. cultural beliefs and customs) with the host environment would impact negatively on the ethnic entrepreneurial growth of the family business. One explanation for the fact that some move beyond this potentially limiting belief is that they realized that growing up in a family of a particular culture and having certain values of importance is no longer sufficient for survival in today's highly demanding business environment.

In family businesses, governance receives family imprinting and sometimes becomes a synthesis (sometimes a compromise) between the family values and the business rule, reflecting all the critical steps in organizational development, the delegation process of managerial activities, the creation of managerial style, the involvement of the family members in the management bodies, and the entrepreneurial succession process. The cultural ties and factors, including identity, help ethnic entrepreneurs to consider business conduct and strategies rather than emphasize margins. As stated in Chapter 2, the spread of such entrepreneurship across national borders may well characterize the next phase of globalization as one merging and extending the historical nexus of cultural identity and trading in novel ways.

ETHNIC ENTREPRENEURIAL GROWTH

Entrepreneurship sometimes generates growth and the *reverse* must also be true – growth sometimes promotes entrepreneurship. It is the prerogative of the entrepreneur to choose the extent of growth. Ethnic entrepreneurial growth can be confirmed to have a direct and positive influence on the variable of perceived good governance. It is clear that if economic behaviour is discretionary, pursuing continued development of the family business is the more entrepreneurial choice than refraining from it; just as founding a business is more entrepreneurial than not doing so. In fact, ethnic entrepreneurial growth may perhaps be best conceived of as a collective term, for the concept of entrepreneurship is the development of new economic activities to ensure growth, which in turn can provide for other family members in need.

The "entrepreneurial capability" of family business members is crucial if growth is what they want to strive for. Immigrant family business members have argued that what makes a successful entrepreneurial family business or family member is their ability to generate growth, think entrepreneurially, act entrepreneurially, and always to be on the lookout for innovative ideas and opportunities to do business and build on what the family already has. Entrepreneurial growth takes a variety of forms: exploitations of scale economics by plant expansions, modernization of the technological base, diversification, and consolidation via mergers and acquisitions, or by other less formal modes of strategic alliance. A central stimulus for a successful entrepreneurial growth strategy is acceptance of the need for professionalization of commercial practice as the business develops from its previous family-orientated culture.

PROFITABILITY

Profitability is an important determinant of perceived good governance. A significant and positive relationship has been found between this and the dependent variable of perceived good governance. Many entrepreneurs seek only to create a job and generate a living for themselves. The opposite of this has been shown to be true for immigrant entrepreneurs. Research indicates that immigrant entrepreneurs would rather grow a business that could support and create a living for many others, and they would also strive towards the adding of value that could result in capital profitability gain, to ensure good governance.

Further research with immigrant family businesses indicates that effort among family members is directed towards the recycling of entrepreneurial capital and talent within the family and their relatives. This is seen to be a well governed system of private responsibility towards the family as a whole and, secondly, a means of organizing and managing themselves for the long haul in order to perpetuate the creation and recognition processes of economic regeneration, innovation, and solid profitability. This can be regarded as a long-term goal to create real added value for their business.

Research has revealed that ethnic entrepreneurs tend to be secretive by nature, and will only really "open up" within their own social enclave. This is a major concern in determining the questions to be asked regarding finance-related issues by an "outsider". However, even for immigrant family businesses, as for all entrepreneurial ventures, the promise of profitability is most probably the single most important motivating factor in starting a new venture. An unprofitable business venture would only be considered suitable if it was established that it was either poorly managed or governed, and that through a turn-around strategy it could be made profitable. Even then, other immigrant elders/entrepreneurs are usually called in for a specialized opinion. In line with profitability, most immigrant entrepreneurs will never indicate to outsiders "how" profitable a business venture in which they find themselves is. Once a business venture is found to be profitable, immigrants and their families will reap profits through hard-earned productivity, thereby promoting good governance.

FAMILY HARMONY

Most family business-related research has failed to recognize family harmony as a variable influencing good governance. Family harmony, commitment, and communication are important determinants of profitability to ensure good governance in immigrant family businesses. Family harmony will increase the dedication needed to govern a business successfully (through long hours of work), in that family business members would thereby ensure the business is profitable, and this action will have a positive influence on good governance. The higher the quality of family harmony within the family, the greater will be the effort to execute risk control, to adhere to and enforce the regulations as stipulated for the internal regulatory environment, and to look after all the stakeholders' interests to ensure good governance.

People universally consider harmonious family living as the most important aspect of their lives. Living and working effectively in harmony is a governance phenomenon in ethnic entrepreneurship, firstly for the entrepreneurs themselves and then for their relatives. The effort to establish family harmony is considered to be a difficult one, especially considering the fact that immigrant family business members spend most of their time together during long hours of hard work. The role of the elders is considered by most immigrants as important to ensure mutual respect and understanding of the knowledge and skills of others, and to coordinate the family business network in such a way that family harmony is a high priority. The idea of "the family" is considered by immigrants as being so powerful in the family business network that the family ideology will present what is "correct and proper" or what is "wrong" in governing their business.

FAMILY COMMITMENT AND COMMUNICATION

The issue of commitment and communication in cultural exchange has become an important one for businesses expanding into foreign markets. Effective family commitment parallels the congruence of goals among participants in the family business. This entails that relatives have common beliefs regarding behaviours, goals, and policies. In the immigrant family business, commitment is seen as a keen desire to continue good family relationships to ensure the family's continuance, or in business, as the explicit commitment to family members as partners to ensure good governance. The literature has also revealed that a culture of open family communication, reinforced by structured processes, is an integral precondition to creating a successful family governance process. A viable family governance process and systems cannot survive in an atmosphere of ignorance and distrust. Communication is achieved through regular family meetings guided by good communication processes for both family and other business matters. Immigrant entrepreneurs indicate that they make use of formal structures to discuss additional family issues, including the performance of the family business or investments, to communicate further educational and mentoring aspects to the younger generations, to establish the need for family commitment and confidentiality, and in matters regarding their progress and the business plan of action. As for all family businesses, the first place to start communication is between the family members themselves about family matters. The second area of open communication requires a regular flow of information from the family company or investment – from the governance structure to the relevant family members. These two communication processes among the family members and between the family and its business structure help create the knowledge and competence required by family and business members alike.

TRUST

There is a significant body of literature emphasizing the role of trust in maintaining good organizational governance, as trust plays an important role in business survival and success and is also an important determinant of family commitment and communication. Research, though, has indicated that trust can have a negative influence on the variable of perceived good governance, especially in family businesses with a centralized authority structure. Immigrant entrepreneurs, particularly of the second generation, have indicated that trust within the family business could become difficult to attain if too much trust is placed in only certain individuals – usually those yielding the most power. The actions of those responsible for the strategic direction of risk control, the internal regulatory environment, and for looking after the stakeholders' interests should greatly influence the level of trust within enterprises. Finally, for family businesses, trust often represents a fundamental basis for cooperation, and potentially provides a key source of competitive advantage. In matters of family business governance, too much or too little trust can, however, be problematic. Based on the research, family businesses are often challenged to develop a governance mechanism that permits the building and sustaining of optional trust. Openness and inclusion creates family trust, and family trust creates well governed open communication, which in turn ensures good governance.

Summary

One of the most formidable obstacles to the stability, growth, and success of a family business is the issue of good governance. Continuity in family businesses requires the development of effective governance structures and processes. Governance structures can monitor both the family and the business system to ensure that they adequately address all the issues associated with entrepreneurial leadership and ownership of a family business. The development of a solid good governance model should not only take into account the need to ensure success of the family wealth or business, but also consider the need to cultivate and honour the human needs of all the family members concerned. Even factors related to the dynamics of human relationships, such as good parenting, can establish the network in which a good governance model can work within the immigrant family business. Governance of family businesses is more complicated than that of a non-family-controlled business, because in the family business, the business, the family, and the stakeholders all need governance. The lack of effective governance of these three groups can be a major cause of organizational problems.

The immigrant family business possesses many features that make its governance a difficult task because the family business typically depicts a complex, long-standing stakeholder structure that involves family members, top management, and possibly a board of directors. Usually, ownership passes from one generation to the next within the family, while the family members of the owner(s) usually play multiple roles in the management and governance of the business. As an intermediary between the family and the business, the board has a crucial role in the family business's governance structure. The role of the board is to add value. It is frequently involved with management, and through its participation in the family, it continuously influences decisions in the business. Therefore, the board of a family business serves a different purpose from that of a non-family business. As an intermediary, it needs to understand and respect the family for its needs, values, culture, and goals, and also the business for its strategic, financial, and managerial needs.

This research has established that the commitment of the immigrant family to the success of the business and its governance can be a very positive force in starting and growing an enterprise. The literature reveals that the assumptions underpinning business and family systems are often antithetical, which creates complex dilemmas for the entrepreneur. The ethnic entrepreneurial career is extremely demanding, fraught with long hours of hard work. Balancing the needs of both the family and the business is not easy. The family has to play a supportive role by providing money, contacts, labour, and other resources, and has to be supportive of further entrepreneurial endeavours to ensure good governance.

More research, however, needs to be done to understand, firstly, how immigrant entrepreneurs and their families adjust to entrepreneurial lifestyle enforcing good governance and, secondly, the role of the family as one of the success factors in enforcing good governance. A team effort is needed by the immigrant familial network, encompassing all members of the business and the stakeholders' network – all the people that share a mutual interest in the ethnic enterprise either from within or outside the immigrant family – to ensure good governance for the family business.

Case Study:
A Chinese Immigrant Family Business in Pakistan

Shehla Riza Arifeen

HuiPing Zhang was born in a village in southern China in 1961. Her father was a cook in a restaurant and her mother was a housewife. She started school in 1968 and graduated from high school in Guangzhou. HuiPing worked for some time for an organization that trained officers. One of her colleagues suggested a former pupil of his, Johnny, an immigrant in Pakistan since 1982, as a potential marriage partner. They corresponded for two years and HuiPing decided to accept Johnny's proposal of marriage and flew alone to Pakistan to get married. She was 27 at that time and married Johnny a week following her arrival. She spoke only Chinese at that time. Their wedding, in 1988, was attended by the small Chinese community in Lahore. Johnny at that time was working for a Chinese restaurant in Lahore as manager/chef. HuiPing settled into her life as a housewife in Lahore and gave birth to her daughter Vicky in November that same year, and her son Jimmy in December, 1990. She gradually adjusted to life in a foreign country, learning to speak a little English and Urdu so that she could communicate with the non-Chinese. Her life was centred on housework and childcare. Johnny and HuiPing became Pakistani citizens in 1990.

In 1995, Johnny decided to set up a small Chinese restaurant in a commercial area of Lahore that did not have one. As Chinese food is popular in Pakistan, it seemed a good opportunity, also given Johnny's experience in managing restaurants and his background as a chef. About the same time, HuiPing also decided to set up a small, ladies-only beauty salon in her home. Her children were going to school, she had more time on her hands, and she wanted to supplement her husband's income. She set up her salon in 1996, after a friend of hers brought back the equipment for the salon from China. Neither business was thriving. In 1999, in order to save money, HuiPing and Johnny decided to run the businesses from the same location and set up home in the same rented premises. Here they managed better as they had cut down costs. The family was able to meet all their expenses and save a bit.

HuiPing would often help out Johnny with his cooking/catering business as well as attend to customers in her parlour, and manage the home and childcare. She had no help in her salon and did all the work herself. This, in fact, turned out to be an advantage because all the customers preferred that she catered to them personally. They waited for her to finish working on a customer to then take their turn. Her customers liked her because she was polite, hospitable, and thorough in her work. Hers was also the only beauty salon in town that would open up early in the morning at 7am or close late at 10pm, if a customer requested an appointment at that hour. Her customers became an important part of her life. They came to replace the family she did not have in the country. They also became a source of emotional support. She felt she could talk to them about her problems and they would give her advice. If she needed some advice about her children's education or health or property or tax issues, she would consult them. She worked long hours but she felt it was all worthwhile, as both her children were in good schools, receiving quality education, and speaking both English and Urdu fluently. In Pakistan, high school education has to be funded by the parents and is expensive. Both her children were very studious and completed their O-levels with excellent grades. Both children received merit-based financial support for their A-levels from a private school. It was a happy time for her even though it was a physically demanding period of her life.

Around 2008, the premises on which they had their businesses was sold to another owner. They were having some problems with the new landlord and felt it was time to look towards buying a small house in which they could have their businesses and save on rent. Their family in China agreed to help them financially. In March 2009, they found a small house in another part of town and moved the salon but not the restaurant. The new house was too small to accommodate both businesses and they were concerned about losing customers from the restaurant business. They decided to keep the restaurant in its current location for a few months, pending a later decision.

Two months after moving into their new home, in May of that year, HuiPing badly burnt her leg and could not walk for a month. Her salon business suffered because of this, as well as the move, and she found she had only half the number of customers that she had previously. Johnny had also been unwell. He had a cough and was not sleeping or eating well. At first, HuiPing thought it was because of the hectic few months they had had – the move, her foot, and so on. By August she was concerned enough to mention his illness to her customers. One of her customers, who was a doctor, insisted that he needed to be admitted to hospital. Johnny at first refused to agree to go to hospital. However, when he discovered lumps in his neck, he had no choice. Dr X (a doctor customer) asked him to come to her hospital (a large government hospital), from where they sent him immediately to a private cancer hospital for tests. By this time, Johnny had become so weak he could not even walk and had to use a wheelchair. His restaurant was closed indefinitely pending test results. The test results came back positive. He was diagnosed with non-Hodgkin's lymphoma. HuiPing could not afford the expensive cancer hospital. Dr X admitted Johnny to her hospital and first stabilized his health and then, once he was stronger, began chemotherapy. The family decided to shut down the restaurant business and save on the rent of the restaurant. All the equipment was either moved to the home or sold. HuiPing says of this period in her life:

When Johnny was in hospital we could not run the restaurant. So we stopped it. He wanted to do it but I think he can't do it. At that time, if some customers wanted to come to me, then I would go home from hospital to do something for the customer. I was mostly running between hospital and home. The children were also very upset. Actually it was a very difficult time for Jimmy as he was in A-levels.

She and the children would take shifts to be with Johnny at the hospital. There were times when Johnny was on his own because the children were in school and she had to go home to serve a customer. The hospital staff was generally accommodating and kind to them. They felt looked after. Furthermore, Johnny took the chemotherapy well, not suffering the after-effects usually associated with the process. The chemotherapy treatment lasted six months. This period was financially stressful as HuiPing became the sole breadwinner. However, Johnny insisted on doing his bit. Once he was out of hospital, Johnny began translation work, travelling even to sites out of town, in between his chemotherapy sessions. This was of concern to HuiPing. She worried about his health but he insisted on doing it. She says: "At times his leg used to be numb and he could not feel anything, yet he would insist on walking and going on this job."

Johnny is in remission now. He only takes translation work off and on. Both their children received scholarships at a local private university. Their daughter graduated nearly two years ago, at the top of her class and is working. Their son is in his last year at university. HuiPing acquired training from another Chinese lady on weight loss massage as her customer numbers had gone down drastically during the period following Johnny's cancer diagnosis. She has passed an exam in China and is a Chinese certified weight loss masseuse as well as a masseuse for back pain, shoulder pain, etc. She says of her future:

I think I will give massages from the house. I do not want to shut the business. It is better than working for somebody. Life has been very hard. It has been a very hard time for me ... I can say that. It has been difficult being away from home. But when you are married, you have no choice. The children are here. I am lucky I have good friends here ... so many good customers that have been helping me.

Chapter 9

Epilogue:
Discussion and Recommendations
for Future Research

Brockhaus (2003) asks the question: "Why do entrepreneurs need a theory of entrepreneurship?" His succinct answer is: "because it enables its user to be efficient". According to Brockhaus (2003), "efficiency" for the entrepreneur means recognizing what kind of information is helpful and knowing where it can be obtained. The efficient entrepreneur uses the theory to translate raw data into usable information and to process the data into categories and variables. A good theory indicates to the user how things and events are related – which are likely to be external causes and independent, and which are likely to be internal results and controllable. A good theory also tells entrepreneurs the probable direction of causality. Therefore, an entrepreneur with a good theory of how entrepreneurship works is practical and efficient. This is crucial because entrepreneurship can be expensive. Real-time failures cost money and the irreplaceable time of many people, as well as their hopes and reputations.

One of the most formidable obstacles to the stability, growth, and success of a family business is the issue of good governance. Continuity in family businesses requires the development of effective governance structures and processes. Governance structures can monitor both the family and a business system to ensure that they adequately address all the issues associated with entrepreneurial leadership and ownership of a family business. The development of a solid good governance model should not only take into account the need to provide seeing to the family wealth or business, but should also consider the need to cultivate and honour the human needs of all the family members concerned. Governance of family businesses is more complicated than that of a non-family-controlled business, because in the family business, the business, the family, and the stakeholder group(s) all need governance. The lack of effective governance of these three groups can be a major cause of organizational problems.

Immigrant family businesses possess many features that make their governance a difficult task because the family business typically depicts a complex, long-standing stakeholder structure that involves family members, top management, and a board of directors. Usually, ownership passes from one generation to the next within the family, while the owners' family members usually play multiple roles in the management and governance of the business. As an intermediary between the family and the business, the board has a crucial role in the immigrant family business's governance structure. The role of the board is to add value. It is frequently involved with management, and through its participation in the family it continuously influences decisions in the business. Therefore, the board of a family business serves a different purpose from that of a non-family business. As an intermediary, it needs to understand and respect the family for its needs, values, culture, and goals, and also the business for its strategic, financial, and managerial needs.

The research has established that the commitment of the immigrant family to the success of the business and its governance can be a very positive force in starting and growing a family business. The literature revealed that the assumptions underpinning business and family systems are often antithetical, which creates complex dilemmas for the entrepreneur. The immigrant entrepreneurial career is extremely demanding, fraught with long hours of hard work. Balancing the needs of both the family and the business is not easy. The family has to play a supportive role by providing money, contacts, labour, and other resources, and has to be supportive of further entrepreneurial endeavours to ensure good governance.

More research, however, needs to be done to understand firstly, how immigrant entrepreneurs and their families adjust to an entrepreneurial lifestyle enforcing good governance, and secondly, the role of the family as one of the success factors in enforcing good governance. It was established that a team effort is needed by the familial network (it encompasses all members of the business) and the stakeholders' network (all the people that have an interest) to ensure good governance for the immigrant family business. At the same time, these efforts must be evaluated through the lens of ethnic values and culture to align with family functionality.

Hopefully, this research has broken new ground and provided an entrance to an entire area of research. The areas covered by this qualitative, case study research – factors that influence good governance for the immigrant family businesses – remain unexplored until now. The findings here provide the foundation and introduction, thereby acting as a basis of comparison for future research in the fields of perceived good governance for immigrant family businesses, the internationalization of immigrant family businesses, and in particular family businesses in a cross-national study. Indeed, the entire good governance experience may well be different when comparing immigrant family businesses from country to country, region to region, and wherever ethnic entrepreneurs exist. There are many cultures whose people are sent to foreign cultures to work for extended periods of time. Clearly, for the family businesses from these cultures, there may be implications in terms of governance experiences, as identified in this research. The cross-cultural aspect of family business governance must now be considered when conducting such research as more and more emphasis is placed on good governance for all businesses concerned. Perhaps these are grounds to be considered with regard to the impact of perceived good governance for non-family businesses as well. For example, how would a family business member fare in a managerial succession in a non-family business? Do they possess certain traits that would make them better managers? What would motivate these individuals, and secondly, would existing family business governance techniques still apply in measuring all the relevant factors in the pursuit of good governance? Further studies and development of what has been established in this study would provide a deeper understanding of this new area of research.

This is the first conceptual study that has developed a theoretical model of how immigrant family-related factors and good governance lead to immigrant family business sustainability. This theoretical model provides a foundation for and introduction into developing a new sustainable immigrant family business theory. Also, this theoretical model acts as a basis of comparison for future research into how good governance impacts sustainability in immigrant family businesses. In doing so, this conceptual study has provided an entrance to an entire new area of research, that of sustainability factors in the immigrant family business.

Sustainability has been an enduring problem for businesses of all shapes and sizes across the entrepreneurial landscape. The ability of the immigrant family business to practice the good governance required for delivering competitive advantage and profitability is the core element for its long-term sustainability. The core foundation of good governance for sustainability, coupled with other mediating variables, presents researchers with a unique perspective from which to study the immigrant family business.

The stakeholders of the governance structure for the immigrant family in order of importance are the family, the founder, the successors, and the advisors. Each can be a significant reason for success and equally the cause of failure, as for any family business. Yet, for the immigrant family business much investigative work and study is still needed to research the impact of entrepreneurship, ethnicity, culture, and family dynamics on 1) how governance structures are formed and function, and 2) the role played by these forms and the functions of governance in immigrant family business sustainability. In further investigations, governance must also be defined in terms of resources and constraints that both support and challenge immigrant family business sustainability.

Bibliography

Abrahams, D., Ando, K. and Hinkle, S. 1998. Psychological Attachment to Groups: Cross-cultural Differences in Organizational Identification and Subjective Norms as Predictors of Worker's Turnover Intentions. *Personality and Sociology Bulletin*, 24: 1027–39.

Adair, W., Brett, J., Lempereur, A., Okumura, T., Tinsley, C. and Lytle, A. 1998a. *Culture and Negotiation Strategy*. Evanston, IL: Dispute Resolution Research Center, Northwestern University.

Adair, W., Kopelman, S., Gillespie, J. and Brett, J.M. 1998b. *Compatible Cultural Values and Schemas in US/Israeli Negotiations: Implications for Joint Gains.* Evanston, IL: Dispute Resolution Research Center, Northwestern University.

Adair, W., Okumura, T. and Brett, J.M. 1998c. *Culturally Bound Negotiation Scripts and Joint Gains in the US and Japanese Intra- and Inter-cultural Dyads.* Evanston, IL: Dispute Resolution Research Center, Northwestern University.

Adendorff, C. and Boshoff, C. 2011. The impact of culture-related factors on good governance in Greek family businesses in South Africa. *South African Journal of Business Management*, 42(2): 1–14.

Agarwal, A., Tripathi, K.K. and Srivastava, M. 1983. Social Roots and Psychological Implications of Time Perspective. *International Journal of Psychology*, 18: 367–80.

Agarwal, P. 1991. *Passage from India: Post 1965 Indian Immigrants and Their Children; Conflicts, Concerns, and Solutions.* Palos Verdes, CA: Yuvati Publications.

Aldrich, H. and Cliff, J. 2003. The Pervasive Effects of Family on Entrepreneurship: Toward a Family Embeddedness Perspective. *Journal of Business Venturing*, 18: 573–96.

Aldrich, H. and Waldinger, R. 1990. Ethnicity and Entrepreneurship. *Annual Review of Sociology*, 16: 111–35.

Anderson, J.C. and Narus, J.A. 1995. Capturing the Value of Supplementary Services. *Harvard Business Review*, 73(1): 75–83.

Aram, J.D. and Cowen, S.S. 1990. Strategic Planning for Increased Profit in the Family Owned Business. *Long Range Planning*, 23: 76–81.

Aronoff, C.E. 1998. Megatrends in Family Business. *Family Business Review*, 11(3): 181–5.

Aronoff, C.E., Astrachan, J.H. and Ward, J.L. 1993. *Family Business Sourcebook II*. Marietta, GA: Business Owner Resources.

Aronoff, C.E., Astrachan, J.H. and Ward, J.L. 1998. *Developing Family Business Policies*. Marietta, GA: Family Enterprise Publishers.

Aronoff, C.E. and Ward, J.L. 1992. *Family Meetings: How to Build a Stronger Family and a Stronger Business*. Family Business Leadership Series No. 2. Marietta, GA: Business Owner Resources.

Aronoff, C.E. and Ward, J.L. 1995. Family Owned Businesses: A Thing of the Past or a Model for the Future? *Family Business Review*, 9(2): 121–30.

Aronoff, C.E. and Ward, J.L. 1996. *Family Business Governance: Maximising Family and Business Potential*. Marietta, GA: Family Enterprise Publishers.

Arrow, K. 1974. Kenneth Arrow on Capitalism and Society. *Business and Society Innovation*, 10: 22–7.

Astrachan, J.H. 1988. Family Firm and Community Culture. *Family Business Review*, 1(2): 165–89.

Astrachan, J.H. and Aronoff, C.E. 1998. Succession Issues Can Signal Deeper Problems. *Nation's Business*, 86(5): 72–4.

Astrachan, J.H. and Keyt, A.D. 2003. Commentary On: The Transacting Cognitions of Non-family Employees in the Family Business Setting. *Journal of Business Venturing*, 18: 553–8.

Astrachan, J.H., Klein, S.B. and Smyrnios, K.X. 2002. The F-PEC Scale of Family Influence: A Proposal for Solving the Family Business Definition Problem. *Family Business Review*, 15(1): 45–58.

Astrachan, J.H. and Kolenko, T.A. 1994. A Neglected Factor Explaining Family Business Success: Human Resource Practices. *Family Business Review*, 7(3): 251–62.

Astrachan, J.H. and Shanker, M.C. 2002. *Family Business Contribution to the US Economy: A Closer Look*. Alfred, NY: The George and Robin Raymond Family Business Institute.

Astrachan, J.H. and Ward, J.L. (eds). 1996. *Family Business Sourcebook II*. Marietta, GA: Business Owner Resources.

Au, K., Chiang, F.F., Birtch, T.A. and Ding, Z. 2013. Incubating the Next Generation to Venture: The Case of a Family Business in Hong Kong. *Asia Pacific Journal of Management*, 30: 749–67.

Auster, E. and Aldrich, H. 1984. Small Business Vulnerability, Ethnic Enclaves and Ethnic Enterprise. In R. Ward and R. Jenkins (eds), *Ethnic Communities in Business: Strategies for Economic Survival*. Cambridge: Cambridge University Press, 39–54.

Ayres, G.R. 1990. Rough Family Justice: Equity in Family Business Succession Planning. *Family Business Review*, 3(1): 3–22.

Ayres, G. and Carter, M. 1995. Family Business in Transition: Why Traditional Tools Fall Short. In *Proceedings of the 1995 Family Firm Institute Conference; Gateway to the Future, October 11–14, St. Louis, MO*. Brookline, MA: Family Firm Institute, 74–84.

Azmat, F. and Zutshi, A. 2012a. Influence of Home-country Culture and Regulatory Environment on Corporate Social Responsibility Perceptions: The Case of Sri Lankan Immigrant Entrepreneurs. *Thunderbird International Business Review*, 54(1): 15–27.

Azmat, F. and Zutshi, A. 2012b. Perceptions of Corporate Social Responsibility amongst Immigrant Entrepreneurs. *Social Responsibility Journal*, 8(1): 63–76.

Barnes, L.B. and Hershon, S.A. 1976. Transferring Power in the Family Business. *Harvard Business Review*, 54(4): 105–14.

Barth, F. 1969. *Introduction to Ethnic Groups and Boundaries: The Social Organisation of Cultural Difference*. Boston, MA: Little, Brown.

Baughn, C.C., Neupert, K.E. and Sugheir, J.S. 2013. Domestic Migration and New Business Creation in the United States. *Journal of Small Business & Entrepreneurship*, 26(1): 1–14.

Baycan, T., Sahin, M. and Nijkamp, P. 2012. The Urban Growth Potential of Second-Generation Migrant Entrepreneurs: A Sectoral Study on Amsterdam. *International Business Review*, 21(6), 971–86.

Beavers, W.R. 1982. Healthy, Midrange, and Severely Dysfunctional Families. In F. Walsh (ed.), *Normal Family Processes*. New York: Guilford, 45–66.

Becker, G.S. 1965. A Theory of the Allocation of Time. *The Economic Journal*, 75: 496–517.

Becker, G.S. 1993. *Human Capital: A Theoretical and Empirical Analysis with Specific Reference to Education*. Third edition. Chicago, IL: University of Chicago Press.

Beckers, P. and Kloosterman, R.C. 2013. Open to Business? An Exploration of the Impact of the Built Environment and Zoning Plans on Local Businesses in Pre-war and Post-war Residential Neighbourhoods in Dutch Cities. *Urban Studies*. 16 May.

Beckhard, R. and Dyer, W.G. Jr. 1983. Managing Continuity in the Family Owned Business. *Organizational Dynamics*, 12(1): 5–12.

Belussi, F. and Sammarra, A. (eds). 2012. *Business Networks in Clusters and Industrial Districts: The Governance of the Global Value Chain*. Abingdon and New York: Routledge.

Benavides-Velasco, C.A., Quintana-García, C. and Guzmán-Parra, V.F. 2013. Trends in Family Business Research. *Small Business Economics*, 40(1): 41–57.

Benson, B., Crego, E.T. and Drucker, R.H. 1990. *Your Family Business: A Success Guide for Growth and Survival*. Homewood, IL: Dow Jones Irwin.

Berembeim, R.E. 1990. How Business Families Manage the Transition from Owner to Professional Management. *Family Business Review*, 3(1): 69–110.

Berrone, P., Cruz, C. and Gomez-Mejia, L.R. 2012. Socioemotional Wealth in Family Firms: Theoretical Dimensions, Assessment Approaches, and Agenda for Future Research. *Family Business Review*, 25(3): 258–79.

Berry, J.W. 1993. An Ecological Approach to Understanding Cognition across Cultures. In J. Altarriba (ed.), *Cognition and Culture: A Cross-cultural Approach to Cognitive Psychology*. Amsterdam: North-Holland, 361–75.

Bertrand, M. and Schoar, A. 2006. The Role of Family in Family Firms. *Journal of Economic Perspectives*, 20(2): 73–96.

Billore, S., Zainuddin, A.H., Al-Haj, N.H.Y.Y. and Halkias, D. 2010. Female Immigrant Entrepreneurship: A Developing Sector in Japan's Entrepreneurial Economy. *Journal of Developmental Entrepreneurship*, 15(2): 165–86.

Bjuggren, P.O. and Sund, L. 2000. Organization of Successions of Small and Medium Sized Enterprises within the Family. In *Proceedings of the International Council for Small Business, 45th World Conference, Brisbane, Australia, 7–10 June* (CD Rom), 1–17.

Bjuggren, P. and Sund, L. 2001. Strategic Decision Making in the Intergenerational Successions of Small- and Medium-sized Family-owned Businesses. *Family Business Review*, 14(1): 11–23.

Blaschke, J., Boissevain, J., Grotenberg, H., Joseph, I., Morokvasic, M. and Ward, R. 1990. European Trends in Ethnic Businesses. In R. Waldinger, H. Aldrich, R. Ward and Associates (eds), *Ethnic Entrepreneurs*. London: Sage, 79–105.

Bonachich, E. 1973. A Theory of Middleman Minorities. *American Sociological Review*, 38(5): 583–94.

Bonachich, E. and Modell, J. 1980. *The Economic Basis of Ethnic Solidarity*. Berkeley, CA: University of California Press.

Bourdieu, P. 1986. The Forms of Capital. In J.G. Richardson (ed.), *Handbook of Theory and Research for the Sociology of Education*. New York: Greenwood Press, 241–59.

Bourdieu, P. 1992. Economisch kapitaal, cultureel kapitaal, sociaal kapitaal. In Pierre Bourdieu, *Opstellen over smaak, habitus en het verldbegrip*, ed. Dick Pels. Amsterdam: Van Gennep, 120–41.

Boutaris, J. 2003. Proposal on a New Dimension of Profit. *Business Strategy for the Bio-environment*, 1.

Bradach, J.L. and Eccles, R.G. 1989. Price, Authority, and Trust: From Ideal Types to Plural Forms. *Annual Review of Sociology*, 15: 97–118.

Brenic, M.M. and Zabkar, V. 2001. *Trust in Cross Cultural Business to Business Relationships: The Case of the Former Yugoslav Markets*. Ljubljana: University of Ljubljana, Faculty of Economics.

Brett, J.M., Adair, W., Lempereur, A., Okumura, T., Shikhirev, P., Tinsley, C. and Lytle, A. 1998. Culture and Joint Gains in Negotiation. *Negotiation Journal*, 14: 55–80.

Brett, J.M. and Okumura, T. 1998. Inter- and Intra-cultural Negotiation: US and Japanese Negotiators. *Academy of Management Journal*, 41: 495–510.

Brett, W.P. 2000. Culture and Negotiation. *International Journal of Psychology*, 35: 97–104.

Brockhaus, R. 1975. I-E Locus of Control Scores as a Predictor of Entrepreneurial Intentions. Paper presented at the Academy of Management meetings, New Orleans.

Brockhaus, R. 1980. Risk Taking Propensity of Entrepreneurs, *Academy of Management Journal*, 23(3): 509–20.

Brockhaus, R. 1982. The Psychology of the Entrepreneur. In C.A. Kent, D.L. Sexton and K.H. Versper (eds), *Encyclopaedia of Entrepreneurship*. Englewood Cliffs, NJ: Prentice Hall, 39–57.

Brockhaus, R.H. 1987. Entrepreneurial Folklore. *Journal of Small Business Management*, 25(3): 1–6.

Brockhaus, R.H. Sr. 1994. Entrepreneurship and Family Business Research: Comparisons, Critique and Lessons. *Entrepreneurship Theory and Practice*, 19(1): 25–38.

Brockhaus, R. 2003. Why Do Entrepreneurs Need a Theory of Entrepreneurship? Available at: http://www.busi.mun.ca/ggorman/b5600/5600reading1.doc [accessed 16 January 2013].

Brockhaus, R. and Dixon, B. 1986. The Level of Job Satisfaction that New Zealand Entrepreneurs Had with Their Previous Jobs. In R. Ronstadt, J. Hornaday, R. Peterson and K. Versper (eds), *Frontiers of Entrepreneurship Research*. Wellesley, MA: Babson College.

Brown, R. 1995. Family Businesses: Rethinking Strategic Planning. Paper presented at the 40th Annual International Council on Small Businesses, Sydney, Australia, June.

Brown, R.B. and Coverley, R. 1999. Succession Planning in Family Businesses: A Study from East Anglia. *U.K. Journal of Small Business Management*, 37(1): 93–7.

Bubolz, M.M. and Sontag, M.S. 1993. Human Ecology Theory. In P.G. Boss, W.J. Doherty, R. LaRossa, W.R. Schumm and S.K. Steinmetz (eds), *Sourcebook of Family Theories and Methods: A Contextual Approach*. New York: Plenum, 419–48.

Buchanan, B. 1974. Building Organizational Commitment: The Socialization of Managers in Work Organization. *Administrative Science Quarterly*, 19: 533–46.

Butler, J.S. and Herring, C. 1991. Ethnicity and Entrepreneurship in America: Toward an Explanation of Racial and Ethnic Group Variations in Self-employment. *Sociological Perspectives*, 34(1): 79–94.

Carnevale, P. and Pruitt, D.G. 1992. Negotiation and Mediation. *Annual Review of Psychology*, 43: 531–82.

Carsrud, A.L., Gaglio, C.M. and Olm, K.W. 1986. Entrepreneurs, Mentors, Networks and Successful New Venture Development: An Exploratory Study. In R. Ronstadt, J.A. Hornaday, R. Peterson and K.H. Vesper (eds), *Frontiers of Entrepreneurship Research*. Wellesley, MA: Babson College, 229–35.

Cassia, P.S. and Bada, C. 1991. *The Making of the Modern Greek Family: Marriage and Exchange in 19th Century Athens*. Cambridge: Cambridge University Press.

Chan, S. and Lee, E. 2004. Families with Asian Roots. In E.W. Lynch and M.J. Hanson (eds), *Developing Cross-cultural Competence: A Guide for Working with Children and Their Families*. Baltimore, MD: Brookes Publishing, 219–98.

Chell, E. 1985. The Entrepreneurial Personality: A Few Ghosts Laid to Rest? *International Small Business Journal*, 3(3): 43–54.

Chrisman, J.J., Chua, J.H. and Litz, R.A. 2004. Comparing the Agency Cost of Family and Non-family Firms. *Entrepreneurship Theory and Practice*, 28(4): 335–54.

Chrisman, J.J., Chua, J.H. and Sharma, P. 1998. Important Attributes of Successors in Family Businesses: An Exploratory Study. *Family Business Review*, 7(1): 19–34.

Chrisman, J.J., Hoffer, C.W. and Boulton, W.R. 1988. Toward a System for Classifying Business Strategies. *Academy of Management Review*, 13: 413–28.

Chua, J.H., Chrisman, J.J. and Sharma, P. 1999. Defining the Family Business by Behavior. *Entrepreneurship: Theory and Practice*, 23(4): 19–39.

Chua, J.H., Chrisman, J.J. and Sharma, P. 2003. Succession and Non-succession Concerns of Family Firms and Agency Relationship with Non-family Managers. *Family Business Review*, 16(2): 89–107.

Chung, H.M. and Chan, S.T. 2012. Ownership Structure, Family Leadership, and Performance of Affiliate Firms in Large Family Business Groups. *Asia Pacific Journal of Management*, 29(2): 303–29.

Churchill, N.C. and Hatten, K.J. 1987. Non-market Based Transfers of Wealth and Power: A Research Framework for Family Businesses. *American Journal of Small Business*, 11(3): 51–64.

Churchill, N.C. and Hatten, K.J. 1997. Non-market Based Transfers of Wealth and Power: A Research Framework for Family Businesses. *Family Business Review*, 10(1): 53–67.

Churchill, N.C. and Lewis, V.L. 1983. The Five Stages of Small Business Growth. *Harvard Business Review*, 61: 30–51.

Cliffe, S. 1998. Facing Up to Succession. *Harvard Business Review*, 76(3): 16–18.

Corbetta, G. and Montemerlo, D. 1998. Managing Succession in Italian Small and Medium-size Family Businesses. *The Family Business Network Newsletter*, 20: 8–10.

Couyoumdjian, J.P. 2012. Who Walks Out? Entrepreneurship in a Global Economy. *International Review of Law and Economics*, 32(1): 158–65.

Craig, J. and Lindsay, N.J. 2002. Incorporating the Family Dynamic into the Entrepreneurship Process. *Journal of Small Businesses and Enterprise Development*, 9(4): 416–30.

Cromie, S., Stephenson, B. and Monteith, D. 1995. The Management of Family Firms: An Empirical Investigation. *International Small Business Journal*, 13(4): 11–34.

Da Vinci, L. 2003. *Country Report on Greece*. Athens: Athens Laboratory of Business Administration.

Dahl, S. 2004. Intercultural Research: The Current State of Knowledge. *Middlesex University Discussion Paper*, 26: 1–22.

Daily, C.M. and Dollinger, M.J. 1991. Family Firms Are Different. *Review of Business*, 13(1): 3–5.

Daily, C.M. and Dollinger, M.J. 1993. Alternative Methodologies for Identifying Family versus Nonfamily-managed Businesses. *Journal of Small Business Management*, 31: 79–90.

Daily, C.M., Johnson, J.L. and Dalton, D.R. 1995. The Many Ways of Board Composition: If You Have Seen One, You Certainly Have Not Seen Them All. Paper presented at the Academy of Management Meeting, Vancouver.

Daily, C.M. and Thompson, S.S. 1994. Ownership Structure, Strategic Posture, and Firm Growth: An Empirical Examination. *Family Business Review*, 7(3): 237–49.

Dalton, D.R., Daily, C.M., Ellstrand, A.E. and Johnson, J.L. 1998. Meta-Analytic Reviews of Board Composition, Leadership Structure and Financial Performance. *Strategic Management Journal*, 19: 269–90.

Dana, L.P. and Light, I. 2012. Toward a Theory of Social Capital in Entrepreneurship. *International Journal of Social Sciences*, 1(1): 35–54.

Dana, L.P. and Riseth, J.Å. 2012. Sámi Reindeer Herders in Finland: Pulled to Community-based Entrepreneurship and Pushed to Individualistic Firms. In C. Karlsson, B. Johansson and R.R. Stough (eds), *Entrepreneurship, Social Capital and Governance: Directions for the Sustainable Development and Competitiveness of Regions*. Cheltenham: Edward Elgar, 358–77.

Danco, L.A. and Jacovic, D.J. 1981. *Outside Directors in the Family Owned Business*. Cleveland, OH: Center for Family Business, University Press.

Danes, S.M. and Brewton, K.E. 2012. Follow the Capital: Benefits of Tracking Family Capital across Family and Business Systems. In A. Carsrud and M. Brannback (eds), *Understanding Family Businesses*. New York: Springer, 227–50.

Danes, S.M., Lee, J., Stafford, K. and Heck, R.K.Z. 2008. The Effects of Ethnicity, Families and Culture on Entrepreneurial Experience: An Extension of Sustainable Family Business Theory. *Journal of Developmental Entrepreneurship*, 13(3): 229–68.

Danes, S.M., Reuter, M.A., Kwon, H. and Doherty, W. 2002. Family FIRO Model: An Application to Family Business. *Family Business Review*, 15(1): 31–43.

Danes, S.M., Zuiker, V., Arbuthnot, J., Kean, R. and Scannell, E. 1998. Business and Family Goals and Tensions. In *Fifth Annual International Family Business Program Association Proceedings*, San Antonio, TX, 23–25 July.

Danes, S.M., Zuiker, V., Kean, R. and Arbuthnot, J. 1999. Predictors of Family Business Tensions and Goal Achievement. *Family Business Review*, 12(3): 241–52.

Dasgupta, D.S. 1998. Gender Roles and Cultural Continuity in the Asian Indian Immigrant Community in the U.S. *Sex Roles*, 38(11/12): 953–74.

Davidson, M.C. 2008. *Dubai: The Vulnerability of Success*. New York: Columbia University Press.

Davidsson, P. 1991. Continued Entrepreneurship: Ability, Need and Opportunity as Determinants of a Small Firm Growth. *Journal of Business Venturing*, 6: 405–29.

Davis, E. and Kay, J. 1993. Corporate Governance, Take-overs, and the Role of the Non-executive Director. In M. Bishop and J. Kay (eds), *European Mergers and Merger Policy*. Oxford: Oxford University Press, 200–216.

Davis, J.A. 1982. The Influence of Life Stage on Father-Son Work Relationships in Family Companies. Unpublished doctoral dissertation. Harvard Business School.

Davis, J. 2001. Governing the Family-Run Business. *HBS Working Knowledge*. Available at: http://hbswk.hbs.edu/pubitem.jhtml?id=2469&sid=0&t = family [accessed 14 March 2012].

Davis, P. and Stern, D. 1988. Adaptation, Survival, and the Growth of a Family Business: An Integrated Systems Perspective. *Family Business Review*, 1(1): 69–85. (Reprinted from *Human Relations*, 34(1980): 207–24).

Davis, P.S. and Harveston, P.D. 1998. The Influence of Family on Business Succession Process: A Multigenerational Perspective. *Entrepreneurship Theory and Practice*, 22(3): 31–5.

Davis, P.S. and Harveston, P.D. 1999. In the Founder's Shadow: Conflict in the Family Firm. *Family Business Review*, 12(4): 311–23.

De Massis, A., Sharma, P., Chua, J.H. and Chrisman, J.J. 2012. *Family Business Studies: An Annotated Bibliography*. Cheltenham: Edward Elgar.

Deacon, R. and Firebaugh, F. 1975. *Family Resource Management: Context and Concepts*. Boston, MA: Houghton-Mifflin.

Deacon, R.E. and Firebaugh, F.M. 1988. *Family Resource Management: Principles and Applications*. Boston: Allyn & Bacon.

Deakins, D., Isaq, M., Smallbone, D., Whitten, G. and Wyper, J. 2005. *Minority Ethnic Enterprise in Scotland: A National Scoping Study*. Scottish Executive, Social Research Justice Programme report, Research Findings No.19/2005. Available at: http://www.scotland.gov.uk/Resource/Doc/54357/0013267. pdf [accessed 16 April 2013].

Dean, S.M. 1992. Characteristics of African American Family Owned Businesses in Los Angeles. *Family Business Review*, 5(4): 373–95.

Dela Rama, M. 2012. Corporate Governance and Corruption: Ethical Dilemmas of Asian Business Groups. *Journal of Business Ethics*, 109(4): 501–19.

Delmar, F. and Davidsson, P. 2000. Where Do They Come From? Prevalence and Characteristics of Nascent Entrepreneurs. *Entrepreneurship and Regional Development*, 12(1): 1–23.

DeNoble, A., Ehrlich, S. and Singh, G. 2007. Toward the Development of a Family Business Self-efficacy Scale: A Resource-based Perspective. *Family Business Review*, 20(2): 127–40.

Dess, G.G., Lumpkin, G.T. and McGee, J.E. 1999. Linking Corporate Entrepreneurs to Strategy, Structure, and Process: Suggested Research Directions. *Entrepreneurship Theory and Practice*, 23(3): 85–102.

Dicks, T.R.B. 1971. *The Greeks: How They Live and Work*. New York: Praeger Publishers.

Djelic, M.L. and Quack, S. 2010. Transnational Communities and Their Impact on the Governance of Business and Economic Activity. In M.L. Djelic and S. Quack (eds), *Transnational Communities: Shaping Global Economic Governance*. Cambridge: Cambridge University Press, 377–413.

Doherty, W.J. and Colangelo, N. 1984. The Family FIRO Model: A Modest Proposal for Organizing Family Treatment. *Journal of Marital and Family Therapy*, 10: 19–29.

Doherty, W.J., Colangelo, N. and Hovander, D. 1991. Priority in Setting Family Change and Clinical Practice: The Family FIRO Model. *Family Process*, 30: 227–40.

Donckels, R. and Frohlich, E. 1991. Are Family Businesses Really Different? European Experiences from STRATOS. *Family Business Review*, 4(2): 149–60.

Dumas, C. 1990. Preparing the New CEO: Managing the Father-Daughter Succession Process in Family Businesses. *Family Business Review*, 8(2): 99–120.

Dumas, C. 1992. Integrating the Daughter into Family Business Management. *Entrepreneurship Theory and Practice*, 16(4): 41–55.

Dunemann, M. and Barett, R. 2004. *Family Business and Succession Planning: A Review of the Literature*. Berwick: Monash University, Family and Small Business Research Unit.

Dunn, B. 1999. The Family Factor: The Impact of Family Relationship Dynamics on Business-Owning Families During Transitions. *Family Business Review*, 12(1): 41–60.

Dwyer, F.R., Schurr, P.H. and Oh, S. 1987. Developing Buyer-Seller Relationships. *Journal of Marketing*, 51(2): 11–27.

Dyer, J.H. and Singh, H. 1998. The Relational View: Cooperative Strategy and Sources of Interorganisational Competitive Strategy. *Academy of Management Review*, 23(4): 660–79.

Dyer, W.G. 1986. *Cultural Change in Family Firms: Anticipating and Family Transitions*. San Francisco, CA: Jossey-Bass.

Dyer, W.G. Jr. 1988. Culture and Continuity in Family Firms. *Family Business Review*, 1(1): 37–50.

Dyer, W.G. Jr. 1992. *The Entrepreneurial Experience*. San Francisco, CA: Jossey-Bass.

Dyer, W.G. 1994. Potential Contributions of Organizational Behaviour to the Study of Family Owned Businesses. *Family Business Review*, 7(2): 109–31.

Dyer, W.G. 2006. Examining the "Family Effect" on Firm Performance. *Family Business Review*, 19(4): 253–73.

Dyer, W.G. and Handler, W. 1994. Entrepreneurship and Family Businesses: Exploring the Connections. *Entrepreneurship in Theory and Practice*, 19(1): 71–83.

Dyer, W.G. Jr. and Sanchez, M. 1998. Current State of Family Business Theory and Practice as Reflected in Family Business Review 1988–1997. *Family Business Review*, 11(4): 287–95.

Ehrenberg, R.G. and Smith, R.S. 1997. *Modern Labor Economics: Theory and Public Policy*. Reading, MA: Addison-Wesley.

Eisenstadt, S.N. 1955. *The Absorption of Immigrants*. Glencoe, IL: The Free Press.

Enderwick, P., Tung, R.L. and Chung, H.F. 2011. Immigrant Effects and International Business Activity: An Overview. *Journal of Asia Business Studies*, 5(1): 6–22.

Evans, A.J. 2012. Ethnic Enterprise Governance: A Public Choice Analysis of Liverpool's Chinatown. *Journal of Enterprising Communities: People and Places in the Global Economy*, 6(1): 28–38.

Fakoussa, R. and Collins, L. 2012. Brothers in Business: The Pakistani Family Business in the UK. In L. Collins, L. Grisoni, J. Tucker, C. Seaman, S. Graham, R. Fakoussa and D. Otten, *The Modern Family Business: Relationships, Succession and Transition*. Houndmills: Palgrave Macmillan, 179–209.

Featherman, D.L. 1993. What Does Society Need from Higher Education? *Items*, 47: 38–43.

Feldman, H.D., Koberg, C.S., and Dean, T.J. 1991. Minority Small Business Owners and Their Paths to Ownership. *Journal of Small Business Management*, 9(4): 12–27.

Ferguson, A. 2001. A Family Feud's Last Episode? *Business Review Weekly*, 23(19), 58(1).

Ferguson, C.E. 1972. *Microeconomic Theory*. Third edition. Homewood, IL: Richard D. Irwin.

Film Australia. (n.d.) *Franco Belgiorno-Nettis: Teachers Notes*. Australian Biography Series 2. Available at: http://australianbiography.s3.amazonaws.com/study/4591_ausbiobelgiorno.pdf [accessed 19 February 2013].

Flemons, D.G. and Cole, P.M. 1994. *Playing with Contextual Complexity: Relational Consultation to Family Businesses. Transitioning from Individual to Family Counseling Monograph*. Alexandria, VA: American Counseling Association Press.

Fletcher, D.E. (ed.). 2002. *Understanding the Small Family Business*. London: Routledge.

Foreman-Peck, J. and Zhou, P. 2013. The Strength and Persistence of Entrepreneurial Cultures. *Journal of Evolutionary Economics*, 23(1): 163–87.

Freiling, J. and Laudien, S.M. 2013. Sustaining Trust as Informal Governance Mechanism: A Competitive Edge for Family Firms? *Economia Marche – Journal of Applied Economics*, 31(2): 9–24.

Gardner, W. and Rogoff, B. 1990. Children's Deliberateness of Planning According to Task Circumstances. *Developmental Psychology*, 28: 480–87.

Gedajlovic, E., Carney, M., Chrisman, J.J. and Kellermanns, F.W. 2012. The Adolescence of Family Firm Research: Taking Stock and Planning for the Future. *Journal of Management*, 38(4): 1010–37.

Geletkanycz, M.A. 1997. The Salience of "Culture's Consequences": The Effects of Cultural Values on Top Executive Commitment to the Status Quo. *Strategic Management Journal*, 18(8): 615–34.

Gersick, K.E., Davis, J.A., McCollom Hampton, M.M. and Lansberg, I. 1997. Choosing the Right Ownership Structure. In M. Fischetti (ed.), *The Family Business Succession Handbook*. Philadelphia, PA: Family Business Publishing, 7–8.

Gibb, A. and Ritchie, J. 1982. Understanding the Process of Starting Small Businesses. *European Small Business Journal*, 1: 26–45.

Goel, S., Mazzola, P., Phan, P.H., Pieper, T.M. and Zachary, R.K. 2012. Strategy, Ownership, Governance, and Socio-psychological Perspectives on Family Businesses from Around the World. *Journal of Family Business Strategy*, 3(2): 54–65.

Goldberg, S.D. 1991. Factors Which Impact Effective Succession in Family-owned Businesses: An Empirical Investigation. Unpublished doctoral thesis, University of Massachusetts.

Golden, W. and Powell, P. 2000. Towards a Definition of Flexibility: In Search of the Holy Grail? *Omega, The International Journal of Management Science*, 28: 373–84.

Grant, J.L. and Kronstal, K. 2013. Old Boys Down Home: Immigration and Social Integration in Halifax. *International Planning Studies*, 18(2): 204–20.

Greenberger, D.B. and Sexton, D.L. 1987. A Comparative Analysis of the Effects of the Desire for Personal Control on New Venture Initiations. *Frontiers of Entrepreneurship Research. Proceedings of the Seventh Annual Babson College Entrepreneurship Research Conference*. Wellesley, MA: Babson College.

Greene, P.G. and Butler, J.S. 1996. The Ethnic Community as a Natural Business Incubator. *Journal of Business Research*, 36: 51–8.

Gregoriou, P., Kontolemis, Z. and Matsi, M. 2010. Immigration in Cyprus: An Analysis of the Determinants. *Economic Policy Review*, 4(1): 63–88.

Greve, A. and Salaff, J.W. 2005. Social Network Approach to Understand the Ethnic Economy: A Theoretical Discourse. *GeoJournal*, 64(1): 7–16.

Grossman, E., Puryear, A., Rogoff, M.S., Lee, R.K., Heck, Z., Haynes, G.W. and Onochie, J. 2008. Sampling Minority Business Owners and Their Families: The Understudied Entrepreneurial Experience. *Journal of Small Business Management*, 46(5): 422–55.

Gubitta, P. and Gianecchini, M. 2002. Governance and Flexibility in Family Owned SMEs. *Family Business Review*, 15(4): 277–97.

Gunn, A. 2012. Immigration and Multi-level Governance in Canada and Europe: The Role of Municipalities as Integration "Policy Innovators". Canada-Europe Transatlantic Dialogue, policy paper.

Gutman, L.M. and Akerman, R. 2008. *Determinants of Aspirations*. Centre for Research on the Wider Benefits of Learning, Institute of Education, University of London. Available at: http://www.learningbenefits.net/Publications/ResReps/ResRep27.pdf [accessed 16 April 2013].

Habbershon, T.G. and Astrachan, J.H. 1997. Perceptions Are Reality: How Family Meetings Lead to Collective Action. *Family Business Review*, 10(1): 37–52.

Habbershon, T.G. and Pistrui, J. 2002. Enterprising Families Domain: Family-influenced Ownership Groups in Pursuit of Transgenerational Wealth. *Family Business Review*, 15(3): 223–37.

Habbershon T.G. and Williams, M.L. 1999. Resource-based Framework for Assessing the Strategic Advantages of Family Firms. *Family Business Review*, 12(1): 1–26.

Halkias, D. 2013. Business and Social Profiles of Immigrant-Owned Small Firms: The Case of Pakistani Immigrant Entrepreneurs in Greece. *International Migration*. Available at: http://onlinelibrary.wiley.com/doi/10.1111/imig.12008/abstract [accessed 17 December 2013].

Halkias, D., Harkiolakis, N., Thurman, P., Rishi, M., Ekonomou, L., Caracatsanis, S.M. and Akrivos, P.D. 2009. Economic and Social Characteristics of Albanian Immigrant Entrepreneurs in Greece. *Journal of Developmental Entrepreneurship*, 14(2): 143–64.

Halkias, D., Nwajiuba, C., Harkiolakis, N. and Caracatsanis, S.M. 2011. Challenges Facing Women Entrepreneurs in Nigeria. *Management Research Review*, 34(2): 221–35.

Halkias, D., Nwajiuba, C., Harkiolakis, N., Clayton, G., Akrivos, P. and Caracatsanis, S. 2009. Characteristics and Business Profiles of Immigrant-owned Small Firms: The Case of African Immigrant Entrepreneurs in Greece. *International Journal of Business Innovation and Research*, 3(4): 382–401.

Halkias, D., Thurman, P., Harkiolakis, N. and Caracatsanis, S.M (eds). 2011. *Female Immigrant Entrepreneurs: The Economic and Social Impact of a Global Phenomenon*. Farnham: Gower.

Hall, A., Melin, L. and Nordqvist, M. 2001. Entrepreneurship as Radical Change in the Family Business: Exploring the Role of Cultural Patterns. *Family Business Review*, 14(3): 193–208.

Handelsman, K.G. 1996. An Exploratory Study: The Management of Family-owned Businesses. Unpublished Masters research report, The Graduate School of Business, University of Cape Town.

Handler, W.C. 1989. Methodological Issues and Considerations in Studying Family Businesses. *Family Business Review*, 2(3): 257–76.

Handler, W. 1990. Succession in Family Firms: A Mutual Role Adjustment between Employer and Next Generation Family Members. *Entrepreneurship Theory and Practice*, 15: 37–55.

Handler, W. 1991. Key Interpersonal Relationships of Next-Generation Family Members in Family Firms. *Journal of Small Business Management*, 29(3): 21–32.

Handler, W.C. 1992. The Succession Experience of the Next Generation. *Family Business Review*, 5(3): 283–307.

Handler, W.C. 1994. Succession in Family Businesses: A Review of the Research. *Family Business Review*, 7(2): 133–57.

Handler, W.C. and Kram, K.E. 1988. Succession in Family Firms: The Problem of Resistance. *Family Business Review*, 1(4): 361–81.

Hansen, E.L. 1995. Entrepreneurial Network and New Organization Growth. *Entrepreneurship: Theory and Practice*, 19(4): 7–19.

Hanson, S.L., Fuchs, S., Aisenbrey, S. and Kravets, N. 2004. Attitudes towards Gender, Work, and Family among Female and Male Scientists in Germany and the United States. *Journal of Women and Minorities in Science and Engineering*, 10(2): 99–129.

Harkiolakis, N., Halkias, D. and Abadir, S. 2012. *E-negotiations: Networking and Cross-cultural Business Transactions*. Farnham: Gower.

Hershon, S.A. 1975. Determinants of the Satisfaction of the Primary Stakeholders with the Succession Process in Family Firms. Unpublished doctoral thesis, University of Calgary, Canada.

Herskovits, M.J. 1955. *Cultural Anthropology*. New York: Knopf.

Hewett, K. and O'Bearden, W. 2001. Dependence, Trust and Relational Behaviour on the Partly Foreign Subsidiary Marketing Operations: Implications for Managing Global Marketing Operations. *Journal of Marketing*, 65(4): 51–66.

Hilb, M. 2012. *New Corporate Governance: Successful Board Management Tools*. Berlin: Springer.

Hill, C.W.L. and Jones, T.M. 1992. Stakeholder-Agency Theory. *Journal of Management Studies*, 29: 131–54.

Hofstede, G. 1980. *Culture's Consequences: International Differences in Work-related Values*. Beverly Hills, CA: Sage.

Hofstede, G. 1983. The Cultural Relativity of Organisational Practices and Theories. *Journal of International Business Studies*, 14: 75–89.

Hofstede, G. 1991. *Cultures and Organisations*. London: McGraw Hill.

Hofstede, G. 2001. *Culture's Consequences: Comparing Values, Behaviours, Institutions, and Organisations across Nations*. London: Sage.

Hofstede, G., Noorderhaven, N.G., Thurik, A.R., Uhlaner, L.M., Wennekers, A.R. and Wildeman, R.E. 2004. Culture's Role in Entrepreneurship: Self-employment out of Dissatisfaction. In T.E. Brown and J. Ulijn (eds), *Innovation, Entrepreneurship and Culture: The Interaction between Technology, Progress and Economic Growth*. Cheltenham: Edward Elgar, 162–203.

Holland, P.G. and Boulton, W.R. 1984. Balancing the "Family" and the "Business" in Family Business. *Business Horizons*, 27(2): 16–21. Reprinted in C.E. Aronoff and J.L. Ward (eds), *Family Business Sourcebook*. Detroit, MI: Omnigraphics, 1991, 493–500.

Hollander, B. and Bukowitz, W. 1990. Women, Family Culture and Family Business. *Family Business Review*, 3(2): 139–51.

Hollander, B.S. and Ellman, N.S. 1988. Family-owned Businesses: An Emerging Field of Inquiry. *Family Business Review*, 1(2): 145–64.

Hoy, F. and Verser, T.G. 1994. Emerging Business, Emerging Field: Entrepreneurship and the Family Firm. *Entrepreneurship Theory and Practice*, 19(1): 9–23.

Huang, Y., Chen, A. and Kao, L. 2012. Corporate Governance in Taiwan: The Nonmonotonic Relationship between Family Ownership and Dividend Policy. *Asia Pacific Journal of Management*, 29(1): 39–58.

Hubler, T. and Schwartz, S. 1984. Non-family Board Members Can Offer New Perspectives for Family Business. *Minnesota's Business*, July.

Huck, P., Rhine, S.L.W., Bond, P. and Townsend, R. 1999. A Comparison of Small Business Finance in Two Chicago Minority Communities. *Economic Perspectives*, (May/June): 46–62.

Hum, T. 2001. The Promises and Dilemmas of Immigrant Ethnic Economies. In M. Lopes-Garza and D.R Diaz (eds), *Asian and Latin Immigrants in a Restructuring Economy: The Metamorphosis of Southern California*. Stanford, CA: Stanford University Press, 77–101.

Hutton-Wilson, D. 2001. Corporate Governance: Critical Challenges for South Africa. *Management Today*, 17(7): 8–13.

IFERA (International Family Enterprise Research Academy). 2003. Family Businesses Dominate. *Family Business Review*, 16(4): 235–40.

Jaidah, M.J. 2008. Explaining Multi-Generation Family Business Success in the Gulf States. Dissertation, Harvard University, Proquest dissertations database [accessed 29 September 2012].

Jean, L.S.K. and Tan, F. 2001. Growth of Chinese Family Enterprises in Singapore. *Family Business Review*, 14(1): 49–74.

Jelinek, M. and Schoonhoven, C.B. 1990. *The Innovation Marathon*. San Francisco, CA: Jossey-Bass.

Jiobu, R.M. 1988. *Ethnicity and Assimilation*. New York: State University of New York.

Johanisson, B. and Huse, M. 2000. Recruiting Outside Board Members in the Small Business: An Ideological Challenge. *Entrepreneurship and Regional Development*, 12(4): 353–78.

Johnson, J.L. and Cullen, J.B. 2002. Trust in Cross-Cultural Relationships. In M. Gannon and K. Newman (eds), *The Blackwell Handbook of Cross-Cultural Management*. Oxford: Blackwell, 335–60.

Johnson, J., Daily, C. and Ellstrand, A. 1996. Boards of Directors: A Review and Research Agenda. *Journal of Management*, 22: 409–39.

Jones, T., Ram, M., Edwards, P., Kiselinchev, A. and Muchenje, L. 2012. New Migrant Enterprise: Novelty or Historical Continuity? *Urban Studies*, 49(14): 3159–76.

Jones, W.D. 1982. Characteristics of Planning in Small Firms. *Journal of Family Owned Business Management*, 20(3): 15–25.

Kar, S.B., Cambell, K., Jimenez, A. and Gupta, S.R. 1995/1996. Invisible Americans: Indo-American Quality of Life. *Amerasia Journal*, 21: 25–52.

Karofsky, P., Millen, R., Yilmaz, M.R., Smyrnois, K.X., Tanewski, G.A. and Romano, C.A. 2001. Work-Family Conflict and Emotional Well-being in American Family Businesses. *Family Business Review*, 14(4): 313–24.

Kashima, E.S. and Kashima, Y. 1997. Practice of the Self in Conversations: Pronoun Drop, Sentence Co-production and Contextualization of the Self. In K. Leung, U. Kim, S. Yammaguchi and Y. Kashima (eds), *Progress in Asian Social Psychology*, vol. 1. Singapore: Wiley, 165–80.

Kashima, E.S. and Kashima, Y. 1998. Culture and Language: The Case of Cultural Dimensions and Personal Pronoun Use. *Journal of Cross-Cultural Psychology*, 29: 461–86.

Katila, S. and Wahlbeck, Ö. 2012. The Role of (Transnational) Social Capital in the Start-up Processes of Immigrant Businesses: The Case of Chinese and Turkish Restaurant Businesses in Finland. *International Small Business Journal*, 30(3): 294–309.

Kets de Vries, M.F.R. 1977. The Entrepreneurial Personality: A Person at the Crossroads. *Journal of Management Studies*, 14: 34–57.

Kets de Vries, M.F.R. 1988. The Dark Side of CEO Succession. *Harvard Business Review*, 63(6): 56–60.

Kets de Vries, M.F.R. 1993. The Dynamics of Family Controlled Firms. *Organizational Review*, 21: 59–71.

Kets de Vries, M.F.R. 1996. *Family Business: Human Dilemmas in the Family Firm.* London: International Thomson Business Press.

Kets de Vries, M.F.R. 1997. The Entrepreneurial Personality: A Person at the Crossroads. *Journal of Management Studies*, 14(1): 34–57.

Khoza, R. 1994. The Need for Afrocentric Management Approach: A South African Based Management Approach. In P. Christie, R. Lessem and L. Mgibi (eds), *African Management: Philosophies, Concepts and Applications.* Randburg: Knowledge Resources, 117–24.

Kidwell, R.E., Hoy, F. and Ibarreche, S. 2012. "Ethnic" Family Business or just Family Business? Human Resource Practices in the Ethnic Family Firm. *Journal of Family Business Strategy*, 3(1): 12–17.

King, R. (ed.). 2001. *The Mediterranean Passage: Migration and New Cultural Encounters in Southern Europe*. Liverpool: Liverpool University Press.

Kluckhohn, C. 1951. The Study of Culture. In D. Lerner and H.D. Lasswell (eds), *The Policy Sciences*. Stanford, CA: Stanford University Press, 86–101.

Knight, F.H. 1921. *Risk, Uncertainty and Profit*. New York: Houghton Mifflin.

Knight, R.A. 1993. Planning: The Key to Family Owned Business Survival. *Management Accounting*, 74: 33–4.

Kogut, B. and Singh, H. 1988. The Effect of National Culture on the Choice of Entry Mode. *Journal of International Business Studies*, 20: 411–32.

Koliopoulos, J.S. and Veremis, T.M. 2002. *Greece: The Modern Sequel*. London: Hurst & Company.

Koopman, A. 1994. Transcultural Management: A Search for Pragmatic Humanism. In P. Christie, R. Lessem and L. Mgibi (eds), *African Management Philosophies, Concepts and Applications*. Randburg: Knowledge Resources, 41–76.

Kotkin, Joel. 1993. *Tribes: How Race, Religion, and Identity Determine Success in the Global Economy*. New York: Random House.

Kreiser, P., Marino, L. and Weaver, K.M. (2001). *Correlates of Entrepreneurship: The Impact of National Culture on Risk-Taking and Proactiveness in SMEs*. Tuscaloosa, AL: University of Alabama, Department of Management and Marketing.

Kroeger, C.V. 1974. Managerial Development in the Small Firm. *California Management Review*, 17(1): 41–6.

Landau, J. 2007. Enhancing Resilience: Families and Communities as Agents for Change. *Family Process*, 46(3): 351–65.

Landolt, P. 2000. The Causes and Consequences of Transnational Migration: Salvadorans in Los Angeles and Washington, D.C. Ph.D. dissertation. Department of Sociology, The Johns Hopkins University.

Lank, A.R., Owens, R., Martinez, J., Reidel, H., de Visscher, F. and Bruel, M. 1994. The State of Family Businesses in Various Countries around the World. *The Family Business Network Newsletter*, (May): 3–7.

Lansberg, I.S. 1988. The Succession Conspiracy. *Family Business Review*, 1(2): 119–43. Reprinted in C.E. Aronoff, J.H. Astrachan and J.L. Ward (eds), *The Family Business Sourcebook II*. Marietta, GA: Business Owner Resources, 1996, 70–86.

Lansberg, I. 1996. The Succession Conspiracy. In E. Beckhard (ed.), *The Best of Family Business Review*. Boston, MA: Family Business Institute, 64–74.

Lansberg, I. 1999a. Independent Directors in the Middle. *Family Business Magazine*, 4(Summer): 43–8.

Lansberg, I. 1999b. *Succeeding Generations: Realising the Dreams of Families in Business*. Boston, MA: Harvard Business School Press.

Lansberg, I. and Astrachan, J.H. 1994. The Influence of Family Relationships on Succession Planning and Training. *Family Business Review*, 7(1): 39–59.

Lansberg, I.S., Perrow, E.L. and Rogolsky, S. 1988. Family Business as an Emerging Field. *Family Business Review*, 1(1): 1–8.

Lazaridis, G. and Koumandraki, M. 2003. Survival Ethnic Entrepreneurs in Greece: A Mosaic of Informal and Formal Business Activities. *Sociological Research Online*, 8(2).

Leach, P. 1994. Are Your Kids Up To Your Job? *Director*, 47(12): 71.

Lee, J. 1996. Culture and Management: A Study of Small Chinese Family Businesses in Singapore. *Journal of Small Business Management*, (July): 63–7.

Levinson, H. 1971. Conflicts That Plague Family Businesses. *Harvard Business Review*, 49(2): 90–98.

Light, I. 1979. Disadvantaged Minorities in Self-employment. *International Journal of Comparative Sociology*, 20: 31–45.

Light, I.H. and Bonacich, E. 1988. *Immigrant Entrepreneurs: Koreans in Los Angeles, 1965–1982*. Berkeley, CA: University of California Press.

Light, I., Rezaei, S. and Dana, L.P. 2013. Ethnic Minority Entrepreneurs in the International Carpet Trade: An Empirical Study. *International Journal of Entrepreneurship and Small Business*, 18(2): 125–53.

Lindblom, C.E. 1959. The Science of "Muddling Through". *Public Administration Review*, 19: 79–88.

Litz, R.A. and Turner, N. 2013. Sins of the Father's Firm: Exploring Responses to Inherited Ethical Dilemmas in Family Business. *Journal of Business Ethics*, 13(2): 297–315.

Liu, W., Yang, H. and Zhang, G. 2012. Does Family Business Excel in Firm Performance? An Institution-based View. *Asia Pacific Journal of Management*, 29(4): 965–87.

Loudon, J.K. 1986. The Liability of Advisory Boards. *Directors & Boards* (spring): 19–20.

Lumpkin, G.T. and Dess, G.G. 1996. Clarifying the Entrepreneurial Orientation Construct and Linking It to Performance. *Academy of Management Journal*, 21(1): 135–72.

Luo, X.R. and Chung, C.N. 2013. Filling or Abusing the Institutional Void? Ownership and Management Control of Public Family Businesses in an Emerging Market. *Organization Science*, 24(2): 591–613.

Maas, G. 1999a. Family Business in South Africa: A Development Model. Paper presented at the Saesba Conference, 30 July–1 August: 1–15.

Maas, G. 1999b. Die bestuur van familie-besighede in Suid-Afrika – 'n Entrepeneurskapsbeskouing. *Werkswinkel*, 1–36.

Mace, M.L. 1971. *Directors: Myth and Reality*. Boston, MA: Harvard Business School.

Maloch, F. and Deacon, R. 1966. Proposed Framework for Home Management. *Journal of Home Economics*, 58: 31–5.

Malone, S.C. 1989. Selected Correlates of Business Continuity Planning in the Family Business. *Family Business Review*, 2(4): 341–53.

Mann, G.S. 2004. *Sikhism*. New York: Prentice Hall.

Mantzaris, E.A. 1978. The Social Structure and the Process of Assimilation of the Greek Community in South Africa. Unpublished MSoc Science thesis, Department of Sociology, UCT.

Mantzaris, E.A. 1995. *Greek Workers in South Africa 1890–1930*. Athens: Syllogikes Ekdosis (in Greek).

Mantzaris, E.A. 2000. A Social History of the Greek Community in South Africa. Unpublished manuscript.

Mars, G. and Ward, R. 1984. Ethnic Business Development in Britain: Opportunities and Resources. In R. Ward and R. Jenkins (eds), *Ethnic Communities in Business: Strategies for Economic Revival*. Cambridge: Cambridge University Press, 1–19.

Martin, H.F. 2001. Is Family Governance an Oxymoron? *Family Business Review*, 14(2): 91–6.

Mattessich, P. and Hill, R. 1987. Life Cycle and Family Development. In M.B. Sussman and S.K. Steinmetz (eds), *Handbook of Marriage and the Family*. New York: Plenum, 437–69.

Mayer, R.C., Davis, J.H. and Schoorman, F.D. 1995. An Integrative Model of Organizational Trust. *Academy of Management Review*, 20: 709–34.

Mazzola, P., Sciascia, S. and Kellermanns, F.W. 2012. Non-linear Effects of Family Sources of Power on Performance. *Journal of Business Research*, 66(4): 568–74.

McClelland, D.C. 1961. *The Achieving Society*. New York: Irving Publishers.

McGivern, C. 1978. The Dynamics of Management Succession: A Model of Chief Executive Succession in the Small Family Firm. *Management Decision*, 16(1): 32–42.

McGivern, C. 1989. The Dynamics of Management Succession: A Model of Chief Executive Succession in the Small Family Firm. *Family Business Review*, 2(4): 401–11.

McGrath, R.G., MacMillan, I.C. and Scheinberg, S. 1992. Elitists, Risk-takers, and Rugged Individuals? An Explanatory Analysis of Cultural Differences between Entrepreneurs and Non-entrepreneurs. *Journal of Business Venturing*, 7: 11.

McGrath, R.G., MacMillan, I.C., Yang, E.A. and Tsai, W. 1992. Does Culture Endure or Is It Malleable? Issues for Entrepreneurial Economic Development. *Journal of Business Venturing*, 7: 441–58.

Miller, D. 1983. The Correlates of Entrepreneurship in Three Types of Firms. *Management Science*, 29(7): 770–91.

Miller, D. and Le Breton-Miller, I. 2006. Family Governance and Firm Performance: Agency, Stewardship, and Capabilities. *Family Business Review*, 19(1): 73–87.

Miller, J.G. 1984. Culture and the Development of Everyday Social Explanation. *Journal of Personality and Social Psychology*, 46: 961–78.

Mischel, W. 1973. Towards a Cognitive Social Learning Reconceptualization of Personality. *Psychological Review*, 80(4): 252–83.

Morokvasic, M., Waldinger, R. and Phizacklea, A. 1990. Business on the Ragged Edge. In R. Waldinger, H. Aldrich, R. Ward and Associates (eds), *Ethnic Entrepreneurs*. London: Sage.

Morris, M.H., Williams, R.W., Allen, J.A. and Avila, R.A. 1993. Individualism and the Modern Corporation: Implications for Innovation and Entrepreneurship. *Journal of Management*, 19(3): 595–612.

Morris, M.H., Williams, R.W., Allen, J.A. and Avila, R.A. 1997. Correlates of Success in Family Business Transitions. *Journal of Business Venturing*, 12(5): 341–422.

Morris, M.W. and Peng, K. 1994. Culture and Cause: American and Chinese Attributions for Social and Physical Events. *Journal of Personality and Social Psychology*, 67: 949–71.

Moskos, C. 1980. *Greek Americans: Struggle and Success*. Englewood Cliffs, NJ: Prentice Hall.

Mueller, S.L. and Thomas, A.S. 2001. Culture and Entrepreneurship Potential: A Nine-Country Study of Locus of Control and Innovativeness. *Journal of Business Venturing*, 16(1): 51–75.

Muncie, J. and Sapsford, R. 1997. Issues in the Study of the Family. In J. Muncie, M. Wetherill, M. Langan, R. Dallos and A. Cochrane (eds), *Understanding the Family*. London: Sage, 7–37.

n'Doen, M.L., Garter, C., Nijkamp, P. and Rietveld, P. 1997. Ethnic Entrepreneurship and Migration: A Survey from Developing Countries. Available at: http://dare.ubvu.vu.nl/bitstream/handle/1871/3362/11597.pdf?sequence=1 [accessed 19 August 2010].

Nadjmabadi, S.R. 2010. Labour Migration from Iran to the Arab Countries of the Persian Gulf. *Anthropology of the Middle East*, 5(1): 18–33.

Naidoo, R. 2002. *Corporate Governance: An Essential Guide for South African Companies*. Cape Town: Double Story Books.

Nash, J.M. 1988. Boards of Privately Held Companies: Their Responsibility and Structure. *Family Business Review*, 1(3): 263–70.

Neto, P., Santos, A. and Serrano, M.M. 2012. Public Policies Supporting Local Based Networks for Entrepreneurship and Innovation: Contributions to the Effectiveness and Added Value Assessment. In I. Bernhard (ed.), *Entrepreneurship and Innovation Networks*. Research Reports 2012:02, Trollhätan: University West, 627–48.

Neubauer, F. and Lank, A.G. 1998. *The Family Business: Its Governance for Sustainability*. New York: Routledge.

Nkongolo-Bakenda, J.M. and Chrysostome, E.V. 2013. Engaging Diasporas as International Entrepreneurs in Developing Countries: In Search of Determinants. *Journal of International Entrepreneurship*, 11(1): 30–64.

Oh, S. and Chung, A. 2013. A Study on the Sociospatial Context of Ethnic Politics and Entrepreneurial Growth in Koreatown and Monterey Park. *GeoJournal*, (April): 1–13.

Olson, D.H., Sprenkle, D., and Russell, C. 1979. Circumplex Model of Family Systems I: Cohesion and Adaptability Dimensions, Family Types, and Clinical Applications. *Family Process*, 18: 3–28.

Osgood, C.E. 1974. Probing Subjective Cultures. Parts 1 and 2. *Journal of Communication*, 24: 21–34 and 82–100.

Parsons, T. and Schils, E.A. 1951. *Towards a General Theory of Action*. Cambridge, MA: Harvard University Press.

Pechlaner, H., Dal Bò, G. and Volgger, M. 2012. What Makes Tourism an Attractive Industry for New Minority Entrepreneurs: Results from an Exploratory Qualitative Study. *Tourism Review*, 67(1): 11–22.

Pederson, H.A. 1950. The Emerging Culture Concept: An Approach to the Study of Culture Change. *Social Forces*, 29: 604–16.

Perricone, P.J, Earle, J.R. and Taplin, I.M. 2001. Patterns of Succession and Continuity in Family-owned Businesses: Study of an Ethnic Community. *Family Business Review*, 14(2): 105–21.

Phizacklea, A. 1984. A Sociology of Migration or "Race Relations"? A View from Britain. *Current Sociology*, 32: 206–18.

Piperopoulos, P. 2012. Ethnic Female Business Owners: More Female or More Ethnic Entrepreneurs. *Journal of Small Business and Enterprise Development*, 19(2): 192–208.

Porter, M.E. 2001. Strategy and the Internet. *Harvard Business Review*, (March): 62–78.

Portes, A. 1995. Economic Sociology and the Sociology of Immigration: A Conceptual Overview. In A. Portes (ed.), *The Economic Sociology of Immigration*. New York: Russell Sage Foundation, 1–40.

Portes, A., Haller, W. and Guarnizo, L.E. 2001. *Transnational Entrepreneurs: The Emergence and Determinants of an Alternative Form of Immigrant Economic Adaptation*. Available at: http://www.transcomm.ox.ac.uk/working%20 papers/WPTC-01-05%20Portes.pdf [accessed 18 February 2013].

Portes, A. and Zhou, M. 1992. Gaining the Upper Hand: Economic Mobility among Immigrant and Domestic Minorities. *Ethnic and Racial Studies*, 15(4): 491–522.

Portes, A. and Zhou, M. 1996. Self-employment and the Earnings of Immigrants. *American Sociological Review*, 61(2): 219–30.

Portes, A. and Zhou, M. 1999. Entrepreneurship and Economic Progress in the 1990s: A Comparative Analysis of Immigrants and African Americans. In F.D. Bean and S. Bell-Rose (eds), *Immigration and Opportunity: Race, Ethnicity, and Employment in the United States*. New York: Russell Sage Foundation, 143–71.

Portes, A. and Zhou, M. 2012. Transnationalism and Development: Mexican and Chinese Immigrant Organizations in the United States. *Population and Development Review*, 38(2): 191–220.

Potter, L.G. 2009. *The Persian Gulf in History*. New York: Palgrave Macmillan.

Poutziouris, P., Wang, Y. and Chan, S. 2002. Chinese Entrepreneurship: The Development of Small Family Firms in China. *Journal of Small Business and Enterprise Development*, 9(4): 383–99.

Poza, E.J. 2013. *Family Business*. Mason, OH: Cengage Learning.

Raijman, R. and Tienda, M. 1999. Immigrants' Pathways to Business Ownership: A Comparative Ethnic Perspective. *International Migration Review*, 34(3): 682–706.

Rajan, R.G. and Zingales, L. 2000. The Governance of the New Enterprise. In X. Vives (ed.), *Corporate Governance: Theoretical and Empirical Perspective*. Cambridge: Cambridge University Press, 201–32.

Rath, J. and Kloosterman, R. 2000. Outsiders' Business: A Critical Review of Research on Immigrant Entrepreneurship, *International Migration Review*, 24(4): 657–81.

Roberts, C.S. and Feetham, S.L. 1982. Assessing Family Functioning across Three Areas of Relationships. *Nursing Research*, 31(4): 231–5.

Robertson, C.J., Diyab, A.A. and Al-Kahtani, A. 2013. A Cross-National Analysis of Perceptions of Corporate Governance Principles. *International Business Review*, 22(1): 315–25.

Rogers, R.H. and White. J.M. 1993. Family Development Theory. In P.G. Boss, W.J. Doherty, R. La Rossa, W.R. Schumm and S.K. Steinmetz (eds), *Sourcebook of Family Theories and Methods: A Contextual Approach*. New York: Plenum, 225–54.

Rousseau, D.M., Sitkin, S.B., Burt, R.S. and Camerer, C. 1998. Not So Different After All: A Cross-Discipline View of Trust. *Academy of Management Review*, 23(3): 393–404.

Rue, L.W. and N.A Ibrahim. 1995. Boards of Directors of Family-Owned Businesses: The Relationship between Members' Involvement and Company Performance. *Family Business Annual*, 1(1): 14–21.

Samovar, L. and Porter, R. 1994. *Intercultural Communication*. Belmont, CA: Wadsworth.

Santiago, A.L. 2000. Succession Experiences in Phillipine Family Businesses. *Family Business Review*, 12(1): 15–40.

Sawin, K.J. and Harrigan, M.P. 1995. *Measures of Family Functioning for Research and Practice*. New York: Springer.

Scase, R. and Goffee, R. 1980. *The Real World of the Small Business Owner*. London: Croom Helm.

Scase, R. and Goffee, R. 1982. *The Entrepreneurial Middle Class*. London: Croom Helm.

Schein, E.H. 1985. *Organizational Culture and Leadership*. London: Jossey-Bass.

Scholten, P.W.A. 2013. Agenda Dynamics and the Multi-level Governance of Intractable Policy Controversies: The Case of Migrant Integration Policies in the Netherlands. *Policy Sciences*, 46(3): 217–36.

Schulze, W.S., Lubatkin, M.H. and Dino, R.N. 2003. Exploring the Agency Consequences of Ownership Dispersion among the Directors of Private Family Firms. *Academy of Management Journal*, 46(2): 179–94.

Schumpeter, J.A. 1934. *The Theory of Economic Development*, trans. R. Opie. Cambridge, MA: Harvard University Press.

Schutz, W.C. 1958. *FIRO: A Three Dimensional Theory of Interpersonal Behavior*. New York: Rinehart.

Sciascia, S., Mazzola, P., Astrachan, J.H. and Pieper, T.M. 2012. The Role of Family Ownership in International Entrepreneurship: Exploring Nonlinear Effects. *Small Business Economics*, 38(1): 15–31.

Scottish Government. 2011. *Scotland's Census*. Available at: http://www.scotlandscensus.gov.uk/en/ [accessed 16 April 2013].

Shane, S. 1993. Cultural Influences on National Rates of Innovation. *Journal of Business Venturing*, 8: 59–73.

Shane, S. 1994. Cultural Values and the Championing Process. *Entrepreneurship Theory and Practice*, 18(4): 25–41.

Shane, S. 1995. Uncertainty Avoidance and the Preference for Innovation Champions Roles. *Journal of International Business Studies*, 26(1): 47–68.

Sharma, P., Chrisman, J.J. and Gersick, K.E. 2012. 25 Years of Family Business Review: Reflections on the Past and Perspectives for the Future. *Family Business Review*, 25(1): 5–15.

Sharma, P., Chua, J.H. and Chrisman, J.J. 2000. Perceptions about the Extent of Succession Planning in Canadian Family Firms. *Canadian Journal of Administrative Sciences*, 17(3): 233–44.

Shen, W. and Cannella Jr., A.A. 2002. Revisiting the Performance Consequences of CEO Succession: The Impacts of Successor Type, Postsuccession Senior Executive Turnover, and Departing CEO Tenure. *The Academy of Management Journal*, 45(4): 717–33.

Shepherd, D.A. and Zacharakis, A. 2000. Structuring Family Business Succession. *Proceedings of the International Council for Small Businesses, 45th World Conference*, Brisbane, Australia, 7–10 June, 1–19 (CD-Rom).

Singh, D.A. and Gaur, A.S. 2013. Governance Structure, Innovation and Internationalization: Evidence from India. *Journal of International Management*, 19(3): 300–309.

Slavnic, Z. 2013. Immigrant Small Business in Sweden: A Critical Review of the Development of a Research Field. *Journal of Business Administration Research*, 2(1): 29–42.

Smith, R. 2012. Local Government Incorporation of Immigrants in Community Economic Development Strategies. Available at: http://ssrn.com/abstract=1853713 [accessed 22 August 2013].

Soares, A.M., Farhangmehr, M. and Shoham, A. 2007. Hofstede's Dimensions of Culture in International Marketing Studies. *Journal of Business Research*, 60: 277–84.

Spiro. 2003. *Personal Tutor in the Greek Language and Greek Custom*. Port Elizabeth: Greek Orthodox Church.

Stafford, K., Duncan, K.A., Dane, S. and Winter, M. 1999. A Research Model for Sustainable Family Businesses. *Family Business Review*, 12(3): 197–208.

Stanworth, M.J.K. and Curran, J. 1973. *Management Motivations in the Smaller Business*. Aldershot: Gower.

Stavrou, E.T. 1999. Succession in Family Businesses: Exploring the Effects of Demographic Factors on Offspring Intentions to Join and Take Over the Business. *Journal of Small Business Management*, 37(3): 43–62.

Stavrou, E. and Swiercz, P.M. 1998. Securing the Future of the Family Enterprise: A Model of Offspring Intentions to Join the Business. *Entrepreneurship Theory and Practice*, 23(2): 19–39.

Steier, L. 2001. Family Firms, Plural Forms of Governance, and the Evolving Role of Trust. *Family Business Review*, 14(4): 353–67.

Stewart, A. and Hitt, M.A. 2012. Why Can't a Family Business Be More Like a Nonfamily Business? Modes of Professionalization in Family Firms. *Family Business Review*, 25(1): 58–86.

Stoy Hayward. 1992. Family Firm Research: The Need for a Methodological Rethink. *Entrepreneurship: Theory and Practice*, 23(2): 31–56.

Strohschneider, S. and Güss, D. 1999. The Fate of the Moros: A Cross-cultural Exploration of Strategies in Complex and Dynamic Decision-making. *International Journal of Psychology*, 34(4): 235–52.

Su, W. and Lee, C.Y. 2013. Effects of Corporate Governance on Risk Taking in Taiwanese Family Firms during Institutional Reform. *Asia Pacific Journal of Management*, 30(3): 809–28.

Sundaramurthy, C. 2008. Sustaining Trust within Family Businesses. *Family Business Review*, 21(2): 89–102.

Sundberg, N.D., Poole, M.E. and Tyler, L.E. 1983. Adolescents' Expectations of Future Events: A Cross-cultural Study of Australians, Americans, and Indians. *International Journal of Psychology*, 18: 415–27.

Sweder, R.A. and Le Vine, R.A. 1984. *Culture Theory: Essays on Mind, Self and Emotion*. New York: Cambridge University Press.

The Sydney Morning Herald. 2010. Transfield Co-founder Carlo Salteri Dies. 13 October. Available at: http://news.smh.com.au/breaking-news-business/transfield-cofounder-carlo-salteri-dies-20101013-16jvq.html [accessed 19 February 2013].

Tagiuri, R. and Davis, J.A. 1982. Bivalent Attributes of the Family Firm. Reprinted in the Classics section of *Family Business Review*, 9(2) (1996): 199–208.

Takyi-Asiedu, S. 1993. Some Socio-cultural Factors Retarding Entrepreneurial Activity in Sub-Saharan Africa. *Journal of Business Venturing*, 8: 91–8.

Thomas, A.S. and Mueller, S.L. 2000. A Case for Comparative Entrepreneurship: Assessing the Relevance of Culture. *Journal of International Business Studies*, 31(2): 287–301.

TransfieldServ. 2012. *Transfield Services Corporate Video 2012*. Available at: https://www.youtube.com/watch?v=er8x8Oe5K-4 [accessed 19 February 2013].

Triandis, H.C. 1972. *The Analysis of Subjective Culture*. New York: Wiley.

Triandis, H.C. 1989. The Self and Social Behaviour in Differing Social Contexts. *Psychological Review*, 96: 506–20.

Triandis, H.C. 1990. Cross-cultural Studies of Individualism and Collectivism. In J. Bergman (ed.), *Nebraska Symposium on Motivation*. Lincoln, NE: University of Nebraska Press, 41–133.

Triandis, H.C. 1994. *Culture and Social Behaviour*. New York: McGraw Hill.

Triandis, H.C. 1995. *Individualism and Collectivism*. Boulder, CO: Westview Press.

Triandis, H.C. 1996. The Psychological Measurement of Cultural Syndromes. *American Psychologist*, 51: 407–15.

Triandis, H.C. 2000. Culture and Conflict. *International Journal of Psychology*, 35(2): 145–52.

Triandis, H.C. and Gelfand, M. 1998. Converging Measurement of Horizontal and Vertical Individualism and Collectivism. *Journal of Personality and Social Psychology*, 74: 118–28.

Triandis, H.C., Marin, G., Lisansky, J. and Betancourt, H. 1984. Simpatia as a Cultural Script of Hispanics. *Journal of Personality and Social Psychology*, 47: 1363–74.

Triandis, H.C. and Singelis, T.M. 1998. Training to Recognize Individual References in Collectivism and Individualism in Culture. *International Journal of Intercultural Relations*, 22: 35–48.

Trimikliniotis, N. 2008. Rethinking Migration, Discrimination and Multiculturalism in a Post-Tourist Society. *Cyprus Review*, 20(2): 13–16.

Turkina, E. and Thai, M.T.T. 2013. Social Capital, Networks, Trust and Immigrant Entrepreneurship: A Cross-Country Analysis. *Journal of Enterprising Communities: People and Places in the Global Economy*, 7(2): 108–24.

Turner, J.H. and Bonacich, E. 1980. Toward a Composite Theory of Middleman Minorities. *Ethnicity*, 7: 144–58.

van de Vijver, F.J.R. and Willemsen, M.E. 1993. Abstract Thinking. *Advances in Psychology*, 103: 317–42.

Van der Heyden, L., Blondel, C. and Carlock, R.S. 2005. Fair Process: Striving for Justice in Family Business. *Family Business Review*, 18(1): 1–21.

Venter, E. 2002. The Succession Process in Small and Medium-sized Family Businesses in South Africa. Unpublished PhD thesis, University of Port Elizabeth, South Africa.

Vidigal, A.C. 2000. Succession Aspects in Hundred-Year-Old Family Firms in Brazil. *The Family Business Network Newsletter* (July/August), 27: 16–18.

Vlachos, E.C. 1965. The Assimilation of Greeks in the United States: With Special Reference to the Greek Community of Anderson, Indiana. PhD Sociology, General, dissertation, Indiana University. Ann Arbor, MI: University Microfilms.

Wadhwa, V. 2006. Are Indians the Model Immigrants? *BloombergBusinessweek*. 13 September. Available at: http://www.businessweek.com/stories/2006-09-13/are-indians-the-model-immigrants [accessed 19 July 2010].

Wadhwa, V. 2012. *The Immigrant Exodus: Why America is Losing the Global Race to Capture Entrepreneurial Talent*. Philadelphia, PA: Wharton Digital Press.

Wagner, J.A., Stimpert, J.L. and Fubara, E.I. 1998. Board Composition and Organizational Performance: Two Studies of Insider\Outsider Effects. *Journal of Management Studies*, 35(5): 655–77.

Waldinger, R.D. 1994. The Making of an Immigrant Niche. *International Migration Review*, 28(1): 3–30.

Waldinger, R. 1996. *Still the Promised City? African-Americans and New Immigrants in Postindustrial New York*. Cambridge, MA and London: Harvard University Press.

Waldinger, R. 1998. Comment. Presented at the International Conference on Nationalism, Transnationalism, and the Crisis of Citizenship, University of California-Davis, April.

Waldinger, R., Aldrich, H., Ward, R. and Associates. 1990. *Ethnic Entrepreneurs: Immigrant Business in Industrial Societies*. London: Sage.

Ward, J.L. 1984. Perpetuating the Family Business. *Director's Monthly*, December.

Ward, J.L. 1987. *Keeping the Family Business Healthy: How to Plan for Continuing Growth, Profitability, and Family Leadership*. San Francisco, CA: Jossey-Bass.

Ward, J.L. 1988. The Special Role of Strategic Planning for Family Businesses. *Family Business Review*, 1(2): 105–17.

Ward, J.L. 1989. Defining and Researching Inside Versus Outside Directors: A Rebuttal to the Rebuttal. *Family Business Review*, 2(2): 147–9.

Ward, J.L. 1991. *Creating Effective Boards for Private Enterprises: Meeting the Challenges of Continuity and Competition*. San Fransisco, CA: Jossey-Bass.

Ward, J.L. 1997a. Growing the Family Business: Special Challenges and Best Practices. *Family Business Review*, 10(4): 323–37.

Ward, J.L. 1997b. Getting Help from the Board of Directors. In M. Fischetti (ed.), *The Family Business Succession Handbook*. Philadelphia, PA: Family Business Publishing, 17–20.

Ward, J.L. and Dolan, C. 1998. Defining and Describing Family Business Ownership Configurations. *Family Business Review*, 11(4): 305–10.

Ward, J.L. and Handy, J.L. 1996. A Survey of Board Practices. In C.E. Aronoff, J.H. Astrachan and J.L. Ward (eds), *Family Business Sourcebook II*. Marietta, GA: Business Owner Resources, 257–69.

Ward, R. 1987. Resistance, Accommodation and Advantage: Strategic Development in Ethnic Business. In G. Lee and R. Loveridge (eds), *The Manufacture of Disadvantage*. Milton Keynes: Open University Press, 159–75.

Waters, T. 1995. Towards a Theory of Ethnic Identity and Migration: The Formation of Ethnic Enclaves by Migrant Germans in Russia and North Africa. *International Migration Review*, 29(2): 515–44.

Watkins, D. and Shen, Y. 1997. Criteria for Board Construction in the Entrepreneurial Firm. Paper presented at the XI Research in Entrepreneurship and Small Business (RENT XI) Conference, Mannheim, Germany, 26–29 November.

Watkins, J. and Watkins, D. 1984. The Female Entrepreneur: Her Background and Determinants of Business Choice – Some British Data. In J. Curran, J. Stanworth and D. Watkins (eds), *The Survival of the Small Firm, Vol. 1: The Economics of Survival and Entrepreneurship*. Aldershot: Gower, 220–32.

Wellalage, N.H., Locke, S. and Scrimgeour, F. 2012. The Global Financial Crisis Impact on Ethnic Diversity of Sri Lanka Boards. *Asian Journal of Finance and Accounting*, 4(1): 52–68.

Wellman, B. and Frank, K. 2001. Network Capital in a Multi-level World: Getting Support from Personal Communities. In N. Lin, R.S. Burt and K. Cook (eds), *Social Capital: Theory and Research*. Chicago, IL: Aldine De Gruyter, 233–73.

Wheelock, J. 1991. The Flexibility of Small Business Family Work Strategies. Paper presented at the Fourteenth National Small Firms Policy and Research Conference, Small Enterprise Development: Policy and Practice in Action, Blackpool, 20–22 November.

Whitchurch, G.G. and Constantine, L.L. 1993. Systems Theory. In P.G. Boss, W.J. Doherty, R. LaRossa, W.R. Schumm and S.K. Steinmetz (eds), *Sourcebook of Family Theories and Methods: A Contextual Approach*. New York: Plenum, 325–52.

White, J.M. 1991. *Dynamics of Family Development: The Theory of Family Development*. New York: Guilford.

Whiteside, M.F., Aronoff, C.E. and Ward, J.L. 1993. *How Families Work Together*. Family Leadership Series, No. 4. Marietta, GA: Business Owner Resources.

Whiteside, M. and Herz-Brown, F. 1991. Drawbacks of a Dual System Approach to Family Firms: Can We Expand Our Thinking? *Family Business Review*, 4(4): 383–95.

Willard, B. 2002. *The Sustainability Advantage*. Gabriola Island, British Columbia: New Society.

Wilson, K. and Martin, A. 1982. Ethnic Enclaves: A Comparison of the Cuban and Black Economies in Miami. *American Journal of Sociology*, 88: 135–60.

Wortman, M.S. 1994. Theoretical Foundations for Family Owned Business: A Conceptual and Research-based Paradigm. *Family Business Review*, 7(1): 3–15.

Yamaguchi, S. 1998. The Meaning of Amae. Paper presented at the Congress of International Association of Cross-cultural Psychology, Bellingham, WA, August.

Yan, J. and Sorenson, R. 2006. The Effect of Confucian Values on Succession in Family Business. *Family Business Review*, 19(3): 235–50.

Yang, X., Ho, E.Y.H. and Chang, A. 2012. Integrating the Resource-based View and Transaction Cost Economics in Immigrant Business Performance. *Asia Pacific Journal of Management*, 29(3): 753–72.

Yasin, N. and Inal, Y. 2012. The Emergence of Immigrant Pakistani Entrepreneurship and Innovation in Northern Cyprus. *International Journal of Business and Management Studies*, 4(1): 133–45.

Zhou, X., Yang, F. and Wu, Z. 2012. Family Involvement, Ethnicity, and Willingness to Borrow: Evidence from US Small Firms. *Entrepreneurship Research Journal*, 2(2): 1–26.

Zhu, H., Chen, C.C., Li, X. and Zhou, Y. 2013. From Personal Relationship to Psychological Ownership: The Importance of Manager–Owner Relationship Closeness in Family Businesses. 从私人关系到心理所有权：家族企业中经理与企业主关系亲密度的重要性. *Management and Organization Review*, 9(2): 295–318.

Zimmer, C. and Aldrich, H.E. 1987. Resource Mobilization through Ethnic Networks: Kinship and Friendship Ties of Shopkeepers in England. *Sociological Perspectives*, 30(4): 422–45.

Zuiker, V.S. 1998. *Hispanic Self-employment in the Southwest Rising above the Threshold of Poverty*. (Garland Studies in the History of American Labor.) New York: Garland.

Index

Page numbers in **bold** type refer to a table. Page numbers in *italic* type refer to a figure.

For Product Safety Concerns and Information please contact our EU
representative GPSR@taylorandfrancis.com Taylor & Francis Verlag GmbH,
Kaufingerstraße 24, 80331 München, Germany

Printed and bound by CPI Group (UK) Ltd, Croydon, CR0 4YY

04/05/2025

01860547-0002